PRISONER #7: RUDOLF HESS

Prisoner #7

RUDOLF HESS

THE THIRTY YEARS IN JAIL
OF HITLER'S DEPUTY FÜHRER

by Eugene K. Bird

THE VIKING PRESS NEW YORK

Published in England under the title of
The Loneliest Man in the World
Copyright © 1974 by Eugene K. Bird and Desmond Zwar
All rights reserved
Published in 1974 by The Viking Press, Inc.
625 Madison Avenue, New York, N.Y. 10022
SBN 670-57831-2
Library of Congress catalog card number: 73-19479
Printed in U.S.A.

I wish to express my grateful thanks to Mr Desmond L. G. Zwar, of Fleet Street, London, without whose literary collaboration this book might never have been written. His help and enthusiasm for the project of filling an important historical gap were untiring.

Eugene K. Bird, 1971

CONTENTS

LIST OF ILLUSTRATIONS

PRISONER #7: RUDOLF HESS

INTRODUCTION

MORE THAN 30 years ago the world was astonished to hear that Rudolf Hess, deputy to Adolf Hitler, had taken a Messerschmitt plane and flown to England to seek peace with the British. Hess flew on his mysterious mission believing he would be given an audience with the King, or at least with the Prime Minister, Winston Churchill. Instead, he was kept in a series of British prisons, and his 'offers' to end the war between Germany and Britain were rebuffed.

Four years passed. And with the war finally at an end, Hess was taken to Nuremberg to stand trial with his fellow Nazis before the International Military Tribunal. At least there, historians assured themselves, the inside story of Hess's dramatic flight would come out. The world would learn just how closely Hitler plotted Hess's trip, despite Nazi propaganda which had blustered about having his Deputy shot if he ever returned to Germany.

Instead, the court – and the world – saw and heard only a pathetic thin figure huddled in the dock reading books and mumbling the odd remark to his neighbour, Hermann Goering. When, at last, Hess had the chance to get up and tell his story, he gave only a rambling dissertation on 'secret forces' and 'evil influences' being used to destroy him. He sat down, and was convicted. Without any further statement of explanation of his acts he went down to the cells to begin his life sentence.

Hess was taken to Spandau Allied Prison in Berlin where he has remained for more than a quarter of a century. A mystery man, a prisoner never allowed to be shown to the outside world; a lonely figure ending his prison days in virtual solitary confinement.

What is the man really like? 'He is quite mad,' said one magazine. 'He howls at night like a dog.' An English newspaper told its readers: 'Hess tries to goose-step around his cell's eight square yards shouting "Heil Hitler!" at the top of his piping and querulous voice.' Was it true that in 1948 an American psychiatrist had found Hess to be schizophrenic, but that his report had been quashed so Hess would not be moved to an asylum?

Nobody at Spandau, a prison run in turn by Russia, the United States, France and Britain, would say. No prison in the world had tighter security than the old red-brick fortress in West Berlin.

But today I am able to answer these questions. As the American director of Spandau I have been closer to Rudolf Hess than any other person. I believe I am the only living person Hess has taken into his confidence since 1941.

Hess had been angered and frustrated by the articles and books that had been written about him over the years. 'Lies,' he often told me. 'And here I am, unable to correct the untruths.' Gradually he began to open up about what *was* the truth. And I took down what he said.

I have talked for many hours with him in his cell, in the Spandau garden where he exercised, and when he lay close to death in hospital. He has eagerly cooperated in at last providing the answer to the enigma that has caught the curiosity of the world for so many years.

Patiently he has gone over his life as a Nazi minister, as Hitler's right-hand man, and as a prisoner. He has talked on a tape-recorder to me, he has answered specific and important questions in writing. And he has given me exclusive permission to publish his diaries and speeches written in longhand, or typed by him over the years.

My strange association with Hess began in 1947 when, as a young American guard officer, I was posted to Spandau. There I watched the seven prisoners who had escaped the hangman's noose, shuffling around the garden at the rear of the prison. I believe I made a vow then that I would write about them. As the years went by and the seven men were gradually reduced to three, I started my diaries about prison life. Finally, when there was just one man left – Hess – my superiors urged me to write a book. 'This is history, Gene,' said a high-ranking officer. 'It must be recorded.'

What finally tipped the balance and caused my private diaries to become a book was the discovery of a cardboard carton that had come, years before, with Hess from Nuremberg. Officials, believing it was just a collection of his private scribblings, handed it to me to burn if I wanted. For three years I left the box unopened.

One night I did open it. I took out pages of close-spaced pencilled notes and thick piles of type written pages, all initialled at the top, 'RH'. Hess had written a full personal memoir of his historic flight and his motives for making it; a diary recording his daily life in Nuremberg awaiting trial, and his thoughts as he faced what he knew could be death.

I told Hess what I had found and he was impatient to examine the papers. During the day we carefully went over every word he had written, and I allowed him to have the files in his cell at night. He told me: 'I give you exclusive permission to publish them in full or in part; I only ask that in the translation nothing of the sense of what I have written should be altered.' I promised that only an academic translator would be used.* But I did far better than that. As the book that follows was being written I had an energetic and competent proof-reader scrutinizing every word – Rudolf Hess himself. His command of English is excellent (indeed he pointed out more than one grammatical error).

It was a risk to Hess and myself to have him working on the manuscript; it was a breach of prison rules, which allowed him to read only censored newspapers and approved books, and certainly nothing about World War II. I broke these rules for a valid reason: in no other way could the world get to know the true story of Hess in Spandau except through me. I was the only man he trusted, and I wished the accuracy of what I wrote of our conversations to be checked and verified by Hess himself. Whatever then appeared in print would be a faithful record of what he had either written or said. All this involved danger of discovery. Had a Russian warder, or even a warder of one of our Allies, found Hess with the manuscript there would have been grave repercussions.

At times Rudolf Hess sat in the visiting-room talking to his wife – with 20 pages of typewritten manuscript stuck in the back of his underpants. He knew his cell was subject to search during his absence.

From our collaboration I hope we have destroyed once and for all the myth of the crazy old man caged in Spandau. He was never an easy man to know. He was for a long time withdrawn and supicious, even capricious, but never mad. I found him often warm and humorous,

* Mr J. A. Arengo-Jones, Senior Language Supervisor for the German Department of the BBC.

enjoying a never-ending love–hate relationship with a fat warder whose brain Hess decided could be easily outwitted. He was very much an intellectual snob.

As we read together, Hess following the words with his forefinger, there were often times when he did not like what he read. He hesitated when the narrative recorded his fits of pique, his obstinacy and his tantrums. But I told him: 'It is very much a warts-and-all book, you have to look at it as a whole.' He would shrug his shoulders and say: 'It is true, I suppose. I cannot object.' And he would take up his pen and scrawl his signature 'RH' on the page.*

He had a complex and intelligent mind, which had pushed its dark secrets down into the depths where they lay purposely forgotten. It would take many hours, and mental discomfort at the same time for the old man, to bring them to the surface again to right some previously published wrong.

He never lost his pride or his sense of self-importance. When he was writing, day after day in his notebooks, about the moon, he genuinely believed that if he was freed his writings would be of world interest. Not because they shed any new light on space-travel, but because he, Rudolf Hess, had written them. I told him his articles might well have a curiosity value because of the circumstances in which they were written, but little more. He shook his head. I was quite wrong.

This then is the end-product of many hundreds of hours sitting, walking and talking with Hess, a legend in his own lifetime. What follows, however, is not legend, but fact. Fact seen and authenticated by Rudolf Hess, once Deputy Führer of the Third Reich.

Lieutenant-Colonel Eugene K. Bird (USA Retd)
US Commandant of Spandau Prison
Berlin 1972

---

* When Hess initialled a paper he often used 'Ru' instead of 'RH'.

1

The Beginnings

THE DOOR TO Hess's Spandau cell swung open to admit its prisoner on 18 July 1947. It was a cell 8ft 10½in long and 7ft 5in wide; painted dark green half-way up the walls and then cream. The curved ceiling was freshly painted white, contrasting with the black floor.

Hess had a simple iron army bed. Under the mattress there was a thick wooden base which he had asked for to help his posture; a mattress wedge propped up the head of the mattress and there were sheets, blankets and a pillow.

Above Hess's head was a barred window overlooking the tops of trees where birds fluttered about and a weak sunshine filtered in. The window was 5ft 4in from the floor and Hess was allowed to stretch up and open it to let air in. Beneath it ran the pipes of the steam-heating system, covered by a ventilated wooden frame. Lying in his new bed, Hess gazed directly at his cell door. His eyes measured it as they were measuring every inch of his cell. He knew later that it was exactly 72¾in high and 34in wide. It had a square, barred peephole through which his guards could keep watch over him. At the end of his bed was his toilet. It had a black seat and a black lid and flushed quietly, with an unusual whirring sound, made that way so that its flushing at night would not awaken the other prisoners, though the noise would have had to penetrate stone walls 23in thick, and a door made of steel.

Hess's eyes travelled up to the 11ft 4in high ceiling where there was a light covered by curved bars to prevent the prisoner from standing on a chair, taking out the bulbs and electrocuting himself. There were two bulbs, a 150-watt to read by and a 40-watt bulb for night inspection of the sleeping prisoner.

Lying on his bed, Rudolf Hess stretched out his left arm to touch the hard, upright wooden chair, then the rough-hewn table with its shelves on which lay his books, medicines and photographs brought from Nuremberg. On his blanket lay an inflatable rubber ring a child might play with in the sea. Hess had it for his chair, to give comfort to his bony bottom.

If in the night he wanted to alert a warder or an aide-man that he needed help, he had to get out of bed and push a small steel button in the wall near his toilet. He tried it. The trigger-mechanism released a painted tin flap from the wall outside Cell 23, alerting the warder sitting outside. The warder rattled his two large keys and two smaller ones, turning a large key once, then once again, releasing the bolt and swinging the door open.

Hess, having found the system worked, grunted and relaxed on his bed. He was satisfied. Muttering, the warder once more closed the heavy door, the steel clanging loudly into place. The bolt was pushed across, the key turned once, then once more in the double-drop lock.

And then there was silence.

What sort of a man did the cell contain? A few yards away in the prison safe in the Directors' room, a heavy file of papers told the story. . .

Rudolf Hess was born in Alexandria, Egypt, on 26 April 1894, the son of a German wholesale merchant. A round-faced boy with direct blue eyes, Rudolf went to a German school in Alexandria, his lessons supplemented by a tutor. His relationship with his parents (he later told psychiatrists) was always good. He was a 'wanted' child, and the Hesses were a well-off family enjoying a distinguished position in a large German community. His first childhood memories were of his brother, Alfred, being born, and of being given a small toy gun-carriage drawn by two horses.

At 12, he was sent off to Germany to attend the Evangelisches Paedagogium school at Godesberg am Rhein, where he was confirmed in the Protestant church, but did not, he said, attend its services. He had been taught by his mother to pray and he preferred to say his prayers 'privately'. At 17 he was enrolled in a business school in Switzerland, and obediently attended – though by now he was sure he never wanted to be a businessman.

Nevertheless, after a year at the Ecole Supérieure, he went to Hamburg to join an export house and serve his apprenticeship for his planned third-generation Hess role as an importer-exporter. In 1914, when the war broke out, he saw his chance to break away. He volunteered and was accepted in the 1st Bavarian Regiment. During fighting on the Western Front he sustained the first of three war wounds, none of them, fortunately, serious. He was commissioned as a lieutenant, and in the first year of the war transferred to the Air Corps where he got his first taste of flying.

By the end of the war all thoughts of a commercial career had been abandoned by the 24-year-old Hess. He entered Munich University to read history, economics, political science and – a vital subject that was to alter the whole of his life – geo-politics, the study of the effect of geographical position on a nation's politics.

Hess's geo-politics professor was Professor Karl Haushofer, a man with unusual political theories and a persuasive manner. Haushofer had been a general in the war and had won wide respect. His lectures were often peppered with references to the influences of astrology and the supernatural on Germany's history. He had a profound influence on the student Hess.

Hess felt keenly about the position in which Germany found herself in the aftermath of war. He was angry about the poverty and the apparent injustice, and he saw in Haushofer's theories a way for Germany to become great once more. He mixed eagerly in the political life of the university and the activities of fellow-students who were not averse to brawling outside it to get their ideas across.

While at university, Rudolf Hess was busy distributing anti-Semitic pamphlets and brawling in the beerhalls with various armed bands he linked up with. In 1920 he went along to a meeting of the Nazi Party, heard its fiery Hitler speak, and was enthralled. Captivated by what the shouting, gesticulating man said, Hess joined the Nazi Party. It was only a short time before Hitler's attention was drawn to new member Hess. In an essay for a thesis the university student had written:

How must the man be constituted who will lead Germany back to her old heights?

Where all authority has vanished, only a man of the people can establish authority. The deeper the dictator is originally rooted in the broad masses, the better he understands how to treat them psychologically, the less the workers will distrust him, the more supporters he will win among these most energetic ranks of the people. He himself has nothing in common with the mass; like every great man he is all personality.

When necessity commands, he does not shrink before bloodshed. Great questions are always decided by blood and iron . . . In order to reach his goal, he is prepared to trample on his closest friends . . . The law-giver proceeds with terrible hardness . . . As the need arises, he can trample with the boots of a grenadier.

When Hess's essay was shown to Hitler he preened. Who could have fitted the description better than himself?

From Hess's point of view, Hitler's utter ruthlessness was to be admired. Who better could have put across the ideas he had absorbed from Haushofer, and which were now part of his life? He gave Hitler his loyalty and faith and followed him with a dog-like devotion.

His first big chance to show his loyalty was in the Munich beer-cellar putsch on 8 November 1923. After its failure, Hess fled to the Haushofer home in the Bavarian Alps. Soon, however, both he and Hitler were tried; Hitler was jailed for five years. Hess got 18 months, and the two found themselves in Landsberg prison, with a view across the river Lech. Here Hitler started *Mein Kampf* and Hess agreed to help edit his manuscripts.

Hess, at 30, had his own burning sense of injustice. 'Germany shall live,' he wrote* to a friend from his cell, 'even if the law should go to the Devil: I think of the days and months I have spent together with my prison comrades behind bars because German judges pay homage to the opposite ideas!'

When Hess and Hitler were released just before the end of 1924, having served only a few months of their sentences, Hess had become in effect Hitler's private secretary: he was still taking down his leader's thoughts for *Mein Kampf*, helping to write propaganda pamphlets. On 20 July 1929 he was 'commanded' (he was told by Heinrich Himmler, SS Oberführer) 'to be the personal adjutant of Adolf Hitler'.

Hess's feelings at the time on Bolshevism are well illustrated by this letter he wrote to Albrecht Haushofer, Dr Karl's son, on the eve of the latter's departure to England:

---

* Letter produced in evidence against Hess at Nuremberg.

Munich, 18 October 1930

Rudolf Hess
Muenchen 39
Loefetzstrasse 8 (Borstei)
Telephone 60909
Postcheck: Muenchen 24918

Dear Doctor

A few further words on the subject of our recent telephone conversation in Berlin which I hope to be able to continue in person soon.

It is possible that in England you will be asked for your opinion about us and about the situation in Germany as a whole. Please reply in much the same way as H. did to *The Times* correspondent (see attached cutting). Give them to understand that we are a rampart against Bolshevism – as is indeed the case. Because of the catastrophic economic consequences of the recent contracts, if the Party did not exist, the majority of those who voted for us would join the radical leftist camp (even the Conservatives would join them out of sheer desperation) and the remainder would not even bother to vote, which again would help the leftists. Our people, too, are the only active element in the struggle against Bolshevism, either as an organ of propaganda or – if it should become necessary – as a physical force. From your own observations you will be able to tell the English what Bolshevism means.

Do not, on the other hand, mention your reservations. However mildly they are expressed, this would not help the only anti-Bolshevik movement but would discredit it in foreign eyes. Even if your doubts were justified, any hope that they might arouse would inevitably be disappointed, and Germany would be beyond help. This moment is the last hope for millions – there is nothing you can put in its place! Do believe me, your doubts are without foundation: I can assure you of this from my own extensive knowledge of the current situation. You have been too much impressed by events in Berlin which, as always, has its own unique role. There the device of infiltrating Communist provocateurs into our ranks was undeniably successful – this was easy enough to do with the hysterical Berliners – but we are already on their tracks and they are being thrown out one by one.

I am not writing this simply on behalf of the Party – I would not bother you on that account alone. I write because I am convinced that not only the Party but the future of Germany itself is at stake, and that the threat of Bolshevism is of crucial importance for the whole of Europe. The National Socialist movement is being assessed abroad – especially in England, where you will probably meet people of influence.

With best wishes,
Rudolf Hess

In 1932 Hitler appointed his adjutant head of the Party's central political commission where he supervised the political activities of the Nazi factions in the State Assembly and helped determine questions of general political strategy.

On 21 April 1933 came a still higher honour: 'I hereby name to be my deputy, the leader of the central political commission, Party member Rudolf Hess, and give him all the powers of attorney in all questions of decision of the Party leadership to be decided in my name – Adolf Hitler.'

Hess was dominating Party control of universities, schools and religious societies. He was busy organizing the labour front, and in 1935 he put his name to the ominous Jewish legislation that was to play such a terrible part in the works of the Hitler dictatorship. Three years later he moved into Hitler's Secret Cabinet Council that was busy planning foreign aggression.

While all this was going on Hess had found time to marry – encouraged by Hitler – Fräulein Ilse Pröhl. Their son, Wolf-Rudiger, was born ten years later.

2

Hess Takes Off

THE EVENTS OF the first nine months of World War II need no repetition here. With the fall of Belgium, Holland – and then France – it seemed certain to Hitler that Britain would see reason and make peace. The odds against them, he said at the signing of the French armistice, were hopeless. He was astonished to see his offer turned down; and was further astonished when, after the punishment of the Battle of Britain, the small island across the channel not only hit back but, at least in the Middle East, began to turn the tide.

As early as 6 May 1941, the American Secretary of State, Cordell Hull, was reading a de-coded message just in from an American legation in neutral Switzerland, in which a spy, code-name 'Donau',★ describing himself as a 'leading figure in the anti-Nazi Movement', reported: 'According to my latest and absolutely reliable reports, Hitler and Hess had a conference about four to six weeks ago at which the former informed the latter that the best Germany could now hope – and must work for – was "a draw". Since this interview,' said 'Donau', 'Hess has been very pessimistic . . .'

Hess had in fact been busy with his close friends the Haushofers, checking out peace 'feelers' and taking steps to put them out on Germany's behalf. He said he had the backing of Hitler. But as the weeks dragged on, Hess decided only a great, bold personal stroke would do.

'Many times,' Hess wrote,† 'in the middle of his greatest victories,

★ The reports made to the Americans by the mysterious 'Donau' are in the Washington archives. They were astonishingly accurate. He forecast Germany's attack on Russia – 'Barbarossa' – and said: 'The attack on Russia (provided a deal satisfactory to Germany is not made earlier) is scheduled for the end of May or early June – just as soon as the Finnish marshes dry up.' The attack in fact took place on 22 June.

† Hess wrote this statement in his Nuremberg cell. It was handed to me, unread, until I opened the box of his papers in 1970.

the Führer expressed how painful it was for him that the war was delaying all his plans for building and developing Germany, to an extent which could not be foreseen . . .

'It was this knowledge which made me decide to fly to England.

'Many people are unable to understand this flight even today. The German people are entitled to learn what the motives were which led someone occupying one of the highest places in the Reich to take so unprecedented a step – so unprecedented in all respects; undertaken without the Führer's permission.

'During the campaign in France, I expressed the opinion to the Führer that in the event of peace being concluded with England, we should at least recover what was taken from us by the dictated peace of 1919; for instance, compensation for the loss of the German Mercantile Marine. The Führer contradicted me. He did not want, on his part, to have a peace treaty comparable to that of Versailles which would bring new wars in its wake. He aimed at a real conciliation between peoples. He said I knew that he had always aimed at an understanding with England. As far back as 1924, when he was imprisoned in the fortress of Landsberg, he had declared that this was the main pillar of his foreign policy, as I would remember.

'He said he had still not given up hope of being able to come to an understanding with England sometime after the end of the war, as soon as the bitterness had died down on both sides. He said that if one desired reconciliation, one must not start by making peace conditions which could be felt to be wounding. He said he had only *two* demands to make of the British:

'1. The fixing of mutual spheres of interest, designed to prevent new causes of friction between Germany and England; and

'2. The handing back of the German colonies.

'The quicker this war came to an end, he said, the better it would be for humanity, the better, above all, for the peoples most closely involved: If the war was to last for a long time, Great Britain would lose her position of power in the world, her Empire would be doomed. But this, he said, would not be in our interest. And he personally would regret it. For this reason too, he had suggested coming to an understanding.

'I kept saying to myself at that time: "If this were known to England, it would perhaps be possible, after all, that the people there would prefer coming to an understanding rather than fighting a war to the bitter end – a war whose outcome was at least uncertain and which was bound in any case to last for years and inflict grievous harm on all participants.'

'But I assumed the British would regard it as being an intolerable loss of prestige even to consider proposals put forward by the Führer with the war in the state it then was.

'It would have been different for them if there had been a reason for engaging in negotiations, a reason recognizable by the world at large.

'*I decided to provide a reason, by flying to England.*

'For a number of reasons I was only able to act upon this decision a year later.

'It was my hope to be able to convice the British Government how senseless it was to continue this war until both sides were exhausted and brought to the verge of breakdown.

'At the same time I wanted to give the British Government an opportunity to make a declaration on the following lines: "*As a result of discussions with Rudolf Hess, the Government now feel that the Führer's offers are sincerely meant. In these circumstances it would be irresponsible to continue the bloodshed without ourselves trying to reach an understanding. We therefore declare our readiness to negotiate.*"'

Hess decided that the moment the weather conditions over Britain were favourable, he would take the newly developed ME 110 which he had been allowed to fly by the designer Willi Messerschmitt and head for Scotland. But weather held him up.

'Only a few days before my flight came a number* of the usual unfavourable weather reports. But this meant I had all the more time to enjoy dear old Augsburg with Pintsch [Hess's adjutant], little realizing that I was looking at much of it for the last time.

'In November 1940† the Führer told me that he wanted to inform me about his plans for the next year. I asked him to please let me state, uninfluenced first, what I would do if I were in his place. I expressed my conviction that Soviet Russia had signed the non-aggression treaty with us only to soothe us, and to enable her to attack us, with better chance of success, at a moment convenient to her.

'My opinion was underlined by reports from news agencies claiming

* Letter to Ilse Hess, 8 May 1947.

† This section from his 'Last Word' written in Nuremberg in October 1946.

Russia was in the process of preparing a military build-up of the greatest size, against Germany, showing all the signs of intended aggression. I considered it impossible that Russia would pass up the opportunity to fall on our back when we were engaged in a war with the Western powers.

'Only by the destruction of National Socialist Germany would the way be paved for the old goal of spreading the world revolution westward. The right moment would appear to be when Germany's army – after landing in England – was tied down in great numbers on the other side of the Channel.

'I therefore would give up the idea of landing in England and, instead, steal a march on the Russians' surely planned attack.

'Attack is still the best form of defence.

'It turned out that the Führer had already decided this course himself.

'I furthermore was of the opinion that it would be possible to come to an agreement with England – in spite of the refusal of such proposals already made by the Führer. After the outbreak of the war between Germany and Russia, the chances would be better than ever.

'England couldn't have an interest in a Russian victory over Germany with England helping Russia.

'She couldn't possibly want to sacrifice hundreds of thousands of British people and her national prosperity only to ensure that a part of Europe, and eventually all of Europe, came under the Soviet sphere of power. The British also knew that the highly developed industry of the Continent, using cheapest manpower and an abundance of raw materials supplied by the Russians, would lead to world markets being flooded with export goods at prices which England could not compete with.

'The war would not be ended by the occupation of the British Isles. England would continue the war with its Empire and probably with the help of America. Our forces would be spread further apart by having to defend themselves against a counter-attack in England as well. This would favour Russia's intentions.

'The Russians would hardly leave us another year.

'I was loath to tell the Führer that I myself planned to fly to England for an understanding. I could not know at that time that it would be impossible to win responsible persons over to the idea of an understanding. Less could I know why this had to be impossible.

'The Führer's decision to steal a march and attack the Russians was justified by the success of the first 1½ years of our fight against them. The final failure was not foreseeable.

'Since I am aware of the means which can steer people by a strange force, I am even more convinced that Russia would have attacked us, as substantially it was part of the plan by the leading criminals of the world working in the background. It shows more than ever that the Führer's plan to beat the Russians was right.'

On 9 May, *the day before* his flight, Hess wrote to a colleague: 'Dear Party Leader Darré, I do not know where you got the information that I am holding a meeting in the middle of this month. I have a rather big trip in front of me and I don't know yet when I'll be back. Because of this I cannot put myself in the position of making a certain time for it and bind myself to that time. After I return I will call on you again.'

On 10 May, Hess 'borrowed' a leather flying suit which he put over his officer's uniform and prepared for take-off. 'He appeared in officer's uniform, without badges of rank,* at flight-control, and signed under his wife's maiden name for a flight from Augsburg to Stavanger in Norway,' said designer Willi Messerschmitt.†

'I flew direct,' said Hess,‡ 'except for the diversions I made in order to hoodwink our friends the British. And I flew entirely alone.

'It was impressive to be flying alone over the North Sea in magically beautiful evening light, strongly affected by the Northern latitudes in which I found myself.

'The numerous small clouds far below me looked like pack-ice on the sea: crystal clear and everything tinged with red. The sky, as it were, swept clean – Oh all too clean! "Continuous cloud cover at 500 metres" the weather report had said. And I had intended if necessary to withdraw into this cover. But there was no sign whatever of any such thing. For some moments I thought of turning back. Then I said to myself, however, "Night landing with this machine is a tricky business."

'And even if nothing happened to me, the Messerschmitt machine was bound to be damaged, possibly beyond repair, and that would be the end.

* In fact his uniform bore the insignia of a captain.
† Messerschmitt gave a full report at Nuremberg on 11 May 1947.
‡ His letter to his wife 21 June 1947 from Nuremberg.

'Whatever else might have happened, the secret would have been out and would have been reported "upstairs", then I really should be finished forever. I said to myself: "Stick it out. Come what may."

'But then I had some luck, inasmuch as it was hazy over England and the haze reflected the evening light, making it impossible to see anything from above.

'I of course went straight for this hazy belt. That is to say I flew at full throttle at a few thousand metres towards the coast and attained a terrific speed. This saved me from being overtaken and shot down by the Spitfire which was coming in behind me. If it hadn't been for this, I would have flown on comfortably at speed, if the concealing bank of mist had not tempted me to "take the plunge". I could not see behind me because I was too confined in my seat and the cockpit window reflected the light too much.

'I greeted England with a wild scream of my engines, flying a few metres above the rooftops of a small township on the coast, my speed being about 750 kms/hr. I was then out of sight of my pursuer since I was certainly invisible from above. Within the mist-bank itself visibility was several kilometres and as clear as one could wish for. You can imagine how careful I was not to get out of that helpful bank of mist.

'I came down lower still to a height of perhaps five metres over the tree-tops, roof-tops, cattle and people (the British airman calls it "hedge-hopping". He was evidently impressed with my achievement!)

'At home this sort of flying was forbidden, although I had tried it out on occasions for short spells and not so radically as this time. Father Bauer* used to say I would fly in through the barn door if I could.

'I thus arrived, pretty much according to programme, almost touching the tops of a medium range of mountains as I flew past, until I reached the west coast and then on to the estate of my unsuspecting host.

'To bale out I went to a height of 2,000 metres. I landed with a parachute ten metres in front of the door of the only farmhouse in the vicinity. That too was good. Because my leg injury practically prevented me from walking.

'The farmer helped me into the house, and as we sat drinking tea in front of the fire, I expected to be taken into custody. I did not have to wait long.'

* Hans Bauer, Hitler's pilot.

When he took off on the Saturday evening, Hess had left behind two letters. One was to his wife. He tucked that away among his young son's toys so it would be found (but not found so quickly that any alarm could be raised to prevent him taking off). The second sealed envelope he left with the faithful Pintsch. It was addressed to the Führer, and Pintsch knew exactly when he was to deliver it.

Pintsch arrived in Berchtesgaden on the overnight train at 7 o'clock on Sunday morning and immediately made his way to Hitler's eyrie, the Berghof, fear grabbing at the pit of his stomach. He waited while the Führer saw several officials and finally was able to get through to Hitler just ahead of Dr Fritz Todt, the Minister of Armaments and Munitions. Hitler took the letter and then – according to an eyewitness – laid it aside unopened 'thinking it was some unimportant memorandum'.

Finally he slit open the envelope while the apprehensive Pintsch waited. His eyes ran over the lines Hess had written . . . 'He had said that his action must not be interpreted as a sign of German weakness; on the contrary, he would lay stress on the military invincibility of his country and point out that Germany did not have to ask for peace,' remembers a former general, quoting Hitler himself.*

The general, Colonel-General Franz Halder, Hitler's Chief of Staff, writing the account in his diaries, quoted by Hess five years later in a letter,† said Hitler was taken completely by surprise by the Hess flight. The Führer immediately summoned Goering and Air-General Ernst Udet to the Berghof and went into deep discussion on the chances of Hess making it in the Messerschmitt, being shot down, or diving into the English Channel. Messerschmitt, the plane's designer, was ordered to await Goering's presence later in Munich to explain himself.

Ribbentrop was hurriedly packed off to Rome to inform the Duce of the shock 'departure'. ('In fact,' comments Hess, discussing Ribbentrop's panic trip, 'I had left word that I would tell the English that Italy was included in the arrangement as a condition *sine qua non*.')‡

Hitler was worried about the use Britain would make of the Hess sensation. Accordingly, the Führer himself dictated the statement that was to be put out through all German propaganda – that Hess was, in fact, mad.

* Otto Dietrich, *Hitler* (Henry Regnery, 1955).
† General Halder's Diaries, quoted by Hess in a letter to his mother, 7 April 1947.
‡ In a letter to his mother, 7 April 1947.

On the day after the flight, the BBC radio broadcast from London beamed at Germany announced that Hess was in Britain. 'Great Britain is the only place where Hess is safe from the German Gestapo. The fact that he flew 1,300 km by plane is enough to show that he is not, as the Nazis claim, "sick from nerves". This distance could only be flown by an experienced pilot and Hess was an experienced pilot. Also the fact that he flew 1,300 km in a fighter plane shows that he never intended to return to Germany. There would not be enough fuel for the flight back. So Hess wanted to flee from Germany.

'This shows us that something must be wrong in the Nazi clique. Hess is not a nervous-disease case; the Führer had appointed him as his successor, and only a few days ago Hess spoke to German workers. During his speech nobody saw any signs of insanity.

'No. Hess has seen where Hitler is leading the German people and made his decision to leave Hitler alone in the mess. This is the truth about the Hess Case.'

Germans who could pick up the British broadcasts secretly through their own country's heavy jamming had learned to trust the BBC. It was a firm rule at Bush House that *nothing* should be put out that was untrue. If that happened none of the London broadcasts would be trusted.

Now they were being told two conflicting theories: Hess was mad; Hess was running away from Hitler.

Hitler angrily got on to Dr Albrecht Haushofer★ on 12 May and ordered him to write a full confidential report on all that had been going on secretly between Germany and Britain to bring about peace negotiations. Haushofer sat down and wrote from Obersalzburg: 'The circle of English personalities which I have known very well for years, and whom I wanted to use to favorably influence a German-English understanding, as the core of my work in England in 1934-38, includes the following groups and personalities:

'(i) A leading group of younger Conservatives (many of them Scottish) including: the Duke of Hamilton, until the death of his father known as Lord Clydesdale, Conservative Member of Parliament; the Parliamentary Private Secretary of Neville Chamberlain,

★ A close friend of Hess, and son of the famous geo-politician, Hess's original teacher.

Lord Dunglass; the present Under Secretary of State in the Air Force Ministry, Balfour; the present Under Secretary of State in the Education Ministry, Lindsay (National Labour), the present Under Secretary of State in the Ministry for Scotland, Wedderburn.

'Close relations connect this group with the Court. The younger brother of the Duke of Hamilton is, through his wife, closely related to the present Queen. The mother-in-law of the Duke of Hamilton, the Duchess of Northumberland, is the highest-ranking private tutor at the Court; her brother-in-law, Lord Eustace Percy, was a member of the Cabinet several times and is today still an active and influential member of the Conservative Party (specially close to the former Prime Minister, Baldwin). There are close connections from this group to important groups of older Conservatives, and to the families Stanley (Lord Derby, Oliver Stanley) and Astor (owner of *The Times*). The young Astor, also Member of Parliament, was Parliamentary Private Secretary to the former Secretary of State for Foreign Affairs, and Home Secretary, Sir Samuel Hoare, now English Ambassador in Madrid.

'Most of the named personalities,' Haushofer went on, 'I have known for years and had close personal contact with them. The present Under Secretary of State of the Foreign Office, Butler, also belongs to this list; in spite of some of his public statements, he is not a Churchill or an Eden follower. There are many connections of those named, to Lord Halifax, to whom I also had personal access.

'(ii) The so-called "round-table" circle of younger Imperialists (foremost colonial and empire politicians), whose most important personality was Lord Lothian.

'(iii) A group of "assistant secretaries" in the Foreign Office. The most important were the Chief of the Middle European Department, Strang, and the Chief of the South-East Department, O'Malley, later Minister in Budapest.

'Hardly any of those listed were not at one time or another for an English-German settlement. Even though most of them thought the war to be unavoidable in 1939, it seemed reasonable to take these personalities into consideration, when one believes that the time has come to examine the possibility of a readiness for peace on the British side.

'That is why, when the Deputy of the Führer, Reichsminister Hess, asked me in the autumn of 1940 about possibilities of access to sensible Englishmen, I suggested concrete possibilities of taking up these connections. I thought the following should be taken into consideration:

'A. Personal contact with Lothian, Hoare or O'Malley – all three of whom can be reached in neutral countries.

'B. Contact by letter with one of my friends in England. For this purpose the Duke of Hamilton came into consideration first, because my relationship with him was so steadfast and personal that I could assume he would understand a letter written even in the most camouflaged words.

'Reichsminister Hess chose the second possibility. I consequently wrote a letter to the Duke of Hamilton at the end of September 1940, and organized its delivery to Lisbon through the Deputy of the Führer. I do not know if the letter reached the addressee. The possibility of the letter being lost between Lisbon and England was not small. In April 1941 I received greetings from Switzerland from the former Völkerbundskommisar in Danzig, and present Vice-President of the International Red Cross, Carl Burckhardt, whom I have also known very well for years. He said that he had greetings from my old English circle of friends to convey to me and that I should visit him in Geneva. Since there was a possibility that these greetings could be in connection with my letter of the past autumn, I thought I should inform the Deputy Führer again, of course pointing out (as I had in the autumn) that I thought the chances for serious peace feelers very slight. Reichsminister Hess decided that I should go to Geneva.

'I had a long talk with Burckhardt in Geneva on 28 April. I found Burckhardt in a certain conflict between his wish to serve the possibilities of a European peace, and his great concern that his name could somehow become public. He expressly asked to keep this event strictly secret. In view of the discretion he had to take, he could only tell me the following: several weeks ago, a "personality" had visited him in Geneva, a man well known and respected in London, and who was close to Conservative circles in the City. This personality, whose name he could not reveal, but for whose uprightness he could swear, had in the course of a long talk expressed the wish of important English circles to examine peace possibilities. In the search for possible channels, my name was mentioned.

'I then informed Professor Burckhardt that I would expect the same discretion as far as my name was concerned. If his contact in London would be willing to come to Switzerland again, and further, be willing to let his name be revealed to me confidentially in Berlin so that the uprightness of the person could be checked in Germany, then I believed that I could agree to another trip to Geneva. Professor Burckhardt was willing to deliver the message in this form: it would let it be known in England that the possibility existed for a confidant from London, after he had revealed his name, to meet a German personality, also well known in England, who was in a position to bring news to the proper German agencies.

'Concerning actual possible peace-talks, several essential points resulted from my own conversation with Professor Burckhardt. Burckhardt was not only in England during the war, but he also had long and detailed talks with Halifax for example, and he often has contact with the English observers in Geneva – Consul-General Livingston, for instance, who also is one of those Englishmen who gains no happiness from the war.

'Burckhardt's impression of the opinions of the moderate groups in England could be summarized as follows:

'(i) England's material interests in the eastern and south-eastern areas of Europe are nominal – with the exception of Greece.

'(ii) No English government which is still able to act will be able to do without a restoration of the western European States.

'(iii) The question of the Colonies will not make any major difficulties if the German demands are limited to the old German possessions, and Italy's appetite can be tamed.

'All this however – and this can't be stressed enough – under the over-riding pre-requisite that a personal trust can be found between Berlin and London; this will be as difficult to find as it was during the Crusades, or during the Thirty-Year War. The dispute with Hitlerism is viewed by the mass of the English people as a religious war, with all the fanatical, psychological consequences of such a point of view. If there is somebody ready for peace in London then it is the native part of the plutocracy, which can work out when, together with the native British tradition, Churchill will be destroyed. While the "foreign" elements, foremost the Jewish, will, for the most part, have already completed the jump to America and the Dominions overseas. Burckhardt's own deepest concern was that if the war lasted longer, every possibility of the rational forces in England forcing Churchill to make peace would disappear, while the entire power to decide over the overseas activities of the Empire would have been taken over by the Americans by that time.

'It would not be possible to have a sensible word with Roosevelt and his circle if the remainder of the native English upper class was shut out.

Albrecht Haushofer,
Obersalzburg, 12 May 1941.'

3

A Secret Drug

THE STORY OF Hess's imprisonment in England has been fully related and documented from the British side, but what was going through Hess's mind? He had flown to Britain genuinely believing that peace might result from his actions. He believed he would be dealing with the highest powers in the land, who would listen seriously to him and act on his suggestions.

Instead, he was imprisoned in an old house. His terms had been rebuffed, even laughed at. Hess, at this time, became convinced there was only one possible answer to this 'craziness' on the part of others: they were all either hypnotized or secretly drugged by some evil power. The evil power was, in his mind, the dread coalition of Jews and Bolsheviks.

'I had the impression,' Hess remembers,★ 'that most of the people who came to me for the first time had first been detained with tea or a meal before they were brought to me. This was also the case with Lord Simon when he visited me for a long conference on the orders of the British Government. He had the typical glassy and dream-like eyes.

'From my observations it can be gathered that people who are in this abnormal state of mind can be forced to put others in the same state. Field-Marshal Milch has said that he had the impression the Führer was not normal in the past years. I would say that the expression of the Führer's face and his eyes *had* changed in the last years; there was an expression of cruelty in it, if not of insanity.

'I am aware that what I have to say about what happened to me in my imprisonment in England will at first sound unbelievable.'

(Hess was sure, by now, that he was being slowly and systematically

★ Hess wrote this in his 'closing statement' he prepared for delivery at the Nuremberg Trial. But he was cut short by the Court and only some of it was delivered.

poisoned at Mytchett Place, and later at Maindiff Court where he was moved in June of 1942.)

'In the spring of 1942 I suffered from a stoppage of the bowels. The doctor gave me laxatives. They did not show the desired effect. Instead, very severe intestinal and stomach cramps started. Other laxatives did not show any other results. Some days later the stoppage was relieved after I had drunk some cocoa. After the next drink of cocoa, the stoppage returned. After repetitious happenings of this I had the suspicion that various medicines were put into the cocoa. I put little test amounts of the cocoa aside, and started experimenting. These experiments proved clearly that one kind of cocoa contained stuff that caused the stoppage, which could not be cured with normal laxatives, the other cocoa contained some antidote.

'The suffering was indescribable. If they had shot me or killed me with gas or even let me starve, it would have been humane in comparison. They began to add acids to the food as well. I found out by leaving a fork in the food; within a few hours the fork was covered with verdigris. The doctor was very embarrassed by this experiment. After meals I could often only sit, or walk bent with pain. In my desperation I scratched chalk off the walls, hoping this would have a neutralizing effect. But it was in vain.

'From time to time a Dr Rees from the British War Ministry came to see me.* He also had funny eyes when he visited me for the first time. He also used to speak of a case of autosuggestion which I had become a victim of. His case was especially grotesque because he was a psychiatrist of great fame. He had no idea that he should have been his own patient and when I told him so he didn't believe it and considered it a bad joke.'

On 21 November 1941, at dinner with some of the doctors, Rudolf Hess gave his first hint that he was 'losing his memory'. He had difficulty remembering words, or what had happened even an hour before, he said.† Two weeks later he said his memory had 'gone completely'. Hess was to remain in a state of amnesia or partial amnesia for almost two years. The doctors had little doubt that it was real.

'My memory failed quite a lot,' wrote Hess later.‡ 'At the same

* Dr Rees saw Hess and examined him 35 times, about 60 hours of interviews in all.
† See *The Case of Rudolf Hess*, ed. J. R. Rees (W. W. Norton, 1948).
‡ In his 'Last Word' statement.

time, I was constantly asked strange questions about my past. If I answered them correctly, they were disappointed. If I was not able to answer them, they were obviously pleased. So I proceeded to increasingly feign a lack of memory. They explained that they could bring back the memory with an injection. Since I had to remain constant in my "loss of memory", I could show no mistrust, and agreed. I had been told that the injection would be followed by a narcosis in which questions would be asked me that were supposed to connect the conscious with the sub-conscious. It was clear to me that they wanted to test in this way if the loss of memory was real.'

On 7 May 1944, after constant persuasion, Hess agreed to submit to an intravenous injection of the narcotic Evipan. He was told that while under its influence, he would remember the past he had forgotten.

At 2045 hrs 5.5 cc of sodium Evipan solution was slowly injected intravenously in the presence of two doctors, and a sergeant and corporal of the Royal Army Medical Corps.*

2110 hrs Dr Dicks (psychiatrist) enters and stands by Hess's bed.

2110 hrs Dr Dicks tells Hess: 'You will now be able to recall all the names and faces of your dear ones. Your memory will return. We are all here to help you . . .'

2112 hrs Groans.

Dr Dicks: What's the matter?

Hess: Pains! In my belly! Oh if only I were well. Bellyache. Water! Water! Thirst!

D: Remember your little son's name?

H: I don't know.

D: Do you remember your good friends, Haushofer . . .

H: No.

D: Willi Messerschmitt?

H: No (groans). Bellyache! Oh God!

D: . . . And all the stirring times with Adolf Hitler in Munich.

H: No.

D: You were with him in the fortress at Landsberg.

H: No.

D: You will recall all the other parts of your past.

H: Recall all the other parts.

* *The Case of Rudolf Hess.*

D': Recall all the great events of your life.

H: All the great events . . .

The session ended at 2215 hrs and the doctors noted afterwards: 'At no point did the patient make a spontaneous remark: the sole unprovoked utterances were groans. This was followed by repeated exhortations that here were all his old doctors eager to help him, but he sat up and said: "Water please, and some food."'

Hess himself says* he knew all the time what was going on – he was *faking* unconsciousness.

'I even let them give me injections against loss of memory. After initially resisting, I had no choice in the matter if I was not to strengthen the already long-held suspicion that I was at least exaggerating.

'Fortunately I was told in advance that it was not certain that my memory would return in response to the injections. But the worst part of it was that the procedure was attended by anaesthetic in which questions were to be put to me designed to "re-unite" the upper and lower levels of consciousness. On this occasion, that is to say in a state of semi-consciousness or daze, the swindle was bound to come to light. But as I've just said, it was impossible for me in the end to do otherwise than to give my consent. I then managed, by the exercise of all the will at my disposal, to retain consciousness – although I was given more of the injection than was usually done – but at the same time I simulated unconsciousness.

'Of course I answered all the questions by saying "I don't know" in the intervals between the words.

'In a low voice, tonelessly, absent-mindedly. VVV.† I only remembered my name which I breathed out in a whisper in the same manner.

'Finally I decided to "come to", looking surprised as I slowly came back into the world. It was a great piece of play-acting and a complete success, at least so far as the deception was concerned. VVV. Now they believed me implicitly. But it didn't help me. My hope that I was to be sent home in the course of an exchange of prisoners remained merely a dream. At various times it was indicated that I would be on board the Swedish hospital ship. But then she sailed away without me, the next time, and all the other times as well.

'How much the doctors were convinced that my loss of memory was

* Letter to his mother from Nuremberg, 5 July 1947.

† VVV was a sign of amusement constantly used in letters by Hess and his wife.

genuine, as a result of the experiments under anaesthetic, is clear from the fact that later on when I decided, for particular reasons, to give up my deception – and that was once in England – the doctors at first would not believe it.

'It was only when I repeated to them all the questions that they had put to me during my "unconscious" state, and when I repeated the play-acting of my "coming to" and put on the mode of speech and tone which I used at that time, it was only then that they admitted how I had pulled their legs.'

Hess's memory remained 'lost' until 4 February 1945, when he admitted to the doctors that his amnesia had been simulated. Dr Dicks wrote in his report*: 'The patient has made a very dramatic recovery from the temporary affection of his memory, which now functions very fully and accurately. I cannot accept his own statement that the memory loss never existed. There was at that time a true partial dissociation of the personality, which permitted the patient to "take in" what was going on around him but caused difficulty of recall. It is a case of preferring to have duped us to having shown temporary weakness.'

But by July 1945, Hess's memory had 'gone' again. Psychiatrist Major D. Ellis Jones wrote on 19 July: 'The loss of memory is again grotesque; e.g. loss of memory of prominent places in Berlin, that he was the Deputy Führer, failing to recognize one nurse who has been here for two years etc.'

Hess's version†: 'Slowly my memory returned fully, even though the brain poison was given to me for at least two years. The latter was the reason that I continued to pretend to have a loss of memory. I kept this up until after the beginning of the proceedings, since I suspected that otherwise I would never be admitted to the proceedings and would never have the chance to make my exposure to the public. Only after the danger appeared that I was not in a state to take part in the proceedings and would have to be excluded, did I admit my manoeuvre. But since I was given a brain poison on each possible occasion in Nuremberg I again took to "feigning a lack of memory" in an increasing manner. Only at the moment I began to make my closing statement did I let my memory "return".'

★ *The Case of Rudolf Hess.*

† 'Last Word' statement.

Meanwhile at Nuremberg preparations were being made for the world's most spectacular trial. In anticipation of Rudolf Hess's arrival from England, his old professor and mentor, Dr Karl Haushofer, was taken into the court offices to be questioned about his former pupil.

Haushofer had himself been in a concentration camp – Dachau. He looked ill when, on 5 October 1945, he was led into the interview room. In the course of his long cross-examination the following points emerged:

Q. In your previous interrogation, you have said that you had a very intimate acquaintanceship with Hess?

A. Yes.

Q. Was he a former student of yours?

A. He was a former student of mine, and I knew Hess long before the National Socialist Party existed.

Q. Did you find him to be an attentive student?

A. Yes. He was a very attentive student but, you see, his strong side was not intelligence but heart and character, I should say. He was not very intelligent.

Q. Did you find that he evidenced interest in the subject matter that you taught?

A. He had a great interest and he worked very hard, but, you see, at that time in Munich there were all those students' and officers' associations, a very strong political movement, and so the young men were always drawn away from their work.

Q. Did you feel that you had a great deal of influence in moulding his ideas?

A. I had a moral influence on him but there was a competition between the political influences and the scientific influences.

Q. But your conclusion is that you did have considerable influence in moulding his ideas as to his future conduct?

A. Yes. My influence was only good as far as he was under my eyes and I could check up on him. I have to honestly say now that up to the time of his flying away he was very much devoted to me and he protected me and my family from bad experiences with the Party.

Q. Were you able to maintain a close intimate relationship with him during all that time?

A. Yes. I tried to point out to him, perhaps, out of twenty things only two that came to my knowledge which I thought were wrong, but otherwise the Party used to tear him away from me.

Q. Was he a man who had great persuasive powers on other people?

A. No. He had no knowledge of human beings and he had often been betrayed by the people surrounding him.

Q. Isn't it a fact that there was a great personal affection for him on the part of Hitler?

A. He had a blind devotion to Hitler and you can say that the relationship from him to Hitler was an obedient relationship.

Q. But I meant in the other direction. Wasn't Hitler devoted to Hess because of a personal friendship?

A. I was always of the opinion that Rudolf Hess was far more devoted to his idol than his idol was devoted to him.

Q. But I have heard that Hitler considered Hess as a great friend for the discussion of philosophy and subjects such as geo-politics.

A. Hitler, who himself was only semi-educated, had noticed that Hess, through his knowledge of books and academic education, was far more educated in these fields than he was himself.

Q. Don't you think from that Hitler was influenced a great deal by Hess?

A. Hitler knew just as little about these things as Hess knew himself, and I am of the impression that Hess, right up to 1935, was convinced that everything would come to a peaceful solution.

Q. But you haven't answered my question. I may not have made it clear to you. I would like to know if, in your opinion, the ideas that Hitler had with respect to matters relating to geo-politics and other matters that come from books, if you don't think Hitler got many of those ideas from Hess.

A. He certainly has been told about these things by Hess, but I received the impression, and I am utterly convinced, that Hitler has never understood these things and he did not have the right outlook for understanding them.

Q. I understand that his ideas on Lebensraum were never completely explained to Hitler.

A. When I formed my opinions on the basis of the English authors and Ratzel and Kjellen and others, Germany at that time was in a very terrible condition as regards frontiers and Lebensraum, and this is why he adopted this conception in many of his speeches, because they were very close to him, but without really understanding them.

Q. But Hitler, being an uneducated man, would talk at great length on the subjects of Lebensraum and geo-politics. Don't you believe he got those ideas from Hess?

A. Yes. These ideas came from Hess to Hitler, but he had never really understood them, and he has never really read about them from the original books. He never read these books.

Q. Did you ever talk to Hitler?

A. Very seldom, because, you see, this was a thing which was often mentioned in your press. My visits to Landsberg were always meant for Hess, he being my pupil.

Q. Isn't it true that Hess collaborated with Hitler in writing *Mein Kampf*?

A. As far as I know, Hess actually dictated many chapters of that book. Hess was able to type, while Hitler was not.

Q. Then, do I understand that you would discuss these matters with Hess and then Hess in turn would discuss them with Hitler and that is how they got into the book?

A. In matters where I saw that neither Hitler nor Hess had any geographical idea, I tried to visit Hess and tried to explain to him the basis of Ratzel's book, dealing with political geography.

Q. Did you find that in all instances that the correct version that you gave would be adapted by Hitler?

A. I always had the impression by his speeches that he never really understood them.

Q. But did you have the idea that he had made an attempt to adopt your teachings?

A. He sometimes made attempts, but, you see, I remember quite well, whenever Hess understood such things and tried to explain it to Hitler, Hitler usually came out with one of his new ideas about an autobahn or anything else which had nothing to do with it, while Hess just stood there and did not say any more about it.

Q. Who would you say had the most influence with Hitler; was it Hess or Ribbentrop, with respect to your teachings?

A. Hitler was never really influenced by Hess very much, but he thought, rightly, that he could count on his devotion, but he really in the end treated him very badly.

Q. Then you believe that the expressions Hitler made were in fact a reflection of your ideas as contained in your books?

A. They were nearly always misunderstood. For instance, he has never really understood the distinction that I made between oceanic and continental policy.

Q. But when you explained that there was a misunderstanding, would you go to Hess and try to straighten him out so they would get your ideas?

A. Yes. Then I tried to go to Hess.

Q. There was always an attempt on your part to try to get your ideas into operation through Hess and to Hitler?

A. I always told him about them whenever I had a feeling that things were being done in a wrong manner.

Q. When you say 'in the wrong manner', you mean contrary to your teachings? You were sincere in all of the things that you taught?

A. I think that whatever I have written, I have written to the best of my capability and knowledge. I have to say here that I am a very incomplete scientist.

Q. When you say that things would go wrong or that Hitler would have a mistaken idea about something, you mean by that that he would do something contrary to what you were teaching?

A. Yes, absolutely contrary to my opinions and my teaching. In order to give a short example: Prague, the breaking of the Munich agreement.

Q. When you would see those things, you would then go to Hess and try to persuade him to have Hitler change his tactics?

A. I have tried that and I have had some very bad experiences and at last, as you well know, I was in Dachau as a result of that.

Q. Why did you go to the jail in Landsberg?

A. Because Rudolf Hess had been my pupil and I am not used to leaving comrades and pupils alone.

Q. What did you talk about?

A. Mainly about his work. I talked to him about geography.

Q. Isn't it a fact that some parts of the book [*Mein Kampf*] were written by you?

A. No. This is not a fact. Usually I am not conceited, but I must say that I could never have written such a bad book.

Q. Are you familiar with Chapter 14?

A. I must honestly say that I don't know it.

Q. In this chapter there is a great deal about Lebensraum and about the need for living space.

A. Naturally, Hess had heard a lot about these matters in my lectures between 1920 and 1924. I had to speak about these things in order to be honest.

Q. Don't you find a great similarity between the contents of the book and your teachings with regard to Lebensraum and such methods?

A. No, I am sure that he did not understand many parts of my ideas as to Lebensraum. For instance, I often pointed out to him that our policy for concentrating people in cities was a wrong one, and I pointed out to him the difference in some of the Eastern countries that were far more thickly populated than our own country.

Q. Did you find anything in the book that was consonant with your teachings, agreeable to your teachings?

A. No. I must say that when Rudolf Hess brought me the book the first time – I think it was in '35, soon after its publication – I was quite unhappy. When I first saw this book I was very much against it, apart from other things also because of his racial ideas. I don't know if the Colonel knows that I have been married to an non-Aryan happily for the last fifty years.

Q. So then from 1922 to 1933 you were in complete disagreement with the principles of the National Socialist Party?

A. I wasn't in any Party, but if I was close at all to any Party it was the Party of Stresemann, the German People's Party.

Q. But during that time you maintained your close friendship with Hess?

A. Yes, that was the old friendship of an old soldier towards a young soldier.

Q. Getting back to the early days, did you cooperate with Hess in the formation of the Party or in the performance of his work?

A. No, never. I never had anything to do with Party organizations. I have never been a member of the Party, and when I was first approached by Hess and he asked me to become a member of the Party, I answered him like this: 'I do not have the inclination to become a Party comrade.'

Q. Hess became number two in Germany, didn't he?

A. I think his burden was far too big for him, not for his heart and character, but considering his intelligence.

Q. But during all this time you counselled him, didn't you?

A. If he asked me about any certain subjects, I gave him honest advice, which was only very seldom adhered to.*

* The above extracts are from the verbatim report on the Haushofer interview. The original is held in the National Archives in Washington.

4

At Nuremberg

ON THE EVENING of 10 October 1945 an army ambulance, escorted by two jeep-loads of guards, sped into Nuremberg Prison. Out of it, wearing his flying boots and an old coat, stepped Rudolf Hess. He looked thin and puzzled. His face and body were bony, the dark eyebrows accentuating the protrusion of his forehead bone. His blue eyes looked haunted and suspicious. He had been flown from Abergavenny to Furth, near Nuremberg, and had apparently had no time to shave. The stubble was showing on his sunken cheeks and his wide, firmly-set upper lip. It had been four years and five months since he had last seen Germany. Now all he had seen of it was a glimpse or two from the ambulance window on the way from Furth.

First he was taken to the search room where his clothes and body were carefully gone over for hidden suicide weapons. On the way to the room he passed Goering who was being brought along the corridor. Hess stopped as their eyes met. He instantly recognized Goering and threw up his right arm in the Nazi salute. He was quickly told that such a salute was banned in Nuremberg. Goering went on his way, smiling.

Hess, his face now expressionless, was taken into the office of the Nuremberg Commandant, Colonel Burton C. Andrus,* who outlined the prison rules to him. Hess merely said: 'They have taken some chocolates away from me in the search room. I want them back. I want to keep them . . . they are poisoned. It is one of the efforts the British made to poison me. I want them for my future defence . . .'

When the formalities with the Commandant were over, Hess was taken off to his 12ft by 6ft stone cell in the huge jail. Along the stone corridors in similar cells were Goering, Schacht, von Papen, Fritzscho, Julius Streicher, Keitel, Jodl, and Doenitz, Sauckel, Speer and von

* Burton C. Andrus, *I Was the Nuremberg Jailer* (Coward-McCann, 1969).

34

Schirach, Rosenberg, Funk, Ley, von Neurath, Raeder, Kaltenbrunner, Frick and Frank, Ribbentrop and Seyss-Inquart. All his former colleagues; the men he had flown away from four-and-a-half years before. What would they say to him, these men who, like him, were getting ready to stand trial for their very lives? Would there be hate? Compassion? Ridicule? Only time would tell.

Quietly, Rudolf Hess settled himself in his cell. He took out a pencil and a sheet of paper, and began writing his diary. It was to tell, with short gaps, the story of his stay in Nuremberg.

Arrived 10 Oct. '45.★ Goering and an old gentleman who is supposed to have been acquainted with me for a long time were brought face to face with me, apparently in order to ascertain whether I would recognize them. I did not recognize them.

13 Oct. I was asked for a signature to a library slip. I stated that I would not sign anything that was not filled out. I made a cross on the slip and then put my signature to it. A few days ago my teeth were examined. At the conclusion of the examination I was to put my signature at the foot of the dental form which specified the teeth found to be defective.

I refused: the dentist had to confirm this in writing. Goering tried for an hour to refresh my memory – in vain. He told me that when I flew to England I should have left a letter behind for the Führer.

17 Oct. Great excitement because I made a fuss because I had not received the things I'd asked for from my luggage. Afterwards I was told that I could make a complaint to the Commandant but that I must not shout at people. American doctor prescribed white bread for my stomach. The promised injection to restore my memory is said to have not yet been administered because judges do not consider it necessary that my memory be restored. I said that it was extremely important for *me*. The doctor said he would do what he could about this.

Have hung up small notices in the cell saying: 'Quiet please. Do not shout at people.' One of the officers who came in said this was a good idea.

18 Oct. The American doctor was quite definite in his assurance that my memory would be brought back by one single injection.

★ Hess had the date of his arrival wrong by two days. Apart from any such correction and the omission of tedious passages, I will let the diary tell Hess's story. As far as possible, it will be uninterrupted, except for necessary inserts. E.K.B.

19 Oct. Indictment handed to me. One hundred pages. I thumbed it through in five to ten minutes and read the headings.

20 Oct. Given long form to fill up (relating to future occupation, religion, whether and why I had left the Church and so on). Only filled in my name.

Notification that trial starts on 21 Nov.

21 Oct. This evening told the officer of the court who is accessible to the accused that I would not appoint defence counsel and it was a matter of complete indifference to me whether IMC [International Military Court] appointed defence counsel for me or not. They wanted me to put this in writing.

22 Oct. Large quantity of blood taken from me for testing purposes. Was not fetched for exercise today. Wrote to the Secretary-General of IMC that I would not appoint defence counsel and that it was a matter of indifference to me whether one was appointed by IMC or not.

Wrote to the Commandant to complain because I had not been shaved for two to three days. American doctor asks me why I have not read the indictment. Said there was no point in my doing so because I would forget the contents anyway. Said I might take a look at it shortly before the trial. Doctor admitted that this was more sensible.

23 Oct. I complained to the military doctor about being *compelled* to take the sleeping draught in the evening when I asked for one. He stands and waits while I take it, instead of being allowed to put it down and swallow it if necessary when required. He said it was an order. American doctor recommends insulin injections to get my weight up before having the injection to restore my memory. I refused. I asked to be given raw apples instead. The doctor said insulin was completely harmless and more natural than vitamins! In spite of this I stuck to my refusal.

Asked if I would like to see my son. I said only after the trial was over. Half an hour later the German doctor came in with a syringe in his hand to give me an insulin injection. I again refused. (Sleeping tablet.)

24 Oct. American doctor came and inquired after my appetite. I said I could hardly be expected to have much appetite in view of the small amount of exercise I got. (Washing list: one shirt, one collar, one pair underpants, two handkerchiefs.) German doctor advises me to try at

least one insulin injection. I replied that I would think about it. He
said the two American doctors only want to do what is best for me.

25 Oct. Weight 65 kilos – lost one kilo.

26 Oct. American doctor comes to tell me I have lost a lot of weight
since 1941, judging by photographs he has seen. I said I was sure I
would soon regain my former weight once I was set free. Weather
in the afternoon was good but I was not taken out into the open air.

27 Oct. Two American doctors came saying they were sure my loss
of weight was a worry to me. They urged me to agree to have
injections; they were quite harmless. I replied that I preferred to get
my weight back by completely natural means; as soon as I were free
I would put on weight again. The doctors said they 'only wanted to
make me feel more comfortable'. I thanked them for their good
intentions. Had no opportunity to get out into the open air.

28 Oct. German doctor says I should reconsider insulin question.

29 Oct. A chair was put into my room. I was told it would be taken
out every evening and brought back again in the morning. I said I
didn't need any chair.

A document was brought to me to read and sign, relating to lighting.
It said everything was being done to protect the prisoners from
harm, and that it had not been possible to save one of the prisoners
who had committed suicide. German doctor measured my height. No
evacuation: constipated.

30 Oct. Was taken to a building next door. Masses of documents in
my handwriting were put in front of me in sealed packets, which I
was told had been brought from England with me. I couldn't remember
anything about the documents or packages. The packets – one of which
I opened – contained samples of medicines and foods which I assumed
to contain harmful substances (poisons). I was assured that the documents – which appear to be of great importance – would be handed to
me after translation, before the trial started. I have not officially handed
over the documents however and have not for instance taken them as
the basis for my defence.

31 Oct. No opportunity for exercise. Weather good. No evacuation.

1 Nov. Ditto. List of documents handed to me. Notification that
IMC had appointed defence counsel for me and that he would be
coming in two days' time.

2 Nov. Lawyer came. Told him I regard the entire trial as a farce and that the judgement would be a foregone conclusion, also that I regard the Court as not competent. Lawyer said there were suggestions in the Press that I might not be fit to stand trial. I replied that I did not wish to be separated from my colleagues and wished to be heard with them and to share their fate.

3 Nov. Lawyer came and I said to him that I had the impression that he also believed my loss of memory was only simulated. A defence counsel who thinks his client does not tell him the truth and has no trust in him cannot expect any trust. The work of defence counsel only makes sense provided there is mutual trust. He replied that he had only wanted to indicate what the Court would assume, and was not giving his own opinion. He added that his position was very difficult in view of the absence of any help from me. He wanted to have time until Monday to reconsider whether he was prepared to take on my defence. He asked whether I knew I was the only one who had been *shackled*, and whether he should enter a plea?

I said no. The shackling was another thing that left me cold.

He talked about my flight to England of which I had, however, no recollection.

American doctor came: I ought to put on weight. Digestion needed putting right. He was in favour of natural remedies, so he wanted to give me some dried prunes. No evacuation.

4 Nov. American psychologist came and carried out a few exercises with me aimed at training my power of concentration and memory. He is convinced that both things will come right and that the stimulus of the trial would have a favourable effect. No evacuation.

5 Nov. German doctor gave me a purgative (tablet) which had no effect. Was given exercise in the prison gymnasium. The sun is shining outside. Psychologist came to me with a number of questions which he read out from a table. The required answers which I had learnt in my youth (geographical terms and the like) were familiar to me. Psychologist said what mattered was that I gradually became able to recall events which had taken place in the recent past. He was convinced that this would happen.

The lawyer declared that he was prepared to take on my defence. I refused to give him a power of attorney; he should get this from the Court.

6 Nov. Cell ice-cold. No heating. Mentioned this to American doctor, who discovers that windows are broken. Will do what he can to see heating restored. (9 am.) Beakers of drinking water stand on the heating pipes which however are cold. No heating on either day or night.

Told lawyer that due to the fact I do not recognize the validity of the Court I would not enter any pleas and would not give my consent to any that he might make (e.g.) appointing a neutral medical expert. I also told him he should not order any newspaper for me without first getting my permission. No evacuation.

7 Nov. Still no heating on. German lawyer showed me an article in a German newspaper about the alleged reasons for my flight to England. Heating and windows repaired. It is warm again. *Evacuation.*

8 Nov. An old gentleman – no American or Englishman, possibly a Soviet Russian – examined me. Reflexes, etc. And put questions designed to test my memory. A woman interpreter whispered to the English doctor that the old gentleman found that some of my answers were humorous.

Shown a film of a National Socialist Congress in which I appeared at various points. I would not have recognized myself unless I had been mentioned. This was a showing for me, personally, and there were some 40 to 50 Americans, and some Russians, present.

9 Nov. Lawyer shows me a report from an English paper about yesterday's film-showing. Cell over-heated in the evening. Tried but failed to open the window. Handed in laundry.

10 Nov. Medical examination by American. More blood samples taken, allegedly in order to find out what my loss of memory is due to. I protest about this. I say my loss of weight is the result of having too little to eat and taking too little exercise and that as soon as I regain my freedom, my weight will go up. I am to get biscuits, sugar, etc., as additions to my diet.

11 Nov. Was photographed with a shield bearing my name. Apparently for a 'Rogues' Gallery'.

12 Nov. In spite of daily pains in stomach and bowels have received no white bread for eight days.

13 Nov. Asked lawyer to write to wife and mother.

15 Nov. Examined by a Paris professor regarding memory. He suggested injections, electric-shock treatment or shock by reunion with family. I rejected the last-mentioned proposal particularly.

16 Nov. Lawyer showed me a report in the paper about my being examined by the medical board and stating that the doctors were considering whether I was fit to stand trial. Letter to my wife sent.

17 Nov. Two of my former secretaries★ were sent in to me. I did not recognize them. One of them brought photographs of home. Both are 'housed' in the prison, although one of them is no longer under detention but works in an American hospital. The interrogating officer who was present attempted to use this opportunity to provoke me by asking me three times how I knew the two ladies were not lying to me. At the third time I said very sharply that he should accept my assurance that Germans of my acquaintance would not lie to me; at which he shouted how did I know that Goering was not, among other things, a common criminal, a pickpocket or the like? To which I replied that it was not usual, in Germany anyway, to appoint pickpockets as ministers.

18 Nov. I notified the officers that I had a declaration to make to a suitable member of the International Military Court. Received no answer.

19 Nov. Communicated my message of the previous day in writing to the Commandant.

20 Nov. Start of the trial. Very tiring. I spent most of the time reading the Bavarian peasant novel *Der Loisl*. Or relaxing with my eyes closed. Nothing that went on at the hearing remains in my memory. Defence counsel told me that the officer on the evening before between 10.30 pm and 11 pm had come to see him in a state of great perturbation. The defence counsel was of the opinion that it was to do with the declaration of the lawyers which I wanted to see before it was issued.

21 Nov. Goering was prevented from making a plea of guilty or not guilty. In my case, in a fit of anger, I merely said very emphatically, 'No!' Hearing monotonous and tiring. Read or slept most of the time.

22 Nov. Hearing as on the previous day. Psychologist asked if I was able to follow. I said I did not intend to. He said I must try to remember something or other of the statements made at the hearing. It was important what the Führer had said to me. I said this was interesting

★ When Hess first saw his wife and son at their 1969 visit he asked: 'How is Hildegard Fath? Please give her my apologies for the way I acted in front of her, way back *then*.' An admission that he was feigning lack of memory and non-recognition.

and important for me personally, and also one day for the German people. But this was of no concern to the rest of the world or to the foreigners present in the court. I was asked about the 'interesting' novel I was reading. I replied that the novel was not particularly interesting but the court proceedings were particularly uninteresting to me. He said the proceedings were concerned with my life. I said that was so, irrespective of whether I listened to the foreigners' talk or not.

In the evening before the start of the hearing, an American doctor and the psychologist appeared in my cell and asked me how I felt. I replied that I did not feel otherwise than I usually did. 'But this trial is a matter of life and death!' I was told. I said I knew this, but I did not regard life as such an important matter. The doctor said most people did. I replied that I differed from most people in this respect. He thought this was a good way of looking at things and that it would certainly help me to sleep well. I replied that I would certainly not sleep worse than usual.

23 Nov. Hearing the same as ever. Childhood memories of a Flemish writer, entitled *Youth*, read out in court.

24 Nov. Trial adjourned for a break. I get photographed in the cell while I am reading. American doctor says to me I might shortly be transferred to a hospital for examination. I said I would agree to this after the trial was over.

25 Nov. The War Criminals' Library, which the German POW Strent (a bank clerk from Berlin) has booked out from the prison library, is very good. Bismarck's thoughts and recollections was not allowed.

On Nov. 24 in the evening the German doctor told me that a sleeping tablet fell out of his hand at the door and that I should put it on the table next morning. I could not find it. Sent von Schirach cigarettes and tobacco, Funk cigars, through the German doctor. The Protestant American Army chaplain asked whether I would care to attend a public service of worship which he had obtained permission to hold and which the defendants were to be allowed to attend, and whether he might visit me in the course of the week. I replied that if I did this, I might give the impression of being so lacking in character, in contrast to earlier times, as to attend a service of worship and to ask for the ministrations of a clergyman because I was facing a death sentence. I therefore asked him not to visit me, glad as I was, in normal times, occasionally to discuss some problem or other with a clergyman. I take it he understood the reason for my refusal. He did not reply and did not look at me in a particularly friendly manner. I thought to myself I wished him the power to maintain the same inner composure as I did.

26 Nov. During a pause in the trial I said to Sauckel, 'There is a Power – call it what you will – which is greater than the power of the Jews.' Sauckel said he believed that was true. Papen and Seyss-Inquart, who were sitting near me, and heard my words, nodded their approval. I went on to say that something like a miracle would happen, and that before our heads rolled!

27 Nov. The psychologist said to Goering that my stomach and abdominal cramps were psycho-somatic in origin. Soon afterwards Goering said to me that the cramps were 'hysterical' and that this was the opinion of the German doctor as well. I replied that he would one day learn the truth. My defence counsel said at the end of today's hearing that the decision would probably be taken on Friday as to whether or not I was fit to stand trial. That the decision would presumably be that I was not. I asked him to point out that I felt myself and regarded myself to be fit to stand trial, and wished to continue to take part in the court proceedings. Counsel and Goering thereupon exchanged knowing looks.

Four o'clock in the afternoon, a special session to decide the question whether I am fit to stand trial. One minute before the start, I said to my counsel that I had decided to say that my memory had returned. He turned away in some perturbation and said: 'Do as you wish.' Whereupon he started delivering a summing-up which lasted about an hour. He argued against my fitness to stand trial because without memory I would not be in a position to defend myself or to provide him with the necessary information to enable him to defend me. Although he was bound to add that I myself regarded myself as being fit to stand trial. He goes on endlessly reading out from the medical reports. I send him a message saying that the whole matter could be shortened by letting me speak. He takes no notice of this but goes on speaking for a long time. After that the prosecuting counsel talk one after the other, likewise at great length, in the course of which they suggest that I may be exaggerating my condition and alleged loss of memory. They likewise read extracts from the medical reports and quote from massive law-books. The judges also have their say and argue to and fro regarding the consequences of my loss of memory and its effect on my fitness to stand trial. One of the judges points out to the American prosecutor Jackson that I apparently wish to be cross-examined. Jackson replies that he does not believe this wish to be genuine and presumably counts on the arguments of the defence counsel in favour of unfitness to stand trial to be stronger than my alleged wish.

After about two hours of argument, the President of the Tribunal submits that I ought perhaps be allowed to speak.

After further argument from his defence counsel, Hess took the microphone, at the same time pulling a paper from his pocket. He began: 'Mr President, I would like to say this: at the beginning of this afternoon's proceedings I gave my counsel a note that I am of the opinion that these proceedings could be shortened if they would allow me to speak myself. What I say is as follows:

'In order to anticipate any possibility of my being declared incapable of pleading, although I am willing to take part in the rest of the proceedings with the rest of them, I would like to give the Tribunal the following declaration, although I originally intended not to make this declaration until a later point in the proceedings.

'My memory is again in order. The reasons why I simulated loss of memory were tactical. In fact, it is only that my capacity for concentration is slightly reduced. But in consequence of that, my capacity to follow the trial, my capacity to defend myself, to put questions to witnesses or even to answer questions – these, my capacities, are not influenced by that.

'I emphasize the fact that I bear the full responsibility for everything that I have done or signed as signatory or co-signatory. My attitude, in principle, is that the Tribunal is not competent – is not affected by the statement I have just made. Hitherto in conversations with my official defence counsel I have maintained loss of memory. He was, therefore, speaking in good faith when he asserted I lost my memory.'

There was a buzz across the court. The President said simply: 'The trial is adjourned.' And the radio and Press commentators dashed for their phones.

Hess's diary described the event: 'I pointed to the message which

I had sent to the defence counsel and then proceeded to read my statement. The faces of the judges, prosecutors and so on were not very intelligent, and some of them sat there with their mouths open. Laughter broke out from the Press box and then the reporters dashed to the doors. The session was adjourned.

Immediately after this a message was sent to me that the Court wished to have the text of my statement for the files. I took my time and first had a meal in peace.

My counsel does not seem to be pleased at all about my action. He said I would achieve the opposite of what I wished to and that now I would certainly be found to be unfit to stand trial. He said he now had to admit that he himself was more convinced than ever that I was suffering from a hysterical and psychopathic aberration. The same applies to my colleague, Goering.

The American doctor, Major Kelley, comes to me. Highly pleased. Saying he had never trusted me completely, but some of his prominent colleagues had been completely taken in. He was bursting with joy and said he must congratulate me on this fine piece of play-acting.

He was going straight to Goering. He must see what sort of a face he made when he heard. He asked me whether I remembered the individual packages which I brought with me from England.

'Of course,' I told him. He asked me what I thought about them. I was still a bit mistrustful, I said.

When I met Goering in the court-room he could not contain himself for astonishment. He was thrilled that the Court should have debated for two hours and then let me make my statement. All the accused had firmly believed in the genuineness of my complaint.

Ribbentrop was so astonished he could not say anything. Goering and Doenitz listened to some 'proofs' of my good memory. I told Doenitz that I had last met him at Wilhelmshaven on the occasion of my Christmas speech in 1939. In the Casino at tea he had been sitting on my right. I had asked him whether he had had other commanders, apart from Prien, who could have sailed to Scapa.

Goering kept on slapping his thigh with glee over the fact that I had so deceived the English and the Americans! He said that he himself had lost the last shred of doubt when he was present when I was confronted with Haushofer and I asked in astonishment how it came about that we were on terms of intimacy.

He also said that I had the ability to look as if I were absent-minded.

In the Standing Orders of the Tribunal it is stated that the accused has the right of cross-examining witnesses, or having them cross-examined by his defence counsel. However, when accused tried to make use of this right, the Court withdrew to discuss the matter, and decided that this would only be allowable where the accused conducts his own defence. Since none of the accused did this, but each was represented by a lawyer, the cross-questioning of witnesses by accused was ruled out of order.

Von Schirach maintained, in conversation with me, that the Führer was mad at the end of his life. Schirach made a number of insulting remarks about the Führer.

2 Dec. The librarian, POW Streng, brought me a supplementary list of books from which I could compile a list so that he could provide me with the books I needed. I made a list of about 20 books. He then brought me a book which I had not included in my list. The POW from Vienna behaved very rudely.

3 Dec. I saw my name on some notes made by Grand Admiral Doenitz. When I asked him about this he said that he had told his defence counsel the story of how I had proved to him that I was in full possession of my memory, by referring to the occasion on which we had first met. I asked Doenitz's defence counsel, a naval judge-advocate, through his client, to lay his newspaper on my place in front of me in such a manner that I could read the paragraph relating to me. He made a point of not complying with this request. Quite independently of this incident, Rosenberg told me that he had the impression that the defence counsel literally hated their clients.

Ribbentrop's defence counsel tells him that the defendants ought to be clear in their minds that the defence counsel are not their clients' 'lackeys'.

4 Dec. My new defence counsel tells me he once represented the Berlin taxi-drivers' union.

8 Dec. Goering said to me that the doctors had told him that my cramps were of a hysterical nature and asked me whether I couldn't do anything about it? I said yes I could – by giving the doctor concerned a good box on the ears. But that was not advisable at the present time. Doenitz agreed with me.

Streicher and I are not on speaking terms. It has been noticed by the Americans.

9 Dec. I asked for my fountain pen back, which I brought with me from England. The doctor has no objection to me having it. I predicted to the psychologist that it would take at least two weeks before I got it, if I ever did. He replied that he was going to pledge his honour as an officer that I would receive it within three hours. I was then asked for the receipt which I had been given for the valuables I had handed in. I could give an assurance that I had never received any such receipt. I was then told that the pen was not in existence.

10 Dec. Food tasted strongly of something as bitter as gall.

11 Dec. Since the food tasted so bitter, my cramps have ceased. I presume this was due to some homeopathic effect.

24 Dec. I spent the morning thinking about the composition of the Senat of the Greater German Reich. The table in my cell is threatening to collapse. But now they have accepted my own suggestion for putting in brackets. Fritzsche had the chance of linking up with the West or the East, but Fritzsche said he thought the only possibility was to link up with the Jews! He stuck to this opinion with great stubbornness.

3 Jan. 46. I complain that I am not allowed to take exercise in half shoes instead of boots. Boots could give me a weak heart. The Commandant says this instruction was issued in order to make it difficult to run away! But the other prisoners were allowed to take their exercise in half shoes.

5 Jan. Schacht tells me that in 1938 he planned an attack on the life of the Führer which unfortunately came to nothing because young officers failed to play their part.

7 Jan. The Press has been saying that it is a pity the Jewish lawyers are not back in business in Germany. They could have defended the accused far better than the present counsel and the whole procedure would have been conducted at a better level.

22 Jan. My defence counsel has broken his ankle. Dr Stahmer, who gave me this news, suggested he took over my defence. I would rather conduct my own defence. Seyss-Inquart's defence counsel tells me my counsel has asked him to take over until my counsel is well again. I tell him I have decided to conduct my own defence. He insisted that this would not be to my advantage but I stuck to my guns. In the

evening the British Lieutenant-Colonel Neave, who is detailed to advise
the defendants, spoke to Goering and asked him to work on me with a
view to getting me to change my mind. Goering said to me next
morning that he had unfortunately had no chance to warn me.

23 Jan. Before I saw Goering, and before the session began, I was
conducted to a room where Neave was present with an interpreter.
He tried to persuade me to give up my decision to conduct my own
defence, since I was unacquainted with legal procedure. N. told me he
would have to see me again during the course of the day, after he had
informed the Court about the communications he had had with me.

28 Jan. I wrote to Dr Stahmer, telling him I had decided to appoint
him my second defence counsel, I myself being the first. Dr Stahmer
refused 'for reasons of colleaguality'.

29 Jan. The *New York Herald Tribune* has published an interview with
my defence counsel and I have lost all faith in my former defence
counsel.

30 Jan. N. wants to know if I still want to conduct my own defence.
Court has insisted that I have a defence counsel. On the afternoon the
Court announced its finding that when one of the defendants has
agreed to accept defence counsel at the beginning of the trial he must
leave his defence in that same man's hands to the end of the trial. It
appoints Dr Stahmer to defend me as well as Goering. Goering is
understandably furious about this. His counsel has too much to do
already and he intends to protest.

1 Feb. Frank told me that the Führer had said to him in Feb. 1942
that he had expected after my flight that the English would have
published extremely damaging lies about what I had allegedly said.
But that in those concerned, something in the nature of the Northern
blood had stirred when they saw how decent I was.

3 Feb. Ribbentrop said he had been present when the Führer was
dictating his letter to Daladier, a few days before the beginning of the
war. He had dictated it straight through in one piece and didn't have
to make a single change in it afterwards. And yet this letter had been a
masterpiece. No one could touch the Führer in this.

16 Feb. A sudden prohibition of conversation during exercise. Likewise a ban on making signs.

17 Feb. The new arrangement is far more far-reaching than it
appeared on Saturday. It begins with the way in which we enter the

court-room. Goering, Hess, Ribbentrop and so on, no longer brought in first but last. So that there is very little time left for us to talk with each other before the session starts. Conversation is supposed to be limited to what is absolutely necessary for the trial.

18 Feb. It will in future only be permissible for short written messages to be passed to defence counsel. All contact between the accused and their counsel is from now on to be carefully checked and tightened up. At the midday meal, each accused will sit at a separate table in one corner of the room. There will only be four accused in each room. Between each accused a guard will stand. There is a ban on all conversation.

19 Feb. Defence counsel had asked for a three weeks' pause between prosecution and defence. The prosecution had conceded one week. The Court today announced the decision that there would be no pause. Defence counsel must give an indication of all evidence they intend to rely on, in advance. And the Court reserves the right to allow or refuse proposed evidence. In summing up, it is said that nothing may be brought up which has not been previously dealt with.

20 May. The prosecution has been charging the accused with breaches of the Versailles Treaty, and conversely, the accused, whenever they try to bring up points against the Treaty are told to shut up.

My cell has been ice-cold for days. Out of doors it is wintry. It turns out that the other prisoners' cells are *heated* and overheated! On Saturday there was only cold food at midday, and the tea was only warm. The tea tasted so much of apothecary [chemical additives] that it was impossible to drink it. I asked the doctor whether I couldn't have some other tea, but in vain. Yesterday evening again only cold food. The others got hot coffee. My tea was not brought. I was told there wasn't any. I then had nothing for 24 hours.

On 24 August psychiatrist Lieutenant-Colonel William H. Dunn said of Hess: 'His recovery during the trial appears to have been closely related chronologically to having been told that he might have been considered incompetent and barred from appearing in court. Following his recovery, he was then exposed, in the court proceedings, to the mounting evidence regarding the crimes and the cruelties of the Party and Hitler. Again he took flight into amnesia to escape the dreadful reality presented. This was gradual, and the early steps were marked by his growing inattention to the proceedings with such behaviour as reading in court which he explained as "an effort to avoid listening to the slander by foreigners" of Germany. Hess knows he is on trial as a war criminal and may be executed. He gives little overt evidence of retaining details of the court proceedings, and yet it must be assumed that those details must be registered in some level of his mind on the basis of the earlier observations. It is impossible to predict when this level of amnesia will lift. But in view of the two earlier episodes it is highly probable that it will – and again possibly with some spectacular display of further claims of simulation or a resumption of his suspicious attitude. It was the considered opinion of the commission of experts* that he was not psychotic and was competent to stand trial.'

Colonel Dunn also told the Commandant what the other prisoners thought of Hess. 'He is considered by his colleagues as an eccentric individual of considerable sensitivity; has a fanatical belief in Hitler and National Socialism. His loyalties and beliefs have been defended since the failure and rejection consequent on his flight to England, by the amnesia which blocked out consciousness and pained reality; or by the vague episode of paranoid nature in which he attempted to find an excuse for the obvious criminality of his associates.' Asked about his flight, Hess told Colonel Dunn that he had no recollection of it. 'When I said that it was my understanding that he had made the flight in an effort to end the war, he said: "If that is true, why am I here as a war criminal?"

'This examiner is strongly impressed with the genuineness of his amnesia but accepts that there are certain conscious exaggerations of it in degree.'

Hess was being urged to go to court for the closing statement, even if he only made the statement that he had nothing to say. He agreed to make an effort.

On 31 August, Hess arrived in court a little later than the other defendants. He sat quietly through the preliminary proceedings and during Goering's speech. Goering later said that Hess had told him just before the court opened that he had no closing statement. So when

* There were three Russian psychiatrists, three British, three American and one French psychiatrist who examined the prisoners.

Goering finished his, he assumed the microphone would be passed along to Ribbentrop. He was astonished when Hess intercepted it.

Hess stood up and asked if he might make a statement seated, because his health was poor. This was granted, and he launched into a long, rambling speech. His first comments were well organized, but he then became less coherent. His words were to be the last he was to speak publicly.

He talked of the 'predictions' he said he had made before the start of the trial . . . predictions that people would make false statements on oath; that some of the defendants would act strangely. He spoke of former political trials where the defendants actually clapped in frenzied approval when their death sentences were passed.

It all pointed to the same evil influence: the secret force that made men act and speak 'according to the orders given them'. When he had rambled on for some 20 minutes, the President of the Court interrupted to say that defendants could not be allowed to make lengthy statements at that stage in the proceedings. He hoped Hess would soon conclude.

Hess did. 'I was permitted to work for many years,' he intoned, 'under the greatest son whom my country has brought forth in its thousand-year history. Even if I could, I would not want to erase this period of time from my existence . . .

'No matter what human beings do,' said Rudolf Hess finally, 'I shall some day stand before the judgement seat of the Eternal. I shall answer to Him, and I know He will judge me innocent.'

Then the Court rose. It had heard the last plea and the final word of evidence and now it would adjourn to consider the verdicts.

Hess was talkative and gleeful, said the psychiatrists, and entirely coherent. He implied again that he had simulated amnesia.

The next day Hess was typing busily in his cell. His high spirits continued despite his continuous complaints about cramps. He talked coherently to the doctors in detail about his flight to Scotland. 'I could find little evidence of memory gaps,' reported Colonel Dunn. 'He made no admission of simulation saying that his memory had been restored since last November, and earlier in England. He called it a "miracle", sarcastically.'

He wrote to his mother on 31 August: 'I hope that you too, like

Ilse, have taken the news that I was again suffering from annesia from the humorous side. You have probably heard in the meantime that my memory has suddenly come back in full: in other words a 'miracle' has suddenly happened as it did once before. Ha, ha, ha for that! On the radio they probably said I was mad, or at least suffering from fixed ideas. Take that too with humour. The General once said: "For the sake of a great objective one must be able to accept being regarded for a time by one's people as a traitor." And I would add: "As a madman." '

Two days later he wrote to his wife: 'I am allowed to have a visit from you, but I have turned it down. It would be undignified.' They would, Hess pointed out, be sitting on opposite sides of a partition. 'We could say that we have seen each other in Landsberg under equally depressing circumstances but there is a big difference. Then there was only a dear German warder sitting there – and he would fall asleep after a few moments.'

But despite his acting in court, he was soberly aware of the enormity of his fate. 'I put up with everything,' he wrote to his mother on 3 September, 'with well-balanced, smiling equanimity. Just as I shall take the Judgement. The Judgement can of course pronounce death, imprisonment or the lunatic asylum. VVV. I depend as ever on my belief in a Higher Power and that it is stronger than all human will.

'In a word, do not take the Judgement too tragically, whatever its terms may be. Here it has now been decided that the accused may receive members of their families *once*; that is to say they may see them and speak to them through a narrow mesh grille with a soldier standing by on either side. I have refused absolutely to receive visitors under conditions which I feel to be unworthy. I do not imagine that you have been thinking at all of coming here; in any case I wanted to inform you.'

But at Hindelang, in the mountains of Bavaria, Ilse Hess had heard the news of the possibility of a visit. She wrote: 'When I heard that permission for a visit had been granted I cabled Seidl at once to see whether you had given permission for me, since I would only come to Nuremberg *with* your permission. Now your letter anticipated Seidl's answer . . .

'My very dear big boy, of course one is like a racehorse which has been trained for years for the start, and which now has this objective taken away at the last moment – but you can rest assured, I do not blame you in the least. I have complete understanding for you and I would have decided in exactly the same way.

'You will understand that I regret our mutual rejection of a meeting for three reasons, even though it is irrevocable:

'In two respects for the sake of the boy,* because he is so bitterly disappointed, since he was so *very much* looking forward to seeing you again which I had so often told him would be possible; although he is naturally imagining the meeting as something very different from what it would have been; the possibility of discussing various masculine problems on which Mummy is not of course competent. I am sorry about this disappointment because the impression which he would take with him could not be equalled by any educative methods or explanations, however clear they might be.

'I regret it also for Mother's sake. And I would have thought that this violent shock would have torn you out of your $5\frac{1}{2}$ years' separation from family and home and would have been good for you spiritually. I have known you, after all, since 1918, and therefore know very well what you have gone through inwardly since 10 May 1941. (And even further back in the time of silent preparation when we were all kept in the dark!)'

During the four weeks of adjournment the tension among the defendants was obvious. They moodily took their exercise and sat worriedly reading in their cells. Soon they would know the worst.

Fifteen days before the verdict Hess was writing† in his cell: 'Don't worry in the least about me, though I reckon for the worst when it comes to the Judgement. I just look at it and smile inwardly . . .

'I very much regret while I was in Berlin I was not able to attend your engagement celebration. But at that time I was concentrating only on my flight. I did not hear anything else . . . see anything else, but the flight. I was, in those days, continually on the jump waiting for better weather.'

Whatever his belief that Destiny would save him from the gallows, he had decided he must be practical. He wrote on 20 September to his bank in Munich, the Bank Goetz, ordering that 1,832 Reichsmarks 10 pfg. be sent immediately to his life assurance company as his life insurance premium, 'so that the life insurance is not cancelled'.

* Wolf-Rudiger was now nine.
† To his sister Gretl.

'In the case of my death, I ask that 80 per cent of the life insurance sum be given to my wife and 20 per cent to my mother, Klara Hess.'

With just four days to go, he wrote to his wife on 26 September: 'Your letter gave me great joy because I now know that you understand, not only my attitude regarding the visit, but that you yourself put your own and German honour higher than all personal wishes and feelings.

'If this sum total of inclinations does not once come to light in the boy, then the whole theory of heredity is no good . . . I wonder, though, how things will look when I am faced with the *practical* tasks of a father. VVV. But I believe I shall not be a disappointment to him. Even if only because father and son will be constantly going on technical expeditions and will be so engrossed with these that educational problems will be forgotten.

'Incidentally, you may assure Wolf that even if I had consented to receive visitors he would not have been able to see me, because minors – in this case sensibly – are not admitted to interviews through grilles.

'As regards your three points, I think that the boy has been sufficiently subjected to emotional impressions and disappointments considering his age and that therefore he should be spared the disturbing experience of seeing me.

'To my consolation and joy, mother also fully understands my attitude in the question of visits. I am very proud of mother too. *I* do not need the family shock – thank God.

'It is marvellous how composed I am, in spite of all the physical discomfort and pain with which I am plagued.'

On 1 October Hess and the others once more filed into their places in the dock. They had just had a pep-talk from Colonel Andrus, the prison commandant, about receiving the verdicts with manly bearing.

Hess was found Not Guilty of War Crimes and Crimes Against Humanity. But he was Guilty of Conspiracy and Crimes Against Peace. He had to wait until the afternoon session for his sentence . . .

'Defendant Rudolf Hess,' said the judge at the afternoon session, 'on the counts of the indictment on which you have been convicted, the Tribunal sentences you to imprisonment for life.'

In the long interim before he was transferred to Spandau, Hess spent most of his time in bitter complaints, as his diary entries show, about the prison regime – verbally to warders, doctors, psychiatrists and in a many-paged letter to the prison governor. The tone throughout was that of an aggrieved man claiming justice. He took vigorous exception to the fact that his counsel had 'brought in a plea for mercy on my behalf. – I state that this has been done without my knowledge and against my will. I regard the entering of any such plea as an undignified act.' To the governor he complained *inter alia* of the reduction of blankets from five to three, the removal of a foot mat, 'the cutting of our hair to the length of 3mm', and the lack of a towel. Light breaks in only occasionally. On 17 January 1947, he notes in his diary, 'One of the doctors who was for a long time in freedom said to me that I enjoyed the greatest sympathy in the world outside of all the prisoners. (I should think so, because of my flight. But what sympathy I shall enjoy in *future*.)' But in general Hess withdrew into himself. He showed no emotion when told of Goering's suicide. He again refused to see his wife.

5

Hess in Charge

THOSE CONDEMNED TO death had been executed: Hess sat in his cell awaiting his transfer to Spandau in Berlin. His mood had completely changed. He was strangely cheerful with his guards, laughing and making jokes about his new prison number. With his background of memory lapses and rumours of mental unbalance, the Nuremberg officials attached little importance to his moods.

There was, however, a good reason for Hess's brightness. He was actually preparing himself for *release*. Determinedly and methodically, he was planning to walk out of Nuremberg and take over the helm of his shattered Germany. Hess was sure in his mind that he was to be the new Führer.

He wrote to his wife on 5 July 1947: 'If I go to Spandau I know it will be hard for you, because you do not know my view of the change of quarters; you do not believe, as unshakeably as I do, in the unchangeability of fate.

'My fate is bound up with absolutely sure conviction that for me there yet awaits a great mission. I have so much evidence of this mission. To doubt it would be the same as doubting that tomorrow the sun will rise.'

Hess had been allowed a typewriter in his cell and spent hours writing with it. Neither the prison Governor, Colonel Burton Andrus, nor his officers took the time to read what he was pecking out on the machine. The trials were over and the pressure was off. What Rudolf Hess had to say was of little concern ...

Hess had no doubt about the importance of his words. He was working out, in an orderly, methodical fashion, the future for Germany. Mad? If what he was doing was a flight of madness then it was the flight that was mad. What he wrote contained much sense ...

Hess began by saying his destiny was to leave the prison as a free man. With the full cooperation of the Allies he was to become 'the new Führer of Germany'. He began first with bulletins that would be published in the Press under his direction. There were specific directives about labour, about food distribution, about liaison with Germany's occupying powers. His tailor was to make a new uniform for the Leader, with flaired breeches and adjustable seams, 'because', wrote Hess, 'I will probably put on weight when I am released'.

'I have,' Hess announced in Bulletin One, 'with the agreement of the Western Occupation Forces, taken over the leadership of the German Government in the area of the Western Zones of Germany.

'I have, therewith, taken over the leadership of the destiny of the German people in a situation which could not be imagined to be more desperate.

'I feel it, and I know everybody feels it.

'Even so, a salvation is possible, every bit as possible as it was after the seizure of power in 1933; even though the situation today is far more serious.

'But even at that time millions had given up hope. Was it not true that a dozen governments had failed because of the difficulties? With every government, Germany went further and further downwards. The decline seemed impossible to stop. In spite of the lack of courage and the predictions of the experts, the decline *was* arrested and it changed to a constant ascension. The change of the fate of our people would have been final if the war had not come.

'Germany's people will not be saved by fighting against one another or by pushing the responsibility one to another, or worrying about things which cannot be changed any more.

'In doing this, they only avert themselves from the problems that they have to solve. The provisions for salvation are that from all sides there will be a line drawn under everything that is past, and that men of goodwill will find themselves coming together to help solve the terrible need of the people and start again rebuilding everything from the beginning. In this sense I appeal to the whole German people. To exclude, from the very beginning, the great mistake, I turn to the mass of my Nationalistic Party members. As understandable as it would be, I do not want them to take any sort of revenge on those who have charged us with slander or backbiting. My wish is that everybody sees in the former opponent a member now of the same big folk community, with the same fate, with the same needs, and the same duty. That duty is to concentrate together, on great aims.

'Everyone should keep in mind that there are elements among us who have an interest in all kinds of clashes with the occupation forces. Everybody must be aware that there is an influence present on both sides which sets people into an abnormal mental condition and can force them to deeds which they would have normally never have been able to commit.

'I call on those who still have enough strength of mind and control over themselves to make it their duty to see that peace and discipline is practised. In the case of provocations they will have to show the provocateurs that they know they are talking with people who are not in their right mind. If the trouble-makers are foreigners, call immediately on the foreign occupation forces and ask them to take steps immediately. Relationships with the occupation forces and their governments must be fully correct. Their orders must be carried out and the German people will be quiet and dignified. The sooner they do this the sooner they will receive help in their hour of need – and the sooner we shall gain a lasting peace for our people.'

Meticulously, Rudolf Hess had drawn up a list of people he wanted immediately released from prisons and camps in which they were being held by the Western Powers, to help him govern the new Germany – his 'Fourth Reich'.

They would include all former Nazi leaders, particularly those who had served in the Reichstag, and their deputies. He would want all the highest State ministers and secretaries. Field-marshals, generals and admirals were on the list.

'By special wish of Rudolf Hess,' he wrote, 'the former Vice-President of the Reichstag, Hermann Esser, who is now in a camp in Ludwigsburg, is to be released and be given a car for fastest possible transport to Munich. Also Direktor Hofwebar, who is in the same camp, should go along in the car.' Munich, he had decided, was to be the new seat of Government and the capital of Germany.

With him in Nuremberg were other men Hess needed. They should 'be told to report to me immediately', ordered Prisoner 125.

They included: Reichsleiter Otto Dietrich, Hitler's former Press Chief; Minister Dr Schmidt; Dr Blohme; SS Obergruppenführer Pohl; Dr Martin, former Police President of Nuremberg; Count Lutz

Schwerin von Krosigk; Minister Funk; State Secretary Fritz Rheinhardt; Fritz Wiedermann; Professor Dr Messerschmitt; Hess's former driver Lipert. He did not forget his imprisoned brother Alfred. He had a job for him. And he had a position for the doctor at his local hospital in Hindelang.

Hess asked for quarters in Nuremberg prison where he could 'receive a great many long-distance telephone calls, telegrams and letters'. He wanted electronic equipment set up, as well as telegraph and radio equipment at his disposal for communicating to the German people. Conference rooms should be made available too.

Occupation troops should be notified that he had ordered that provocation by Germans would be kept to an absolute minimum. Orders should be sent off to the German railway management to give free tickets to all travellers on their way to meet him in Munich. 'If I have not the power to order the railways to do this then it must be done by the occupation forces.'

The new Reichstag would number about 500 men. There would be no women. These men would of course need quarters, so garrisons would be taken over to accommodate them. 'Esser will immediately move to see the American Commandant in Munich and confer with him.'

He had an important job for his prison companion Baldur von Schirach. Many buildings would be needed in Munich, and it was von Schirach's job to secure them.

German police would be recruited and armed with small arms such as pistols, machine-pistols and light machine-guns. They must be clothed and fed properly and be given good boots and blankets. 'I would like Reichsminister Speer,' he wrote of the man occupying a cell along the passage, 'to be assigned the job of lessening the crisis that exists in Germany. He must be given all the help necessary to set up feeding stations and transportation, to issue blankets and field-kitchens. At every large railway station there should be a kitchen to give food to soldiers who are on their way home.'

Hess would need a limousine for himself and three accompanying cars for the trip down to Munich. One of the cars would be for Speer, the others for other important figures released from Nuremberg. 'If possible,' wrote Hess, 'I want German cars.'

Then came a personal note: 'I wish to be given back the one hundred

English pounds and the several thousand Reichsmarks which I brought back with me from the United Kingdom and which were supposedly "lost" in the prison. The £100 is the payment to me as a prisoner-of-war, under the terms of the Geneva Convention.'

All of his private papers should be returned to him – including his Nuremberg diaries.

He would appoint a liaison man, who, he hoped, would deal with one liaison man from the Western Occupation Forces who would have power of attorney for the others.

'I have prepared releases to radio and the Press: In the name of Rudolf Hess, the following should be made known:

'1. Rudolf Hess has given the Vice-President of the German Reichstag, Hermann Esser, the order to call together as soon as possible the members of the German Reichstag. He [Hess] will then speak personally to explain the entire programme of the new government.

'2. Rudolf Hess gives the order to Speer to help the German people in getting all food and kitchen equipment and transportation together. This can only be done by working together with the Allied Forces.

'3. German folk police will be trained and will protect the German people from trouble-making minorities and from looting and stealing.

'4. Control of Press and radio should be changed so that it speaks for the majority of the people and not for the minority. It will not be controlled as it was under Hitler where nothing appeared unless it was approved by Goebbels.

'The Leader of the German folk police has been named but not written down yet. [Hess left a space for the name.]

'I ask our editors who are ready for work to give me by telegram the following information: name, address and age; where and for whom they wrote; in what field they wrote – politics, economy?; and what title they held in their last job.

'Press and radio have made attacks against former outer and inner opponents. They must stop this immediately. It is not their mission to keep old wounds open, or to open new ones.'

He went on: 'On the order of Rudolf Hess all district gauleiters and high officials of the Nazi Party should report to their former offices as soon as possible and take up the jobs they formerly had – members of their staffs as well.'

On Jews. 'If Jews ask or plead or request to save themselves from the rage of the German population and wish to go into protective camps this should be fulfilled. In this way everything should be done to save the Jews from acts of violence and also from unauthorized persons entering the camps.

'It is up to them to make their lives as nice as possible to their own taste, within the camp. The situation in such a camp must be as humane as possible. Otherwise the occupation forces will have to be asked for food and other necessary items for the people in these camps.'

All precautions should be taken by the police for his protection when he arrived at the first meeting of the Reichstag. 'A full guard should be mounted so that all precautions can be taken against the assassination of Rudolf Hess.'

Hess had apparently no knowledge of the cremation and scattered ashes of the 11 colleagues who had been condemned to death. For he wrote: 'Honour guards should be put on the graves of the eleven martyrs who were hung in Nuremberg, until they can be put into one communal grave so they can have one common honour guard. There should also be honour guards on the graves of Himmler, Ley, Rust, Hildebrand, etc. The soldiers Goering, Keitel and Jodl shall have their medals put into their caskets – certainly the Great Cross of Goering and the Ritterkreuz of the two others. Also notify their families that they can be buried in uniforms with all their ribbons. For all the others, only the Party honour badges are to be put into their graves.

'Radio programmes should be no Nationalistic circus. Not too much march music, but good music; also gay music, but no jazz and dance programmes. Certain beloved programmes should be re-introduced, also the folk concerts, with some changes. Rudolf Hess has listened to the Berlin programmes from England on the radio and found that for weeks it was the same old programmes with the old used-up pieces. It should be of a higher level than it has been to now. Rudolf Hess does not want nasty cabaret with its nasty jokes; he wants a lot of gay items, but at the same time, it should be dignified. He wishes to see the first programme before he gives it his approval . . .'

On a new constitution. It was too early at this stage to draw one up. The fate of the people was the important matter. 'Later the people will tell me if they are content with my leadership and will back me up as the Führer.

'I talked once about the title "Führer" with the Führer. It went so closely with his personality that I would not find it right to use it myself too much. It should die with Adolf Hitler. Hitler wasn't for that at all. He said the title should be kept and that every one of his successors should use it.

'I will fulfil this wish of the Führer for a certain time, but I cannot call myself "Führer" until I am Führer to the whole of Germany.'

Finally, he had prepared the oath his followers would swear on taking office: 'By God the Almighty, I swear to be truthful and obedient to Rudolf Hess, to perform the duties of the National Socialist Reichsrat* to the best of my ability. And especially to be absolutely silent about any matter that has been spoken here.'

And now he had arranged his Parliament, this is how he planned to address it:

'TO THE MEN OF THE GERMAN REICHSTAG'

'I think of the dead. The dead whom our people had to sacrifice in their millions in the years of desperate struggle for its freedom and its bread.

'And I think of those who died after the end of the struggle because we lost freedom, and with freedom lost our livelihood.

'Above all, I think of the *one* among the dead: the originator and leader of the National Socialist Reich, Adolf Hitler. In my pain I feel united with them here, and with millions outside whose fidelity has remained unshaken. I think of the many men who have deserved well of people and country, who had to die because they were condemned to death; first and foremost of my eleven comrades who became the victims of the Nuremberg Trials, with the Reichsmarshal Goering at their head.

'At the same time I think of all the other Germans – women, girls and boys among them – who also died in the course of the appalling judicial murders; judicial murders for which the judges were as little responsible as the condemned were for the crimes with which they were charged.

* The Reichsrat was the lower house of parliament.

'There are many gaps in your ranks, the ranks of the leaders of the Movement gathered together here in the Reichstag. Some of them fell, often in the defence of territory committed to their care, some of them voluntarily by their own hand, some of them murdered under the guise of judicial convictions. Among these are many names well known to the whole of our people and who worked with devotion for the nation in war and peace.

'I think of all who in the last days of the war and after it, elected to end their own lives. I name – as representative of other wives who could not be restrained from dying with their husbands – the wife of the Führer. I think of Frau Goebbels as a mother who shared her husband's fate with five* children. The mothers took their children with them when they died by their own hand, because they could no longer bear to watch them starving . . .

'Cruel fate decreed that the Founder of the National Socialist Reich had to die, faced by the apparent certainty that his creation was destroyed forever. The Führer died a voluntary death. He took it upon himself to die because he had no choice.

'He could not expose himself to undignified treatment. He could not submit to the jurisdiction of judges who had no right to try him. Anyone else could, but he could not. He – the Head of the German State. He could not, even if he had been able to foresee the final defeat of Germany.

'If he had continued to live, this would not have benefited the nation, for he would have shared the fate of those who died in the Nuremberg drama. He would thus not have been able to take part in the revival of the National Socialist Reich if he had tried to save himself for this purpose.

'Nor would the Führer have been able to use the International Court for the purpose of making out a convincing case for the German cause for all the world. The more convincingly he spoke, the more mutilated would have been the reports that reached the public. Many of the accused at Nuremberg spoke very impressively – and what did the world hear? Worse still, mental pressure could also have been brought to bear on the Führer, and as a result he like other prisoners and witnesses would surely have been reduced to a condition in which he would have made false charges against Germany. He, who had the

* In fact there were six children.

most authoritative voice of all, would have done serious harm to the Reich. All in all, the offensive treatment of the Head of the German State would have provided a spectacle which must have been intolerable to the nation. There would have been no compensating advantage.

'The spectacle would have been all the more intolerable since this Head of State was one of the most significant personalities in the history of the world. And that, not as a destructive force. No. That of a creative, building or constructive force. History will one day recognize this.

'The figure of the Führer will stand like a beacon over the centuries. Adolf Hitler will be honoured as one of the greatest pathfinders and benefactors of mankind.

'If my captivity was decisive for the future in this respect, it was also in another respect: the desolate solitary confinement compelled me to "think", in preparation for later "action". It was thanks to the lonely hours I spent in prison that I was able to collect my thoughts on the planning and carrying out of the reconstruction and on the solution of the many problems which awaited us.

'I devoted myself to exhaustive thinking about the future, because I carried within me the conviction that the day would come when I would be free again, the miraculous day for our people. *The turning-point!*

'This certainty was rooted in my belief in an Almighty Power which guides events in a way that makes sense and that brings each into inter-relationship with each other purposefully. I knew that for the sake of a task allotted to me I would be saved from danger of a kind I had never thought I might have to endure. It could not have been without deeper meaning that I became inured to powerful poisons, inured to the effects of mental compulsion that enabled me to recognize the existence of a secret of such decisive influence on the course of history.

'The Führer once said in a speech during the war that the fulfilment of great tasks entailed the bearing of great sufferings. I was not spared the sufferings, physical and mental. Completely cut off from the outside world, as it were chained and gagged, I was compelled to watch how Fate dealt with my Germany. And all the time I knew that I would bring salvation if only I regained my freedom and was able to enlighten the enemy peoples as to the crimes committed against them as well and as to how they have been misused.

'Since the spring of 1942, since my knowledge hardened into certainty, I knew, among other things, that Germany would lose the war and would lose it because its wartime leadership and its armaments industry would be increasingly mismanaged and would come to a standstill.

'What I had foreseen came to pass. I was powerless to do anything about it or to do anything to ward it off, or even to issue any warning. I kept on making fresh plans of escape. I kept on making fresh attempts, right up to an attempt which borders on the extreme limit of what could ever be undertaken. All in vain! Each fresh plan, each fresh attempt was accompanied by the highest hopes and ended in deepest disappointment.

'It was at the trial – if anywhere – that I would be able to address the public.

'My statement did in fact have the effect of enabling me to continue to stand my trial. Not that I intended to defend myself; I refused to do this expressly from the very start. I went on record as saying I would not listen. I disputed the court's right to sit in judgement on Germans. On the other hand, I aimed to make use of the framework of the trial as the forum before which to make my accusation in the eyes of the world.

'However, steps had been taken to prevent this. My revelations could only be convincingly presented in the course of a long speech; I was prevented from having a chance to do this. The statement regarding my memory would probably require only a few sentences. I wanted to use the answer to the question of whether I felt myself to be guilty – the answer was restricted to "Yes" or "No". I tried to get permission to speak independently. This was ruled to be out of order.

'Both my defence counsel and some of my fellow accused had been trying for weeks to persuade me to desist from making a final statement. "Keeping silent," they said, "would be an impressive demonstration."

'They only stopped acting like this when I appeared to agree. When I then nevertheless made use of my right, one of my fellow accused kept on talking throughout my speech in an attempt to confuse me and to break my train of thought; he urged me to stop, although he must have been aware that my conclusively proved revelations could be of immeasurable importance for his fate and that of his fellow sufferers. And indeed for the faith of the nation.

'The majority of the accused were clearly likewise under the influence of the external coercive agent.

'*The executions resulting from the Nuremberg Trials are judicial murders.* The judges were aware of this. After the death sentences had been passed, I clung to the hope that the miracle of the great turn of the tide of Fate would occur before the sentences were carried out. In vain.

'Perhaps the enormity of executing completely innocent persons, some of whom bore names of world renown, had to be enacted before the eyes of humanity, in order that humanity should recognize fully how immeasurably great the crimes and how unscrupulous the criminals were.

'The repercussions of the death of the eleven will be as great as those of their martyrdom. For they did in fact suffer martyrdom. Everything that could be done to break the prisoners' nerve and to increase their mental anguish was done. They nevertheless maintained in the highest degree a manly bearing and suffered their bitter fate with heads unbowed. Torn hither and thither for months on end between hope and despair, but never breaking down, they all faced what seemed to them a certain fate with admirable courage. For weeks on end they looked certain death in the eye. Upright, they took the last hard road to their death, each one of them a hero.

'Only one of them – Hermann Goering – kept the means of anticipating execution at the last moment by committing suicide. The fury and disappointment shown by the opponents of the German people, as evidenced in the Press and radio, confirm how right he was to act as he did to prevent the intended spectacle of the hanging of the German Reichsmarshal. The effect of the appalling treatment meted out to my fellow prisoners must have been all the greater since I was unable to convince them that their captors were insane.

'I on the other hand was sure of this. I was thus able to brush off all efforts to insult me or to break down my resistance, as being the behaviour of pitiful, sick persons into whose hands I had for the time being fallen.

'I am, in principle, of the opinion that a person's honour cannot be injured by actions or utterances of another person. Anyone who attempts to do this injures his own honour. A person's honour can only be harmed by dishonourable behaviour on the part of the person concerned.

'In this connection I wish to make the following statement: My defence counsel entered an appeal for a revision of the judgement found against me. It was then put about that I had made an appeal for "mercy". In the first place an appeal from judgement is not a plea for mercy; secondly, my defence counsel's action was taken without my knowledge and against my will.

'Behind hunger, cold, murder and despair, Bolshevism raises its ugly head. It is only with the Bolshevization of Europe that the objective would be reached, which was the purpose of the war. The rule of Bolshevism is the rule of the Jew.

'Two world wars and twice the same result: Jewish power increased. Does it need much political farsightedness to recognize that World War III is already being prepared? The new world war. This time the fronts will be, on one side the Bolshevists, and on the other the Anglo-Saxons. Who will win? That side will win in whose favour the secret agency is employed.

'The real instrument of power in the hands of the Jew is the Bolshevist. It is proved by the fact that for years a Jew has been at the head of the research department of the United States Atomic Power Organization. Is anyone going to believe that this Jew, hitherto completely unknown among scientists, has suddenly been put in this high position where all the secrets relating to the future war must be available? The atom bomb will be the main weapon of the Jewish-Bolshevist war leadership in spite of the fact that it is also in British and American hands.

'The Soviet Union will probably use it first and be able to destroy everything in the West. They have the best possible excuse for doing so because they can say the West used it first. The Anglo-Saxon countries will be the first to go under – I, Rudolf Hess, have warned you!'

6

Spandau

SPANDAU PRISON IS red-brick, high-walled and ugly. It was built in 1876 in an outer suburb of Berlin as a military stockade, and used later as a civilian jail for long-term prisoners. Until 1947 it still boasted an execution chamber with a guillotine, and sloping tiled floor to carry away the blood. It had 132 single cells, five punishment cells and 10 large cells which could each take 40 prisoners.

Facilities also existed for the strangulation, by hanging, of eight prisoners simultaneously.

Before the Allies took it over in November 1946, it held 600 prisoners. During the Nazi regime, it had been used as a clearing station for political prisoners on their way to concentration camps. Now it was going to hold some of the very men who had sent them there.

Through its 20ft high green doors had passed the Jew, the 'undesirable', the Pole, the anti-Nazi. They had been herded over the cobbled yard between the entrance and cell-block to disappear inside, the rattle of keys and crash of steel doors ringing in their ears.

Some had gone to the small cells (9ft by 8ft) in the main block itself. Others had been led down the steel spiral staircase, with its almost arty wrought-iron steps, to the death cells; cramped, low-ceilinged and secure. Cells built *within* cells.

As the seven war criminals who had been sentenced to jail waited at Nuremberg, Spandau was getting ready for them. Their files had been sent ahead from Nuremberg. And they had been measured for their new prison uniforms so that they would be ready on their arrival. The jackets had already been adorned with their prison number on the back, and the trousers with it on each knee. It was not – as myth has long since had it – by chance that they got their particular numbers.

Above all, the Spandau Prison had to be secure. Nobody was going to be ever able to get inside illegally, and certainly no one was going to get out. A 10-foot-high barbed wire fence was put up around the whole prison. Mid-way between that, its strands running between poles two yards apart, electricians and carpenters put up an electric fence six feet high. It carried a 4,000-volt charge that would bring a frizzling death on contact.

Five high guard towers, built then of wood,* went up at strategic places on the perimeter of the wall. Spotlights, operated from the towers, swept through 360 degrees, and could light up every inch of the wall. Orders to the guards manning the posts were clear. 'I will fire my weapon only in the following circumstances:

'Against persons who have gained entrance into the courtyards by force or other illegal method; in self-defence and then only when serious injury to my person is threatened by a prisoner attempting to escape; when the escape of a prisoner cannot be prevented by other means. If it is necessary to direct shots at a prisoner they should be aimed to disable and not to kill; and all cases of use of force or firearms will immediately be reported to the officer-of-the-day.'

As the prison would now house only seven men, only one section of the block had to be prepared. It was decided to remove the guillotine and use the execution chamber as the operating room. The hooks were removed but the pole from which they hung was left. To minimize risks of suicide, the cells had been stripped of all protruding objects on the walls, and an engineer was sent to Nuremberg to study the cell accommodation there so that it could be copied at Spandau. When he came back the lighting conduit in the cells was removed and even the heating pipes covered.

Spandau was to be run by the Four Powers, each taking a monthly turn to supply the guards. Each appointed a director. Britain's months were January, May and September; France was in charge in February, June and October; the USSR, March, July and November; the US, April, August and December. When a country was in charge its director automatically became chairman of the directors for that month. The directors were responsible to the Legal Committee of the Allied Kommandatura, the governing body of the Occupying Powers in Berlin.

* Later six concrete towers were built.

On 18 July 1947 a Dakota landed at Berlin's Gatow airport in the late afternoon sunshine. As it came to a halt a black Royal Air Force bus, with bars in its windows and corrugated steel sides, drew up beside it.

From the plane, each manacled to a US soldier, stepped the seven men who would now be the sole inmates of Spandau.

Baldur von Schirach, the 40-year-old former Nazi Youth Leader, climbed into the bus. A tall, superior man, hair brushed back from his forehead, an air of aloofness about him, he had been given the prison number 1. He had 20 years to serve.

Beside him sat Karl Doenitz, 56, the one-time Commander-in-Chief of the German Navy. Like von Schirach, Doenitz had little time for those who had been his inferiors. Was he not, at the end, appointed Head of State, succeeding Hitler? Doenitz, face expressionless, waited for the bus to depart. His prison number was to be 2. His sentence: 10 years.

Old Konstantin von Neurath – 'the Baron' – 74, every inch the professional diplomat, former Reich Protector of Bohemia and Moravia, was to be Number 3. He had 15 years.

Erich Raeder, 71, former Grossadmiral of the Navy, and later Admiral Inspector of the Navy, found little time for his fellow Naval prisoner. For his age he was in reasonable health except for a hernia and his old arterio-sclerosis. He stepped down gingerly to the bus and climbed in. He would be known in Spandau now as Number 4. He was to be there for life.

Now Albert Speer, 42, a neat, fit-looking man, had been Hitler's architect and later head of armaments. At the trial he had freely admitted his guilt in supporting Hitler. Tall, with thick black eyebrows contrasting with his thinning hair, Speer faced 20 years in jail. He was to be Prisoner Number 5.

Walter Funk, 57-year-old former President of the Reichsbank, got into the bus and, as always, huddled himself into a round untidy ball. He was complaining again, as he always was. Funk had been sentenced to life imprisonment. He would answer to the name: 'Number 6'.

Finally, the lean, almost cadaverous Hess, aged 53. His hunted eyes glanced about the bus and the airfield. His jaw was set sullenly. Gone was the cheerful man who had compiled his message to the German people in the final days at Nuremberg. He was paranoiac now, the doctors said. He faced imprisonment for life. He would always be known simply as: 'Number 7'.

The driver started the motor, and with an escort of jeeps, armoured cars and lorry-loads of soldiers before and behind, the bus started off.

Fifteen minutes later the high green gates of Spandau swung open to allow it in. They swung closed again and the prison's new inmates stepped down. Handcuffs were unlocked and in a straggling line they made their way into the chief warder's room in the cell-block. There, on the painted and polished cement floor they stripped, were led back across the passage to bathe and then escorted into the medical aide-room. After a thorough medical examination the prisoners were handed their new grey convict garb, bearing the numbers by which they would be addressed for as long as they were in Spandau.

The warders had taken away their possessions and carefully listed each article in the inventory book. Funk was concerned about his 1,575 Reichsmarks, his gold, monogrammed cuff-links and his gold collar-buttons. Hess asked that great care be taken of his historic flying suit, helmet and boots. Only personal photographs were allowed to go with them to their cells.

Each cell was identical. Bare-walled, with a table, a chair and a bed. One by one as they entered, Hitler's colleagues took off their soft grey caps and looked around them. The first task was to read the Spandau regulations.

Hess, who had been used to a typewriter and unlimited paper in Nuremberg, found that he would write and receive not more than one letter – of four pages maximum – every four weeks; that he could not speak to any of his fellows unless specially authorized to do so.

He would work every day, except Sunday and German holidays, on cleaning the prison, getting rid of debris, land cultivation or 'necessary tasks'.

Each prisoner, he noted, was allowed one visitor for a visit of 15 minutes in each two calendar months. Meals would be eaten in the cells and there would be no knives or forks; only spoons.

A prison library would provide books 'according to the reasonable desire, character and aspirations of the prisoner'.

'Each day,' said the regulations, 'the prisoners will rise when called (at 6 am), will dress and put their cells in order.' They would then be led, under guard escort, to the washroom where they 'will strip to the waist and wash'. They were allowed one hot bath each, weekly. While they were about their ablutions, their cells would be searched.

Between 6.45 am and 7.40 am each day, breakfast would be taken. Between 8 am and 11.45 am the cell passage would be cleaned. At midday, on Mondays, Wednesdays and Fridays the prisoner barber would shave them, and if necessary, cut their hair.

Between 12.00 and 12.30 pm, lunch would be eaten in the cells . . .

When dinner arrived the first time on the brown, rubber-wheeled trolley, and his cell door was opened for him, Hess leaned across and took the plate farthest away. That way he could be reasonably sure, he said, of foiling any plot to poison him.

Spoon in hand, he settled down on his hard chair to eat his meat and vegetables and finish reading the regulations. 'Punishment for offences committed in prison,' he read, 'may consist of the cancellation of privileges, the cutting off of light in the cell for a period of up to four weeks, reducing of food which will be replaced by bread and water; deprivation of furniture and clothing; and, in special cases, fettering.'

As Germany's fallen leaders settled into their new prison surroundings, Hess became restive. The man who had read his way through almost every available book in Nuremberg was already worried whether there would be enough for him to read in Spandau. After a written request, he stood before a midday meeting of the prison directors to put his problem before them. 'I need special books on scientific material,' said No. 7, standing stiffly to attention, grey cloth cap in hand. 'Do you think it could be made available?' The prisoner was told to submit a written list and inquiries would be made. Next came Doenitz. He said he needed instructional books so that he could learn French. The French director said he would see what he could do.

The seven were imprinting their own individual characters on their cells, as an official visitor reported after a tour. 'This morning I visited Spandau Prison,' he wrote. 'The building is not too bad. Rather gloomy, but not as gloomy as I had thought. There is quite an adequate operating room, a clean, well-equipped dispensary, a library in which the range of books is distinctly limited.

'The first cell we visited was that of Hess. I was somewhat shy, for

I never like to impose on people's misery, so my remarks to Hess were merely: "Good day. How are you?" However Hagen (a prison expert) was much more at ease and asked him how he was and how much he liked the food.

'Hess remarked: "I'm much better today since the Americans took over." Hess then said he was having difficulty with his eyes as the light in his cell was directly overhead. He wondered if he couldn't have a reading-lamp or glasses. The French Governor told me that this was an old complaint of Hess's; that he had been given reading glasses but never wore them.

'Hess was much older-looking than I expected, greying a little, thin and pale. Hagen told him that he had recently seen his signature scrawled on the wall of his former cell in the Tower of London. But he disclaimed all knowledge of this. I had been told that Hess was moody and inclined not to talk. I found him much more amiable than I expected.

'We next went to the cell of von Neurath. He was a very polite, elderly gentleman. He seemed to have good manners. He was all smiles as we merely exchanged a few words of greeting.

'I next entered Speer's cell. He was extremely pleasant. I remarked that I had heard that he had made a number of drawings. He said: "Yes." I said I would like to see them. He showed me the plans he was making for his "dream" house, a charming suburban villa with about four bedrooms and two baths. He had street elevations and garden elevations, floor plans, all phases. It was quite charming and the draughtsmanship was wonderful. Speer, I believe, is only condemned for 20 years. It is quite possible he will build this house. The thought of it keeps him going.

'Doenitz was the next one we called on. He requested permission to ask a question, then launched into a complaint about the fact that he was only allowed one letter a month from his family and that they were not permitted to receive newspapers with the exception of the weekly church newspaper. That is one of the most prevalent complaints.

'Schirach was our next call. I was told he was likely to give us more trouble than anyone. I must say he was the most complaining. He might, if given the opportunity, do away with himself. On the other hand, his was the most neat and artistic cell. It was quite remarkable that within the space of a room which has only a bed, a table, a chair and a WC a man can impress his personality so very vividly.

'Each cell had a different atmosphere. Speer's had an artistic disarray, von Schirach's was extremely neat, his table had been painted a bright red, his pipes* were arranged neatly, even his washing things were extremely neatly arranged. Neurath had a lot of photographs of his family on the wall. Each one was quite different. Some time ago the prisoners were given paint and allowed to paint their cells if they wished.'

From snatches of conversation picked up by the warders, it seemed that the seven had an uncanny, up-to-the-minute grasp of what was going on in the outside world. Various members of the staff were suspected as 'informers' until it was realized that their source of information was the toilet. In the switchover from Nuremberg nobody had thought to order toilet paper. Instead, the prisoners were using sliced-up pages of newspaper on which they read their daily news. The newspaper was quickly banned and toilet paper ordered.

The prison's first breach of security was logged at 10.45 pm on 9 August. A pear was thrown up from a near-by fruit and vegetable garden and it shattered the window of tower No. 3. The guards searched the area with spotlights but the assailant had fled.

---

* Von Schirach particularly favoured English Dunhill pipes.

7

The Warders

WARDER WALLY CHISHOLM stood, flat-footed, attentive, listening to No. 7's complaint. Round-faced, and wearing a British RAF-style forage-cap, Chisholm gave no hint to Hess of what he was thinking. 'I will pass your request on to the authorities concerned,' he replied in his correct German.

Then, in his rubber-soled shoes, he padded purposefully off to the chief warder's office. A man with simple, Scottish country tastes and faultless manners, the bespectacled Chisholm had been brought by the British from duty in a Chinese jail to head their team of warders when the move to Spandau was made. He was always ready with a smile; anxious to please. He showed that he was meticulous – even to the point of fussiness – in his reporting of requests or misdemeanours. 'I remain,' he always wrote, 'your obedient servant, W. Chisholm.' But it was not all hard work . . . Off duty in his quarters, Chisholm was gradually building up a valuable collection of stamps from all over the world. And the Spandau Allied Prison offices were a rich source.

At all times, when the prison opened to receive the seven, there were to be five warders on duty. A chief warder and three others in the cell-block, a fifth on the main gate. Most were career-warders brought by the Powers from jails in their own countries. There was to be no room at Spandau for amateurs. Until regulations were later altered, they all carried truncheons.

Outside the cell-block the security of the prison was the responsibility of the soldiers of the Power in charge on that particular month.

Each military detachment had two officers, two sergeants, six corporals and 44 privates; they guarded Spandau on a 50 per cent off, 50 per cent on duty basis. Sentries were armed with automatic weapons and tear-gas bombs.

Once a sentry had climbed up his ladder into the guard tower there

was no threat of being overpowered by escaping prisoners or intruders.
He simply pulled his ladder up after him.

To penetrate Spandau's defences a visitor had to go to the main
gate (the term 'main' being unnecessary – there was only one) and
show a pass signed by all four directors. Once the warder, peeping at
the card through a small barred window, was satisfied, he would open
the door which was part of the gate itself and sign the visitor in. A
system of code rings on a bell then opened further inner doors.

On the day the prisoners arrived, Harvey Fowler, Warder Chisholm's
American opposite number, was on duty. It was for the rather meek,
balding little Fowler a big day in his life. Like Chisholm he did his
duty well, asked no favours and expected none in return. The prisoners
knew they were dealing with a professional.

With the Russians they knew it was going to be different. From
the start they were shown the roughness and rigidity of rule-following
that they had expected. While other Allied warders wore soft-soled
shoes to deaden the sound of their footsteps at night on the cement
floor, the Russians wore boots. Funk was complaining already that
their noise, their frequent spotlight inspections of his cell while he was
asleep, and their loud voices were driving him mad. The Russians had
an extra task: they meticulously wrote down every word that was said
while they were on duty, and any incident, no matter how trivial, that
caught their attention. Their dossiers on warders, prisoners and officials
was massive.

Any irregularity they observed – such as other warders 'dozing off'
in their chairs outside the cell doors – was reported immediately to the
directors, who discussed it at their formal Thursday meeting.

In the late morning on the same day each week the directors met,
with interpreters and, sometimes, stenographers, around a cheap
wooden table in the main block. That table was to see, in the worst
of the Cold War, the only verbal contact between East and West.
When the Soviets walked out of high-level diplomatic meetings, we
at Spandau kept on; arguing, discussing, sounding each other out.
Meetings sometimes went on all afternoon and into the evening and
harsh words were spoken. But the Four Power representatives at
Spandau stayed talking together. When long-winded arguments had
to be tediously translated into Russian or French there was just a
calendar at one end of the room and a large map of Europe at the

other to occupy the waiting director's interest. In one corner stood a safe with the prison keys in it and an old hat-stand stood next to it. There was nothing else.

From Cell No. 19, on 8 January 1948, came word from prisoner Funk. Doctors had diagnosed acute bladder pressure and only surgical drainage would relieve it. But Funk's message said: 'I will not be operated on in Spandau while the operating theatre is in the condition I know it to be in.' The prisoner was often in excruciating pain and had been catheterized many times. Now only surgery under anaesthetic could help him.

The old execution chamber that had been turned into an operating theatre certainly was not ready. It needed an instrument sterilizer, a large sterilizer for bowls, instrument tables and an instrument cabinet. If a surgeon came from outside to operate he would have had to bring his own instruments, towels, surgeon's clothing and dressings. But the Russians insisted: on no account would Funk be allowed to *leave* prison to be operated on outside. Any one of the Four Powers could veto a proposal and therefore the idea of taking Funk to an Allied hospital in Berlin was out. The British, on the other hand, insisted: 'You cannot operate on a man against his will. If you do, it constitutes – under British law – an assault.'

As the argument went on, equipment was being scrounged from all over war-damaged Berlin. When the theatre was at last ready, Raeder had a successful hernia operation and the removal of his right testicle. Funk agreed finally to have his surgery. He wrote to the directors: 'After the last treatment of my prostatic illness I request the directors of the board to see to it that I shall be operated upon. During the last treatment I again had to suffer unbearable pain in spite of morphia and cocaine. These pains, and the after-effects of poisons and narcotics that were given to me in the form of pills within the last few months have brought on a physical and mental weakness such as I have never felt in my life.

'From what I was told by the physicians treating me in the prison there is no doubt that my ailment is continually growing worse; and in the case of continuance of my present state, my bladder and kidney ailment will become chronic. An operation might suddenly become inevitable in case of complete retention of urine, endangering my life; then an operation might become extremely risky, not leaving much hope. [This was the opinion of the French physician.]'

It was decided to operate. The doctors diagnosed Funk's condition as benign prostatic hypertrophy (excessive growth of tissue), chronic urinary retention and polynephritis. The operation would take place under a spinal anaesthetic.

Funk was taken into the theatre which in its former days had seen so much death. He was strapped down to the operating table. And as he glanced around him at the surgeons, he saw, for the first time in three years – a woman. She was Nurse Aseglio, assistant to the French surgeon. As Funk lay trembling on the table, her dark eyes smiling at him over her mask, she gave him a reassuring wink.

Preparations had already been made in case of Funk's death. His clothes had been measured and a joiner was preparing a pinewood coffin. A coffin large enough for the elderly von Neurath should he die first. If Funk died he was to be cremated and the ashes brought back to the prison. They would be placed in a safe in the main office and guarded by a representative guard from each nation until they were to be disposed of. The box which had held the ashes would be burned in the presence of the four directors. There was to be no chance of any relic becoming a future Nazi memorial.

Funk had been allowed to write a will, and a final letter to his wife to be delivered upon death. A cable announcing his death had been prepared . . .

Funk's frightened eyes shifted from Nurse Aseglio to the surgeon, Guinchard. The operation began at 10.40 am. It went on until 11.30 am.

When it was all over the surgeon was bitter about the conditions under which he was forced to operate. 'There was no blood-pressure or pulse reading taken throughout the surgical procedure, and there was a marked laxity of aseptic technique by the professional personnel.' Funk, despite the drama, appeared in 'good condition following the surgical procedure'.

For eight days Funk lay recovering in a hospital bed brought in from the French sector. On the third and sixth day his condition was critical. He was heavily guarded throughout his illness, but he had the comfort of nursing by Mademoiselle Aseglio. As he got better and a prison officer went to his bed to see him Funk hurled a full urine bottle at him. 'I am not on view for curious people!' he shouted.

When Funk recovered he went back to Cell 19; but it was not long before he had further worries in his mind. During the Nuremberg trial Oswald Pohl, Chief of the Economics Office of the SS, whose responsibility was handling his organization's transactions, alleged that Funk had had business deals with the SS concerning the delivery of the valuables of dead Jews. He described a party he said was held by Funk after an inspection tour of the Reichsbank vaults where the valuables were kept in safes.

A letter from the Land Commissioner of Bavaria arrived asking for Funk's interrogation. In particular the Commission wanted to know about Foreign Exchange funds which had 'disappeared'. 'It is alleged that in the beginning of 1945 the former Reichsminister and President of the Reichsbank effected the agreement of Adolph Hitler to displace the gold and foreign exchange funds of the German Reichsbank. One hundred tons were displaced into potash works in Thuringia. On 8 April 1945 this treasure fell into the hands of American occupying troops. About the middle of April, the remainder of the gold reserve of the Reichsbank, namely 728 ingots, each of 25 kg, furthermore banknotes for more than one milliard Reichsmarks and 25 hundred-weight of other currencies and jewellery, were shipped to Bavaria.

'These valuables, perhaps with the exception of the matrixes, were buried, close by the Wolkensee; probably after conferences by W. Funk and Colonel Pfeiffer, commander of the school for mountain riflemen at Mittenwald. After the . . . dig, one sack filled with Swiss francs was returned to Funk's adjutant. It appears to be possible that this adjutant embezzled the sack of Swiss francs. An officer of the mountain riflemen received from the exchange funds provided to be buried 404,480 dollars and £405 English, for Pfeiffer, the adjutant of former Reichsminister Lammers. Later on, about the middle of August 1945, on the order of Pfeiffer and Rauch, Bulcher delivered these valuables to the American Corporal Newmann. Whether Newmann delivered these to his office is not known.

'In order to escape from imprisonment, Funk fled from his residence to Berchtesgaden. It is possible he considered a flight to Switzerland. Funk allegedly had three sacks, with foreign currencies in one with two gold ingots, each of about 25 kg, with him . . .

'To throw light on the facts, the interrogation of the former Reichs-minister Funk would be necessary.' The writer, Dr Albert Roll, enclosed a questionnaire to be submitted to Funk.

What was the truth? It was never discovered.

The US authorities examined the letter from the Land Commissioner requesting Funk's interrogation but decided: 'US policy has reached the stage that we no longer have an interest in the possible recovery of the property involved.'

On the question of Funk's Reichsbank deposits, that had been dealt with at the trial and so far as Spandau was concerned, it was now a dead matter.

8

The Prisoner Hess

WHAT OF THE man reading in Cell 23? Had Rudolf Hess been correctly evaluated in the past? Was he in the same state of mind he was in when he was being tried at Nuremberg? Had his psychological problems changed since he had arrived in Spandau?

Dr Maurice Walsh, an eminent United States psychiatrist, was asked by the Four Powers to examine Hess in depth to find the answer to these questions. At 10 am on 25 May 1948, Hess was led into the room where prisoners talked through a grille to their visitors.

Around a plain wooden table sat an array of medical officers and interpreters. Colonel F. T. Chamberlin, the American medical representative, sat at the right, on the far side of the table; Dr Walsh sat next to him; next to Dr Walsh sat the British medical representative; the French medical officer sat next to him. At the end of the table sat the Russian medical officer, with the Russian interpreter next to him. The American interpreter sat near the end of the table opposite Colonel Chamberlin. The French director of the prison stood in the room away from the table with an interpreter, with the Russian director near by.

Hess took a chair opposite Dr Walsh. 'He was thin,' Dr Walsh remembered, 'but his general condition was better than I expected from his photographs in Brigadier Rees's book.'*

At 10 am, Dr Walsh began the interview by asking Hess about his general medical symptoms. ('It was decided to speak directly to the prisoner in German in the beginning of the interview, even though the interviewer's German is not perfect,' said Dr Walsh, 'to establish as much rapport as possible under the circumstances.')

Hess was affable and pleasant, said Dr Walsh, during the interview which lasted two hours. 'He answered most questions promptly.

* *The Case of Rudolf Hess.*

80

Certain questions involving his political life and opinions which were asked (merely to elicit his attitude towards his environment past and present) were answered with the polite statement that he preferred not to discuss these subjects.'

Had he taken medicines with him on the flight to Scotland? Hess's thin, bony face, highlighted by thick black eyebrows, considered the question. 'Yes. I took several homeopathic medicines with me.' Why homeopathic medicine? He believed very small doses of homeopathic medicine were effective in maintaining health.

Was he in ill-health before he flew? No. He was in perfect health before the flight to Scotland. Nevertheless, he admitted to the doctor he had taken small doses of homeopathic medicine; along with allopathic and naturopathic medicines, homeopathy enjoyed a great vogue at the time in Germany. 'Homeopathic medicines can be used in either of two ways – to prevent disease or treat it. I used it for the former purpose.'

Had not the great responsibility of being the second person in the Reich caused him nervous stress? 'Except for short periods, important events such as the pending declaration of war, I never felt under pressure. Only on these rare periods did I have difficulty in sleeping.'

Q. Why did you fly to England?

A. In an attempt to stop the war and save useless destruction of human life.

Q. Was the idea of the flight your own, or was it planned in conjunction with others?

A. It was my own idea. It was not discussed with anyone.

Q. How long did you have the idea before the flight? Hess shook his head, he could not say.

What was the German Reich's attitude to the flight – had not the German Government issued a statement to the effect that Hess was of unsound mind when he took off?

Hess thought for a moment as the translators interpreted the question from the English (now being used) which he clearly understood. Yes, he said, from his reading of newspapers while in England he had found that this was so. But he regarded this as an attempt by the then German Government to explain the fact that they had not been informed of his mission earlier, and to explain its failure.

He had often been informed by the Führer, he said, that any effort to prevent loss of life was justified and that he interpreted this as justifying his flight. If his flight had succeeded in its purpose it would not have been disavowed by those in power in Germany.

Had Hess hoped to negotiate personally with the English King? He had not; but he had anticipated negotiating with high British Government officials.

Asked if he felt he had a 'divine mission' to fly to England, he said he did not believe the mission was divinely inspired; there was a Supreme Being who did, however, guide human affairs and their ultimate outcome.

'The prisoner,' said Dr Walsh, 'was asked what his position was in the German Reich at the time of his flight. He answered that he was the second person in the German Reich next to the Führer. What, then, about Goering? What position had he held? He answered that Goering also occupied the second position, but in a different sector. He was in charge of social affairs and Goering industrial.'

Was Hess suspicious at the time that Goering was trying to take his place? No, he said quietly, he was not.

Then was his position and influence in the then German Government waning? Emphatically no, said Hess. It was not.

Was he – because of the position he occupied – insecure? No. So long as he was thought worthy of the position he would continue to hold it.

Was he depressed, or elated, before he took off?

He had noticed no depression or elation, he said, illustrating the extremes with a wavy, horizontal line in the air made by his hand.

In England, he agreed, there was some depression. But that was due to the failure of the flight to accomplish its purpose.

'Was the depression enough to make you cry?' 'No. It was not,' said Hess stiffly.

What about his two suicide attempts in England? Surely he was depressed when he tried to put an end to his life? He agreed that he had been depressed, and 'emotionally upset' at the time of the attempts. But this was a reaction to his failure to stop the war, and to a certain extent, his imprisonment.

And his memory?

'Perfectly normal.' 'Have you ever lost your memory for past events?' 'No.'

An aerial view of Spandau: the garden is on the left, with the tall poplar that Doenitz planted

The visitors' room at Spandau

The cell-block corridor: the open door is that of the cell Hess occupied
before he was taken to hospital

The Directors' table – the only
place in the world where Russia
and the West still kept talking
during Cold War crises

The tiny Spandau chapel made
when two cells were merged
by removing a wall

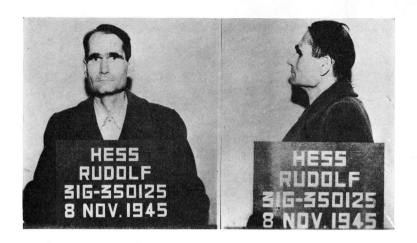

Photographs taken while Hess, von Schirach and Speer were
awaiting trial at Nuremberg

ief Warder Wally Chisholm, who took
r as Director in the absence of the
tish Director, Colonel Ralph Banfield

The author, Colonel Eugene K.
Bird, American Director of
Spandau Prison

The prison library stacked with books belonging to Hess and
prisoners released from Spandau

The old chapel harmonium, first
used in Nuremberg and later
played by Funk when he gave
recitals for his fellow prisoners

A Soviet guard marches out of Spandau after completing duty

A changeover ceremony

A guard-tower on the Spandau wall: it is impossible to penetrate the tower from outside unless the occupying sentry opens a trapdoor

'What about in England where you lost your memory for past events?'

'So far as I am aware,' replied Hess, 'my memory was perfectly normal while I was in England.'

But *twice* it had been recorded that he had lost his memory, insisted the psychiatrist. Hess shook his head. If that occurred it was probably related to his imprisonment and the failure of his flight.

'The prisoner was reminded that at the time of the Nuremberg Trial he had stated that the episode of amnesia which had occurred at that time had been feigned. He stated that this was correct and that he had pretended to lose his memory for a time, and later to have recovered it,' said Dr Walsh.

Why had he done it? Hess said he considered it expedient for legal reasons connected with his trial, to pretend that his memory was lost; and later, for legal reasons to pretend that he had regained it.

Did he believe in a 'Master Race'? Hess smiled. He had never used the expression. 'These expressions were employed by German propaganda for foreign consumption. They were not used in Germany. Anyway, I do not believe in this concept.'

What did his colleagues in the prison think of his flight? 'I am forbidden to talk to them. They can think what they will about it.'

Hess said he did not 'hear voices' – except those from his immediate environment. Nor, he said smiling, did he have 'visions'.

Colonel Chamberlin then said it was not the doctors' intention to humiliate or embarrass him by the question, or to invade his privacy. But had he experienced sexual desires during his present imprisonment?

Hess smiled across at the doctor. He experienced what he assumed to be normal sexual desires, appropriate to a man of his age. But at present he could do nothing to satisfy them.

Asked whether he had a son, Hess said he did and that he was nine years old. He expressed no emotion when speaking of his wife and child.

When the questioning appeared to be at an end, Hess asked if he might make a statement. 'With considerable dignity and with great emphasis,' said Dr Walsh, 'he stated in a very formal manner that he regarded his present imprisonment as dishonourable and unjust. He said that he and his comrades were at times insufficiently fed and were made to do hard labour, which was contrary to the sentence of the Nuremberg Tribunal. He also requested that he should be set at liberty.'

The interview had taken just two hours. Hess was led back along the corridor to his cell and Dr Walsh went to write his report.

'Obviously,' he wrote, 'a two-hour interview does not permit a very extensive survey, particularly in front of so many witnesses . . .

'In the first place it is my definite opinion that Rudolf Hess is *not psychotic* at the present time. No evidence of hallucinatory delusion or illusional trends were secured. His mood was considered to be essentially normal at the time of the interview. No evidence of paranoid colouring of Hess's mental outlook was encountered. His intelligence is obviously superior.

'Hess obviously made great efforts to impress the undersigned with his sincerity and normality. He was most courteous and responsive, looking directly into the eyes of the interviewer while speaking. He did not give the impression of being grandiose or of over-estimating his own importance, but, rather an impression of some humility, considerable quiet self-assurance, was gained.

'In summary, the impression was gained that Hess is an individual of superior intelligence with schizoid personality traits, and that he has no psychosis at the present time; but there would appear to be adequate evidence that he has experienced at least two episodes of hysterical amnesia and depression with suicidal attempts. Both apparently occurred at a time when he was exposed to strong emotional stress.

'There was no doubt of the basically psychotic nature of his psychiatric illness, or that he had experienced recurrent psychotic episodes for several years past.*

'This was indeed an astonishing situation. The former second highest officer of a modern state was found to have a chronic and extremely severe psychiatric disorder which should have incapacitated him from any post of responsibility for the lives and health of human beings! How was this possible in a contemporary state? This was indeed made possible by the fact that the leader of the state, Adolf Hitler himself, as clearly shown in his numerous published writings and pronouncements, also was schizophrenic and had experienced psychotic

* Dr Walsh published the latter part of his report – from this paragraph onwards – in the *Archives of General Psychiatry* in October 1964.

episodes; with a last lapse into frank psychosis at the time of the collapse of his brutally homicidal plans for the domination of Europe and ultimately the world.

'But how then was it possible that persons with such severe psychiatric illnesses should have gained control of this modern nation which had one of the highest literacy rates in Europe?

'Indeed the seductiveness of the schizophrenic has not been commonly realized. There exist in most, if not all humans, areas of incomplete maturity in the personality, which are liable on proper stimulation to regress to earlier developmental levels. This regression can be facilitated by contact with the type of thinking and feeling which can be quite fluently expressed by certain narcissistic or schizophrenic individuals. It is unquestionably true that in all periods of history individuals with this type of psychiatric disorder have succeeded in capturing the allegiances as well as the imagination of large numbers of people. This represents a serious danger to the stability of government and the safeguarding of human life and therefore must be taken into account, together with economic, sociological, political, and anthropological factors, in the maintenance of world peace and the prevention of war.

'I, too, during my interview with Rudolf Hess became aware that I was being seduced by his narcissism in the same manner. It is of course precisely this seductive attraction which gained an audience for narcissistic leaders such as Hitler, or for some of the disturbed leaders of fanatic movements and less scrupulous politicians who have attracted masses of followers. Since many of these people are either psychotic, or nearly so, and are unable to have relationships with others except as narcissistic objects, the danger for the peace of the world if such individuals are allowed to come into a position of power is evident.

'*It was thus a matter of concern for me when the Surgeon of the Berlin garrison informed me that I should omit any reference to mental disease from my report of Hess, stating that the political situation between the United States Government and the Russian Government was tense, and that war could break out at any moment, which appeared true.** It was difficult to see why a frank report on Hess would contribute to this result, but I was informed that the Russians would react unfavourably to a

* The italics are the author's.

report attributing Hess's behaviour to mental disease, since they wished to believe that he and the other leaders of the Third Reich in captivity could and should be held fully responsible for the crimes committed while they were in power.

'I wish only to comment in this communication on the fact that a serious distortion of historical fact can result if the psychiatrist who has submitted an altered report on the psychiatric examination of a public figure *does not correct his report after the emergency has passed*, and where no violation of human rights or of the privacy and dignity of the individual can exist.'

Hess left the cell-block after his interrogation to take his exercise in the garden, the large, tree-dotted expanse at the rear of the prison.

When the seven had arrived it had been a jungle of waist-high weeds and overgrown shrubs which had been uncultivated for years. Stripped to the waist, they had begun the task of clearing it so they would have a path to walk along, and small plots to tend individually.

Though he wrote enthusiastically of 'sweating like a nigger' and helping to plant tomatoes, carrots and cabbages, Hess was never an enthusiastic worker. He complained that he had to take part in the planting of tobacco 'for the slaves of nicotine'; mostly he refused to work at all. Once, he was found fast asleep in the sun in the prison barrow.

The Russians agreed to extend his period of exercise if he would work, but Hess was adamant. He told the warders he would rather stay in his cell. 'Even if he watered the plants a little, or raked a few leaves, we could call that work,' said the Soviet director hopefully.

But Hess said it was below his dignity even to carry a pail of water. 'What would the people outside say if they saw me,' he told a visiting general. 'They might see me from some of these high buildings around the prison* and then they would really think I was crazy. No, I'm not going to do anything of that nature.'

Actually it was a debatable point as to whether the directors had the *right* to force Hess to work. The Legal Branch examined the situation and said: 'The wording of the sentence was – "Hess, on the counts of the indictment on which you have been convicted,

* From nearby high buildings around Spandau, from time to time long-range photographs were taken of the prisoners in the garden.

the Tribunal sentences you to imprisonment for life." ' It had neither sentenced the prisoners to solitary confinement, nor hard labour. The Russians always insisted that though the sentences did not specifically say so, the crimes for which the prisoners had been convicted called for hard labour with solitary confinement.

9

Bayonets in the Kitchen

AS THE FIRST buds of spring appeared on the dozen trees in the garden and the war criminals got down to hard work in the open air, the simmering conflict over how much they were to be given to eat* burst into the open.

Medical officers and directors had argued with each other for months about the amount of calories the seven needed. While they were only working in the cell-block during cold weather making envelopes, the US agreed that they should be given Category Three rations. But when they were out doing hard, manual work, said the Allies, they were entitled to Category Two calories – 1,999 per day. Anything less constituted a starvation diet and could actually cause death through malnutrition. It would be inhumane to give them less. Spandau's prisoners – unlike prisoners in other Berlin jails – could not receive food gifts from outside. Von Neurath had just received, for instance, a parcel of sugar and sardines for Easter and that had been sent back.

The Russians not only disagreed with Category Two rations but found even that amount was being exceeded. The Soviet director said he himself had weighed meals one day and found them 500 grams over the limit.

Bitter charges of discourtesy, and 'reflections on other directors in front of staff' flew across the directors' table. Then the squabble came to a head. An order from his superiors came to the US director:

'It has come to my attention that we, as representatives of the US, are guilty in permitting certain inhumane treatment of war criminals now interned in Spandau Prison. It appears that due to

* A typical 1947 menu: *Dinner*-stew, dessert (usually canned fruit), bread and ersatz coffee; *or* vegetable soup, a small amount of meat with gravy, boiled potatoes, an apple, ersatz coffee.

Russian obstruction, Russian vetoing and Russian interference at the prison we have been unable, even during the months of American chairmanship, to carry out the prison agreements in the humane manner and in the spirit in which the agreements were originally made.

'Therefore you will immediately put into effect the following measures:

'1. You will liberally and in a humane manner interpret these agreements which have been signed by us and by the other three Powers concerned in the care of these prisoners.

'2. Those changes in diet which were authorized, whereby those prisoners suffering from diabetes were to be given substitute food . . . those prisoners suffering from anaemia were to be given small quantities of additional food, are to be immediately put into effect during our chairmanship.

'3. You will obtain and ensure distribution to these prisoners . . . small quantities of butter, jam, meat and powdered milk. Under no circumstances will this additional issue of food exceed 1,000 calories, and will be approx. 500 calories per day.

'The purpose of this additional food will be to arrest the deterioration of the physical condition of the prisoners who are continuing to lose weight under the present harsh conditions and who are approaching a point beyond that of expected malnutrition.

'You will permit prisoners when in their cells to sit or lie in their beds as they see fit, at any hour of the day or night.

'You will permit the prisoners to speak to each other within reasonable limits when they are together. For security reasons conversations should be checked to ensure that they are not of a political or security threatening nature. You will permit prisoners to have one visitor for 15 minutes every two months. The visitors will be permitted to bring two food packages: each package not to exceed two kilos in weight and no prisoner to receive more than two packages per month.

'You will provide a minimum amount of recreational facilities as determined by the US medical adviser, Colonel Chamberlin. This recreation will be consistent with normal prison practice and could possibly include "horseshoes" for outdoor exercise as well as magazines or books of a non-political or non-security nature . . . possibly even checkers, which would require permitting two prisoners, under supervision, to relieve monotony, which otherwise contributes to mental and physical deterioration.*

'I will not permit this order,' said the US Commandant of the Military Government, 'to be vetoed by Russian obstruction or Russian delay.'

Colonel Maxwell Miller, the US director at the time, was quick to put his orders into operation. He put two soldiers with fixed bayonets in front of the kitchen door to make sure there was no interference with the food arrangements. Then he put a CID man in civilian clothes *inside* the kitchen to make sure the food was prepared the way he wanted it to be. The plain-clothes detective then followed the brown, rubber-tyred food trolley around the cells to see that the prisoners got their meals due to them.

The Russians were furious. It was, they said, a unilateral introduction of new regulations and they would make an immediate report to their superiors.

Spandau stood uneasy. What would happen? What would the Russians do when in March it became their turn to run the prison? They could, reasoned the Allies, do several things: They could impose drastically harsh measures which could result in irreparable damage to the health of the prisoners. They could remove the prisoners by force from Spandau. They could refuse, by virtue of their numbers of guards, representatives of the Western Powers their right to enter the prison. And they could refuse to remove their guard at the end of their Russian month in charge.

That left the Western Powers the following courses . . .

They could refrain from interfering with the system so long as it was within the regulations.

They could give the prisoners additional packages of food in the three shift periods out of four when their warders were in a majority in the cell-block.

They could take action *before* the Russians took over in March, either by removing the seven to a different building in the Western sectors of Berlin and denying the Soviets any participation in their control. Or, using as an excuse the repair of the prison, take them by air to a Western zone of Germany.

* In the end the prisoners were not allowed to play 'horseshoes', checkers or any other game.

Or, they could inform the Soviets that Spandau was 'closed' and hand the prisoners over to the Allies by whom they were first captured.

The confrontation by the Allies succeeded. Apart from protesting, the Russians took no dramatic action. The weights of the prisoners in February, the French month, and March, the Russian month, told their own story:

	4 Feb	15 Feb	3 Mar	21 Mar
Von Schirach	65.2 kg	62.5 kg	61.8 kg	61.2 kg
Doenitz	64.7 kg	63.6 kg	62.5 kg	61.6 kg
Von Neurath	67.8 kg	68.0 kg	65.7 kg	64.5 kg
Raeder	55.6 kg	56.2 kg	54.2 kg	55.5 kg
Speer	78.0 kg	76.5 kg	74.7 kg	73.0 kg
Funk	67.4 kg	68.1 kg	65.5 kg	64.5 kg
Hess	66.1 kg	65.3 kg	63.9 kg	63.0 kg

Russian soup, complained Raeder, had very few vegetables in it . . .

The sun is already shining through the bars of Hess's cell window, picking up specks of dust floating lazily in the imprisoned air. He lies awake, listening.

Outside, there is the dull noise of traffic as the suburb of Spandau makes its way to work. In the passage near his door he hears a chair scraping and the rattling of keys.

A bolt is thrown back and Hess hears the key turn once, then once more. He closes his eyes instinctively against the presence he knows so well. The Russian warder, overnight stubble on his flabby cheeks, rasps at him. 'Come on, No. 7. Get up.'

He hears his fellow prisoners' doors being unlocked one after the other. Another day has begun. Another day off the sentence of Speer and von Schirach. Another day that will make no difference to his own life sentence.

They are shaking Funk, huddled as always, like a mole under the grey bedclothes. 'I am sick!' he screams. 'You pigs. You keep me awake all night with your noise. Why don't you just shoot me!'

It is Monday. Wash-day. Shaving day. The visit of the barber with his seven accounted-for razor-blades, his accounted-for shaving brush and cream, his accounted-for towel, barber's sheet and clippers, his accounted-for comb, brush and powder. At the store he duly checks every item from a small black note-book so that he can check it all back in again when he is finished.

Von Schirach gropes in his packet of pipe-tobacco: cheap, pungent Union Leader, made in America, in a red and yellow packet. His Dunhill pipe has burned pounds of it. Speer decides he needs a haircut and absentmindedly touches his thinning temples.

Speer's door is unlocked and he follows the rest over to the wash-room – Cell No. 10, directly opposite that of Hess. Dentures are taken out, held under taps and scrubbed. Faces are reddened with the friction of rubbing and cheap soap. And one by one they shuffle back again into their cells, muttering to one another before they go inside.

From the end of the passages comes more key-clanking as the steel door is opened and the breakfast trolley is wheeled in. On the 3ft by 2ft scratched brown top is bread, jam, margarine and a great jug of coffee. Raeder holds his enamel cup and the steaming liquid is poured in, 'Danke,' he says. 'Thank you.'

Today it is Speer and von Neurath who will do the washing. Two prisoners must take the duty week about. They try hard to get fourteen sheets and seven pillow-cases clean under the shower, but the result is always grey sheets and roughened hands.

It is now suddenly dull and raining outside. 'No garden today,' says the chief warder. Instead tables are dragged into the passage and the prisoners' wooden chairs are brought from the cells. From piles of paper, with brushes and glue, they sit, round caps on their heads, mechanically making envelopes. Dip, brush, fold, stick together. Dip, brush, fold, stick together . . . And the pile in the bags at their feet grows bigger.

Funk whispers across to old von Neurath. 'She's coming today.' 'Who?' 'My wife of course, Louise.'

In the afternoon the warder makes his way down the corridor to the 'envelope factory'. 'Number 6! Come along . . .' Funk follows, still shaky from his operation; a crumpled, bald little man with head on an angle and fear in his eyes.

Frau Funk is there waiting. She sits at a partition table in front

of a large square of Plexi-glass;★ a greying, worried woman, upright
on the hard-backed chair, gazing ahead of her. As Funk enters, twisting
his cap in his hands, she half rises to her feet. But the warder and the
prison director standing ready to monitor every word of the visit
motion for her to sit down. Funk, too, sits down.

'How are you, Walichen?' she asks. 'And your headache?'

Funk: 'It's all right. Take off your hat and let me see your beautiful
hair.' (She does so.)

Frau Funk: 'You also look well. How are your pains?'

Funk: 'The eye doctor has been giving me injections in the eye-
lids, they have a cocaine base. Now the French doctors are doing
likewise. It is much better. Only when I'm in the sunlight it hurts.
Fortunately there are trees and I can place myself in their shade. As
for my other illness, it is very well. They have to give me treatments
only every fifteen days.'

Frau Funk: 'At the time of my arrest they took all my jewellery.
It was never returned. I miss the Leichel picture. I would have liked
so much to have it back. They wanted to confiscate my personal
valuables. They said they came from France. In order to keep them
I had to have certificates as to where I bought them. Now there
are whole companies who are searching everywhere in the area for
gold which was buried.'

Funk: 'All they had to do is ask S——. It was he who was in charge
of the gold transports.'

Frau Funk: 'At the beginning of the occupation an adjutant of
Eisenhower came to see me. He wanted me to tell him the whereabouts of the buried gold. I did not bury any. I could not inform
him.

'Would you like to read the memoirs of Churchill?'

Funk: 'No. Nothing at the moment. I have too much to read.'†

Frau Funk: 'You have gained weight. You look better than you
did at Christmas.'

Funk: 'That was the result of my operation.'

Frau Funk: 'Dietel sends his regards. His wife has just returned
from the Argentine. I am going to appeal to the King of Sweden.

★ This glass was in later years removed.

† The prisoners now had a library. They could take four books – a dictionary, a novel,
a Bible and a religious book–to their cells.

He promised you that he would do all he could for you. And he can be very useful for you.

'Dietel will get you four pipes. I will come back for our wedding anniversary . . .'

The warder glanced at his watch and nodded to Funk. 'All right. Time is up.' Quietly, three feet apart and unable to touch each other, Funk and his wife stood for a moment looking at one another. Then Funk turned, and with a wave of his hand, was gone.

Hess had been adamant. He would have no visits from his wife. 'I do not wish any visits,' he said, 'whether they are important or otherwise. Not while I am in this prison.'

He was also in trouble. He had been found guilty by an inquiry of the directors, of insubordination. No. 7 had refused to get up from his bed, refused to go to work (despite his enthusiastic letters to his wife: 'This year I am not specializing in tomatoes, but in turnips and marigolds . . .'). Hess's punishment was to spend all but one hour a day – for 15 days – in a special punishment cell at the far end of the corridor. He would not be allowed to read or write, and would have only one hour a day exercise. With a shrug of his shoulders the heel-clicking, otherwise subordinate Hess went off to begin it.

Unknown to Hess, a drama was taking place farther along the cell-block corridor . . .

On the morning of 26 October 1950, a load of horse manure was carted in from the near-by British barracks for the prison garden. Speer, the architect of Hitler, was now the architect of the Spandau garden and he had pleaded for weeks that he needed it.

In the warm sunshine, a few days later, he, von Schirach, Doenitz and Raeder were spreading it. As they worked in their light uniforms, a warder moved surreptitiously towards the heap, stayed a minute or two and then moved away again.

Later in the afternoon, as Funk was back in his cell cleaning up, the warder entered. 'No. 6,' he said to the former President of the Reichsbank, 'I have something for you.' He showed Funk the paper-wrapped package. 'It is a rare plant that is considered absolutely reliable when rubbed on the chest as a cure for bronchitis. It must be used three times a day.' Funk excitedly took the package and opened it. He had in his hands a fresh, smelly 'horse apple'. The tubby little man who loved jokes – preferably smutty ones – roared with laughter.

'Oh very good,' he said. 'Very good.' Then he whispered: 'Why not pass it on to von Schirach?' Von Schirach, stiff, rather imperious, would be just the man. The warder quickly agreed.

Quietly, as von Schirach was out of his cell having his wash before the evening meal, the American warder Owens crept in. He quickly placed the unwrapped dung between von Schirach's bed and his mattress. When the Russians came on duty at 16.00 hours it would be interesting to see what happened. For nothing that should not be in a cell escaped the Soviets.

At 16.15 the usual search began. Von Schirach's bedclothes were thrown off his bed and a Russian warder ran his fingers systematically between bed and mattress . . .

The result was pandemonium. Guards came running. The chief warder was called. The directors were alerted. And a full-scale inquiry began. The 'exhibit' was deposited by the poker-faced Russians in empty Cell No. 28 and a guard placed over it.

After days of questioning – and days of guarding the solitary 'apple' – the culprit was found. At a special meeting of the directors, during which the dung was placed on the table, he was named as Warder Owens. The US director proferred his 'profound apologies'. And nine days after the trouble began, the Case of the Smuggled Horse Apple was closed.

10

That Man Adenauer...

ALLEGATIONS OF HARSH treatment of the prisoners could often be found in the more sensational German magazines and newspapers – but they had to be officially ignored.

When they came, however, from a stern, wrinkled old gentleman in Bonn who had certain power – at least on paper – then they had to be answered.

Dr Konrad Adenauer, the Federal Chancellor of Germany, listened sympathetically to tales of cruelty passed along from the prisoners' wives. He wrote on 21 June 1950 to the Chairman of the Allied High Commission: 'According to reliable reports the treatment of the prisoners at Spandau has considerably worsened during the last few months and now shows features that must be termed exceedingly harsh . . .

'Light beams are now again, as during the first years, "for checking purposes" directed at night at regular intervals against the prisoners in their cells so that their sleep is being continuously disturbed and almost made impossible. The prisoners are prohibited to use their beds – except from 10 pm until 6 am. At all other times the prisoners are forbidden to lie down or even sit on their beds. This applies also to those prisoners who are weakened through illness or infirmity.

'The extremely small and narrow cells contain – apart from the bed – nothing but a table and a wooden stool without a back. There are no further articles of furniture. Prisoners have nothing to sit on except the said stools.

'The prisoners, who during the last year were permitted occasionally to talk to each other, have been subjected to an absolute prohibition to speak. They are not even permitted to talk to each other during the walking exercise which takes place twice daily in the prison yard. On these occasions the prisoners must silently and at the prescribed distance from each other walk in a circle around a tree. Before and after each exercise a thorough search of their bodies is carried out by the guards. The prisoners . . . are now strictly prohibited to do any reading. Those prisoners (for example von Neurath, now 77 years old) who are unfit to work, sit, except for the walking exercise, all day long on their wooden stools, without having anything to do or to read. Food in the prison,which had somewhat improved during the British and the US months, has become very bad again and deficient. It had always been bad during the Russian month. No food parcels or other gifts are ever handed to the prisoners. They are always confiscated.

'There is only a French clergyman available to look after the spiritual needs of the prisoners. German clergymen are never admitted. The Pope some time ago had his blessings transmitted to one of the prisoners. The prisoner was never informed of this, but heard it only when his daughter visited him. For humanitarian reasons, I feel compelled to ask, on behalf of the Federal Government, the Governments represented on the Allied High Commission to cause conditions in the military prison at Spandau to be investigated and to take steps to ensure that penal practice be adapted to the principles prevailing in all civilized countries.

'I beg your Excellency to accept the assurance of my high esteem.'

Immediately the Adenauer letter arrived at the Commission, answers from Spandau were demanded by the Commission office. When the information was received from the prison, the Commission's General Committee met to consider the Adenauer letter. He was to be told that contrary to his 'information' it was neither prohibited for the prisoners to use their beds during the day, nor were they forbidden to talk or read, that their cells were furnished not with stools, but with straight-backed chairs; subject to censorship, they were entitled to procure from outside any books of interest to them.

Their food was quite adequate during the months of management by the Western Powers and even during the Soviet month the regular amount of calories was provided.

'With respect to the lighting of the cells,' Dr Adenauer was told, 'periodically during the night for security reasons, in the interests of the prisoners, the frequency with which this is done is to be reduced to a minimum and bulbs are to be covered with shades. An approach will be made to the Soviet authorities with a view to reducing the power of the bulb. Or at any rate that they should be tinted.

'The High Commission does not consider it advisable to request any modification of the provisions concerning their spiritual assistance, which the prisoners otherwise consider satisfactory. Furthermore, it does not appear to be possible to organize the reception of food parcels.'

Funk, however, claimed he was still being tormented by night inspections of his cell when his light was turned on. When he went to bed he began sticking adhesive tape over the light switches. Why had he done it? asked the Soviet director. 'The French director, Major Darbois, has given me permission to do it,' Funk assured him. At the directors' meeting Major Darbois denied giving Funk permission; as a punishment for lying Funk was denied books from the prison library for three days.

The alleged 'war of nerves' against the prisoner in Cell 19 was still apparently going on weeks later. Funk wrote to the directors about his acute 'nervous disease'. 'This aggravation,' said the pencilled note, 'is caused by sleeplessness which shatters the nerves more and more due to increased disturbance during the night by the switching on of the ceiling light of the cell.

'The so-called night-light is so bright* that I am able to read without difficulty. It is not only switched on by warders four times during the last week but twice more by the controlling Soviet chief warder when the Soviet team is on duty; that is up to six times per hour. Every hour, when the warders are being relieved, the cell will be lighted up sometimes for 10 minutes. Moreover, the light switches in the cell corridor make such a cracking noise during the nocturnal silence that when they are switched on or off I am mostly frightened out of my sleep; this means 14 times cracking at each of the four to six lighting up times per hour.

'As I have received opiates every night for two years the fearful awakening by the light noise is accompanied by a frightening oppression and palpitation of the heart. My head is deafened and my body paralysed and I cannot fall asleep again. The nocturnal lighting up is a torture . . . and I beg the directors urgently to release me from

---

* There were two bulbs in the ceiling of each cell; one weak one for inspection purposes, a stronger one for reading.

these horrible torments; and to decide, according to the order of the duty doctor which is affixed to my cell-door, that lighting up of my cell between 10 pm and 6 am will not be carried out without there being a special reason.'

A few weeks later Funk's aggravated nerves became too much for him. As the Soviet warder switched on his cell inspection light Funk flew out of bed in a rage and abused him. Other warders arrived and he also abused them. The British director – at the resultant directors' inquiry – asked why it was necessary to switch the prisoner's light on at 5 am, which was then broad daylight. The Soviet director said his warder could not see the prisoner. It was decided to warn Funk that any future conduct along the same lines would be severely punished. Physically and mentally, the little financier was cracking. He had constipation, headaches, retention of urine, spasms of pain, and a recurrence of his diabetes.

He was 60. He suffered from hypertension and pulmonary emphysema (fluid in the tissue of the lung), as well as his other ailments. However his heart was healthy and the doctors were not worried about his immediate future.

At the same time as they examined Funk, they found that 74-year-old von Neurath should be kept to a minimum of physical activity. He had hypertension and the doctor recommended mild sedation.

During the medical checks a neuro-psychiatrist made a two-hour examination of Hess, now 56. He found 'passive aggressive reaction', 'negative attitudes', and 'passive obstructionism' in No. 7. On the other hand he saw 'a very intelligent man with great will-power'. Said the psychiatrist: 'He continues to gain by the attention he receives and the interest displayed in him. He probably derives much satisfaction by his perennial successful perseverance in this "disturbance" which "baffles and be-devils his environment".

'It is impossible to state at this time,' Dr Hans Lowenbach went on, 'how much of the reaction is conscious and how much has become unconscious "habit" after all these years. There was no suicidal preoccupation.'

And Funk? 'A generally cheerful attitude with rare and sudden moments of sadness; unpredictable outbursts of anger and subsequent embarrassment and apologies. Characteristic memory disturbances (failure for names and recent memories), good and emotional and vivid memories for recent events. Loquaciousness; disturbances of nocturnal sleep, sleepiness in the daytime. His symptoms are brought further into focus by the fact that he has to live on his intellectual and emotional capital without new acquisitions.'

How much was Rudolf Hess's misbehaviour – now a fact of life at Spandau – merely a cry for attention? Did he now crave it? He had been investigated so often psychiatrically that he was almost certainly the world's most mentally examined patient. In Britain the best psychiatric men available had sat down with him for many days trying to work him out; Dr J. R. Rees had spent a total of *60 hours* with him. Again in Nuremberg he had been the centre of attention. An international team of some of the best doctors in the world had tried to find the answer to the Hess riddle. And in Spandau he was continually being examined.

Whenever there was a lull in attention, it appeared that Hess would be sure to misbehave. This is an extract of the warders' 'occurrence book' for December 1950:

December 3rd. 0645 hours. Breakfast served to all except Funk and Hess. Hess refused to get up and wash or fetch his breakfast, complaining he was sick. Told twice to get up, he refused in a most insubordinate manner.

0730 hours. Funk and Hess resting. The day before Hess had again refused to leave his bed, even to wash and eat. He states that his sickness is so severe and so painful that he is not able to get up.

December 8th. The US warder Owens and the English warder Read carry out a search of the cells. From Hess's cell two slices of white bread and a portion of butter are removed. [In the book are references to frequent refusals of Hess to get up out of bed.] The directors' meeting has decided that a notice would be fixed at the door of Hess's cell which authorized the warder to remove Hess from his bed with force if he considered it necessary and right.

December 15th. 0600 hours. Hess refused to get up. Breakfast served to all prisoners except Hess.

0730 hours. Prisoners except Neurath and Hess detailed to clean cell section. Hess refused to get up and obey any orders.

1005 hours. Breakfast for Hess. The day before Hess had again

refused to get up for the Soviet warders. The Soviet warder Baldin
gives orders to remove him from his bed.

December 18th. Hess says he is sick and cannot help with the cleaning.
Mattress removed from the bed of Hess as this is only way, it is
believed, to get Hess up and out of bed. Hess refused to get up and
requested light so he could read. This request refused. Hess complains
again next morning of pains, and states that he cannot get up. Whereupon he is removed again from his bed. After a little resistance he
leaves the cell to go and wash himself. He is grumbling and protesting.
Bullen believes to have heard the word 'Schwein' (pig). Punishment: He
has been deprived of library books for 15 days, writing paper for
15 days, bed and bedclothes to be removed during normal working
hours. No lights to be permitted in his cell except for the purpose of
security checking, 30 minutes in the evening at mealtime and for such
time as considered necessary for eating, cleaning out his cell and
washing. Hess was warned that in the event of further insubordination
the thought of solitary confinement would be considered.

At night Hess's groans and moans were beginning to seriously disturb
his fellow prisoners. He was repeatedly examined by the doctors who
could find no medical reason for his pains and cramps. In the end he
had to be moved to a cell at the far end of the corridor, as far away
as possible from his colleagues. But that remedy did not last long.
Hess was now keeping the warders awake, so he was moved back again.

The French director was worried enough about Hess to call the
attention of the directors' meeting to the problem. Hess, he said, was
spending more time in bed than ever before; he was not getting the
exercise and fresh air he needed. His behaviour was getting pro-
gressively worse.

Just as suddenly as he had sunk into his 'difficult period' Hess
recovered from it. He was alert, confident – and even sometimes
cheerful – the next weekly meeting was told. He had also gained
weight. The meeting thought Hess's improvement might not be entirely
unconnected with disciplinary measures he had been threatened with.

As Walter Funk played next day his beloved Bach on the chapel
organ, his five fellow prisoners sat quietly inside the double cell that

had been set aside for worship. His sixth comrade, Hess, sat as always, outside in the corridor.

The whole prison came to a standstill as Funk gave his weekly recitals on the ancient, foot-pedal harmonium. Warders drifted nearer, and stepped lightly. The chapel – two cells with the dividing wall removed – had seven hard-backed chairs and three small tables, one of them made into an altar. It was draped in a purple cloth on which stood two round, squat candlesticks with fat white candles in them. Between the two stood the bible. On the wall was a rude, wooden cross, a metre high, and nearby, two etchings by Dürer. On one of the tables stood an old vase. But it held no flowers.

All the prisoners – except Hess – were Protestants, Speer by far the most devout. Hess said he believed in God but would not be 'preached at'. He had attended only one service in the chapel but would talk seriously and at length with the Lutheran pastor. 'I believe in God, but in my own way,' Prisoner No. 7 told him.

As Christmas drew near Pastor Nicholas sought the usual permission from the directors to conduct his Christmas Eve afternoon service, from 2 pm until 5 pm. He asked for a wreath to be allowed on the wall, and a religious picture. Funk would again play the hymns and carols.

It was their fourth Christmas in Spandau as they filed quietly from their unlocked cells into the chapel. And as the strains of Funk's organ reverberated through the cell-block each prisoner was aware of the atmosphere around him and what it did to him. Old squabbles – particularly between Raeder and Doenitz – were put aside and greetings exchanged. And down in the kitchen, the chef was busy preparing for the morrow. His instructions read:

'*Menu*. Christmas Day, 1950; Breakfast: Scrambled eggs, toast, butter, jam, coffee.

Dinner: Turkey, dressing, cauliflower, celery strips, bread or rolls, butter, coffee, tea and milk.

Supper: Soup, crackers, lettuce and tomato salad, bread and butter, coffee or tea.'*

Heavy with the Christmas fare, the old brown trolley made its

---

* This compared with a normal day's prison fare: *Breakfast* – omelette made with two eggs, bread, butter, jam, coffee, milk and sugar. *Lunch* – green beans, salad, eggs, vegetable soup, prunes, bread, butter, coffee, sugar. *Supper* – braised beef, mashed potatoes, carrots, pears, bread, butter, cheese, coffee, sugar.

rubber-tyred rounds. At each cell as it stopped, Christmas greetings were exchanged. And that night the seven retired to bed with their books, more than a little bloated.

Those who had always maintained a protective attitude to Hess were worried about his obstructionism and what the New Year would bring for him. The warders said openly that they feared one day someone would lose his self-control and beat him up. One British warder shook his head: 'All the psychiatrists in the world wouldn't make any difference to No. 7. There's nothing wrong with him that a good kick in the pants won't cure.'

Nevertheless the outward signs of his 'attacks' were there as evidence that *something* was going wrong in his mind or body. At night in his cell, or seated in the garden in the sunshine, Hess would suddenly begin his loud, honking moaning, clasping his stomach. His face would grow pale and his forehead break out into beads of sweat. A warder, however, convinced he was faking his attacks, went into his darkened cell one night during an 'attack'. He talked to Hess without switching on the light. Then, staying inside the cell, he closed the door as if he was leaving. The moment Hess heard the door close, he said, his groans instantly stopped. The warder opened the door again as though he was coming back and the groans began again.

Albert Speer, who was as close to the distant Hess as any of us were, said he believed the 'attacks' were psychosomatic. Speer had a long, serious talk with US Army psychiatrist Dr Robert Levy. He told Levy that he did not believe Hess had deteriorated intellectually over the years. He had always been considered 'peculiar', but there was no obvious increase in his peculiarities. Speer said Hess went for weeks without social contact with the other prisoners, but recently he had made some small attempts to have connection with them. He would discuss with them subjects like skiing, technical problems, and his son, of whom he was very proud. They would not discuss the past very much because they had said everything that was to be said about it in the first couple of years.

Hess would also sometimes discuss flying and his flight to England.*

* His flying suit, helmet and goggles always stood only a few yards away from him in the store-room.

Speer did not find it so odd that Hess would not see his family. 'We all remember them as they used to be and we don't like to have to see them under such circumstances.' Sometimes Hess talked about what it would be like when he 'returned to normal living', despite the fact that he had a life sentence. Hess had never said anything to him about 'hearing voices' or having 'mystical or unreal feelings'. Since the Nuremberg Trial, Speer recalled, Hess had frequently complained that his food was being poisoned. Speer had offered to exchange his cream or sugar with him so he (Speer) would 'get the poison instead'.

While the other prisoners were inclined to treat Hess rather roughly, said the psychiatrist, Speer made an effort to try and treat him as a human being. He would sometimes be paid for his trouble with a certain amount of arrogance. To those who were brusque with him, Hess was courteous.

'The other day,' said Speer, 'it was one of the prisoner's birthdays. I knew that Hess would not remember, so I reminded him on the morning of the birthday. He turned to me as though I were one of the aides from the old days and said: "Why didn't you tell me of this before?" '

When it came to a discussion of a complicated technical problem it was Hess, admitted Speer, who was faster than he was in grasping the facts.

The psychiatrist left Speer and went to chat to Hess, 'a grey, ageing, stiff-looking man, whose manner was distant, giving an impression of weirdness'. Hess said he was having bad pains now every night, and pointed to his right lower chest. It was untrue, said Hess indignantly, that he stood around naked in his cell (as other prisoners had reported). But it did help to get cold air on to his pains.

'How do you get along with the other prisoners, Hess?' asked Levy. 'Well . . . we are all comrades.'

11

Cell Secrets

RUDOLF HESS WAS not to be found today in his cell. He had been obstinate again about getting out of bed on the previous morning. Hess drew his bony knees up to his chest and shook his head. He was not getting out of bed. The warders had orders not to argue with Hess. With a deft tug the striped grey mattress was pulled from beneath him and Hitler's former deputy found himself on the cold cell floor. He was taken off to Punishment Cell – appropriately numbered – No. 7.

In the other cells the six prisoners stirred as Spandau's morning began. Their whole lives were an automatic obedience to the daily schedule. They had no clocks or watches in their cells, but they could instinctively time each physical process that slowly whittled away the days, weeks and months of footsteps, rattling keys, voices.

6 am: 'Right No. 4! Get up!' 'Come on No. 6!' Morning ablutions. Handing over of spectacles. Making up of beds.

'6.45 am: Breakfast. 7.30 am: Work begins under instruction of chief warder. 11.15 am: Work stops. Personal search and wash,' said the schedule.

11.30 am–12.15 pm: Midday meal. Rest, write . . . smoke or read until 1.30 pm. Then work again until 4.45 pm.

4.45 pm: Cease work. Personal search and wash.

5 pm: Evening meal. 5.45 pm–6.15 pm: Enter library cell and exchange book through Librarian Raeder.

6.15 pm–10 pm: Rest, read, write, smoke, evening ablutions.

10 pm: Return spectacles, lights out, retire . . .

Saturday: 8–9 am: Change of clothing and bed-linen. 9–10 am: Exercise. 10–11.15 am: Bathing. 2 pm–3.30 pm: Divine service. Recorded concert on first and third Saturday of each month for 30 min.

3.30–4.45 pm: Exercise, rest, read, write and smoke.

Sunday: 8 am–4.45 pm: Rest, read, write letters, smoke, exercise.

Shaves and haircuts: as needed, given by medical orderly Boon or Proost on Mondays, Wednesdays and Fridays between 9 am–11 am.

On the surface the routine was monotonous, dull, and wasting. But in their small worlds of 9ft by 7ft there was plenty going on . . .

Speer was busy writing his memoirs, a practice specifically forbidden by the directors. Nevertheless the tall man with the quiet, perceptive manner was putting down on paper the story of his life and having it smuggled out of the prison, chapter by chapter, to his publishers. Every page of paper the prisoners were handed was stamped with the Spandau seal and recorded in the office so it could be checked off when it reappeared as a letter. Speer was not using *official* paper; he had recently had his cell painted and the painters had put down paper to protect the floor and the sparse furniture; Speer was able to keep some of the paper and secrete it away. In his neat, tidy handwriting he was getting down the story of his rise to favour with Hitler and his ultimate control of German armament production. As he finished each page he strapped it around his leg with a rubber band, underneath his trousers. Before routine searches he was able to switch the manuscript's hiding-place before it was handed to the man who was to smuggle it out of the prison.

Speer's conspirator was Proost, the Dutch aide-man, who said while he was a POW of the Germans it was due to Speer that he was treated well. He now had a chance to return the favour.

Speer had one uncomfortable moment during a cell inspection, when the rubber-band snapped and the pages of one chapter fell about his ankles. It was not, however, noticed.

It was no secret that German publishing houses and mass-circulation magazines were negotiating through intermediaries with the prisoners for their life-stories. Von Schirach had an agreement with a magazine to write his memoirs for 500,000 Deutschmarks. But he waited until he was released before he began 'his duty for the sake of history'.

At night, when all was still, and (the directors believed) serene in the cell-block, things were going on that would have turned them grey. An American warder one night managed to smuggle in bottles of wine, hidden, like Speer's book, in his trouser-leg. Quietly he passed the wine around from cell to cell. Prisoners who had not tasted alcohol for 10 years became quickly intoxicated with the merest gulp. 'The Russian warder was due on at midnight,' explained someone who saw it happen, 'and everyone was worried. Von Schirach was still singing!' From their cells the prisoner's comrades told him to 'shut up or we'll all be in trouble', and von Schirach eventually quietened down.

It was soon after that a ban was put on Communion wine. The Russians refused to see that it was an integral part of the religious service: they could see only its intoxicating properties and the pastor had to be told that it was disallowed.

Old von Neurath also had a smuggler working for him. He had always craved chocolate and he was able to find a willing conspirator among the 32 warders and 18 United Nations displaced persons who worked in the cell-block. Twice he was caught: the first time an inquiry at which every warder was questioned pinned the suspicion down to one man, but nothing could be proven.

The second time chocolates were found hidden in his cell the directors' meeting became heated. 'The prison is not a house of miracles and Neurath is no conjuror,' snapped the French director. 'Someone brought that chocolate into the prison-block.' The Soviet director urged that Neurath be severely punished for having smuggled chocolate. 'He is an old man, and sick. And he was in the garden when it was found,' said the British director from the end of the table. The Soviet director was not to rest merely because discussion of the hidden chocolate had been postponed to another meeting. He interviewed Neurath in his cell and the prisoner admitted that he had eaten some chocolate and hidden the rest. He refused to give the name of the man who had passed it to him.

He was becoming old and fumbling and had deteriorated mentally and physically, said the US director. He was no longer able to dress himself properly. It was the opinion of the US prison physician that one of the night checks on his cell during which he had to stand outside for up to 20 minutes in the cold corridor could kill him. The search for the chocolate smuggler was then dropped.

When cells were suddenly searched at night they were left a mess. Often it took an hour for the prisoner to get his belongings back into order. Schirach had in his cell two pairs of socks, one pair of shoes, two pairs of slippers, four towels, two face-cloths, one pair of pyjamas, one pullover, a jacket, a pair of trousers, underclothes, cap, braces, shawl, four blankets, two pillows, two sheets, a crucifix, two cups, an eye-patch, a soap-bowl, a denture bowl, a fountain pen, pencil and a calendar.

When it was all upturned he naturally sometimes became angry.

While Hess was in the punishment cell Speer would volunteer to sweep out Cell 23 while he was away. Although Speer had no real time for Hess he would go out of his way to take care of him and protect him when he thought he was having a hard time.

The years were gradually taking their toll of the seven. It showed in their faces and in their regular medical reports. Doenitz had pains in his right hip and hands and was having infra-red treatment; von Neurath had headaches and dizziness and was being given daily infra-red treatment on his left hand. Hess was given a hot-water bottle to clasp to his abdomen when his 'attacks' came on and warned that if he still refused to eat his proper meals he would become seriously ill. The doctors had checked thoroughly his heart, stomach and kidneys and all organic diseases were ruled out. Hess refused, however, to have a barium test of his intestines. As early as August 1950, an X-ray had shown a large gastric bubble in his stomach which elevated the left diaphragm and pointed to a suspected gastric ulcer. 'No,' said Hess, in his high, edgy voice. 'It is far better to merely abstain from nourishment. That will cure me.'

Funk was regularly having urethral dilations under a local anaesthetic. They took place every 10–12 days and gave him relief. Dr Otto Churney, present while one of them was taking place, came away from the aide-room and said: 'When I went in he immediately began talking in a loud, very excitable manner, waving his hands and stating that he could not sleep. He feels, he said, that the urethral treatments are another way of extending his torture.' Funk had, in addition to his difficulty in passing urine, headaches and insomnia.

Raeder, at 74, was complaining of pains in the leg and hip and was given massage and infra-red treatment. He was granted the use of a stick to help him in the garden on wet and slippery days. The younger Speer, then 45, was complaining of constipation. The doctor who checked him found that a recent attack of phlebitis (inflammation of the vein) had left him with his left thigh and leg larger than the right.

Von Schirach's chief complaint was that he was getting coffee late in the afternoon and that it was keeping him awake. His coffee was discontinued at night and given him in the morning.

Conditions in the prison were improving. Private toilets had been installed in each cell and new shower baths put in the bathroom. Heating throughout the cell-block kept cells at a comfortable temperature. And a Miele washing-machine costing 620 Deutschmarks had been installed for the prisoners to do their laundry.

But Frau Louise Funk suspected all was not well in the prison. She wrote* indignantly that 'the execution of punishment in Spandau is diametrically opposed to the conception of the civilized world of conditions prevailing in penitentiaries and prisons. The conditions,' said Frau Funk, 'may only be compared to the dungeons of the Middle Ages you read about in thrillers.' She pointed to 'cruel torment of flashing lights in prisoners' eyes . . . in conjunction with modern mental cruelty and cleverly thought out rules of control', which were ruining the prisoners mentally and physically.

'It is worse than a death sentence,' accused Frau Funk, 'for the men are buried alive – physically and mentally.' The Spandau authorities showed the High Commissioner a verbatim record of her last visit with her husband.

Frau Funk: How is your health?

Funk: I consider that Colonel Guinchard who is treating me is one of the best surgeons. He has made some nerve injections; few doctors or surgeons have successfully carried out this kind of therapeutics. It is sometimes very dangerous, as an affected nerve can sometimes have serious consequences.

Frau Funk: I have brought you some warm clothing as well as some fur-lined boots, as you are wearing a light suit.

Funk: Do you know, I am reading a book by Tolstoy, *War and Peace*, in two volumes? This book has always impressed me deeply. If you only knew how painful this light is . . .

Frau Funk: Put something over your face.

Funk: I place a handkerchief and some black eye-flaps on my eyes, but in spite of this it is painful.

(At this point Captain Mironov, the Soviet censor, interrupted. He

* In a letter to the US High Commissioner for Germany, 20 January 1953.

reminded the speakers that it was forbidden to mention any questions concerning the prison.)

Funk: Why! It is not possible to speak! (And he began shouting loudly.)

Frau Funk: Calm yourself! (She then went into a fainting fit.)

As she recovered she said: You know I have seen your friends, and they all ask to be reminded to you.

Funk: Would you have any news from my best friend . . . the one I helped financially previously?

Frau Funk: Don't mention him. He is not very interesting. When in need he did nothing for me, and now I do not want to hear of him.

Funk: I hope you have a good journey. You will be in Frankfurt tonight. Goodbye.

Frau Funk: Goodbye. Keep well.

Albert Speer, the architect who would have transformed Berlin, was busy working with a small pile of stones and two wooden planks in the garden. The hands that had traced the plans for Germany's new architectural skyline were now fashioning two crude seats under the garden trees. One by one, as he worked, Speer's six comrades filed down the iron steps into 'Speer's Garden' . . . 'Speer's Garden of Eden'. It had been a wilderness the day they arrived. Now there were tidy paths, borders around each garden plot, shrubs and trees. Speer had dedicated himself to the garden. He worked in it, drew in it, and every day dreamed in it.

And now he was walking around the world in the garden.

It took Speer on average 215 steps to walk completely around the path. Converting this into metres and kilometres he started out on his trek from Berlin to Prague. Slowly he made his way to Vienna and the Black Sea and using maps and geography books from the library plodded across the Bosporus and the Turkish mainland to Baghdad. He walked on to Asfahan, Teheran, Samarkand and Delhi. Many months later he was in Mandalay, Peking and Vladivostok. Speer would consult the Russian warders about ice conditions and where the sea was likely to be frozen. He would record not only his progress at night in his cell, but historic and geographical landmarks. He would write in his note-book: 'Covered another 15 kms today.' And the line on his world map would grow a little longer.

As a meticulous architect Speer had also worked out that he got more exercise in his confined cell by walking around it rather than up and down. 'Why do I do this?' Speer would say. 'It stops me going crazy.'

No other prisoner was as easy to work with or as placid as Speer. Quite suddenly, however, for no obvious reason, Speer would turn on the placid chief warder Wally Chisholm and abuse him. There would be a flare of tempers and shouting and at the end of it Speer would be put on punishment. The puzzled warders could not believe it. Speer the model prisoner suddenly gone berserk? It was the only way Speer *could* remain such a model prisoner. 'If I did not let off steam like this occasionally, I would go crazy. I do it on purpose and I know I will be punished. It is the only way,' he told me, 'to stay sane.'

The bewildered Chisholm was called in to face the directors about the garden, which was his responsibility. 'There are roses, lilacs and currants planted,' accused the Soviet director. 'Why?' 'There are one or two gooseberry bushes and one or two rose bushes,' replied Chisholm uneasily.

'I was in the garden,' said the Russian. 'And I counted them. That garden is for vegetables.' Chisholm was ordered to remove the flowers. And at the same meeting there was the problem of the Spandau invaders that had to be solved. Rabbits were burrowing under the wall and getting into the garden and damaging it. After a long discussion the directors of Spandau Prison decided that the answer was *snares*. And jail-minded, they added: 'When the rabbits are caught, they are to be confined in cages.'

The kitchen was able to have fresh beans, cauliflower, kale, cabbage, celery, tomatoes, beet, potatoes, leeks, salads, pumpkin, parsley and onions from the garden. And even succulent strawberries. Sadly for the seven who grew them, it was against the rules for a prisoner to eat a strawberry. They were a luxury. Even when the walnut trees shed their nuts and a prisoner stuffed a few in his pocket he was on a charge. Even Hess had the gardening bug for a short time. He got hold of some sunflower seeds and scattered them wildly as he made his way around the garden path. When they came up the sunflowers, like the lilacs, were removed.

In November the garden was a blanket of white, with just the beaten-down track along the path for the prisoners to enjoy. Doenitz and von Schirach, in the winter of 1952, began a snow-fight and were joined by the American warder Owens. All three were castigated for it.

Soon it got too cold even for the walks, and exercise had to be taken in the prison block itself. And the seven men of Spandau were huddled up together with their books, their private enmities and their aches and pains.

12

Release

SPANDAU'S LEAST DIFFICULT prisoner, Baron Constantin von Neurath, who had been Hitler's first Foreign Minister, had now become incapable of work. He was told by the doctors that he had to avoid walking fast; and that one of the younger prisoners like Speer or von Schirach should help him up and down the iron staircase when he went out into the garden. If he became excited in any way, the directors were warned, it could prove fatal.

On 31 March 1952 he had a violent attack of angina pectoris – a suffocating pain radiating from the heart – and when the warders found him he was close to death. They sent out an urgent call to the Soviet medical officer on duty, but he could not be located. Telephone calls were made to the Soviet barracks and headquarters and the guards were all asked to help. But it was two hours before the search for the Russian was abandoned and the British doctor arrived at von Neurath's bedside. The prisoner gasped out that he had been given a capsule of nitro-glycerine to keep by him after a similar attack a month before, but he had used it up. He was just getting over this attack when, three weeks later, he was transferred to the prison sick-room with 'flu. Again he recovered from his illness and was able to go back to his cell, even joining in the basket-weaving in the cell-block corridor.

However in July the following year his condition once more became precarious. His heart had become enlarged, and at times beat rapidly. He had high blood pressure and the Royal Army Medical Corps doctor who examined him said he could only expect to live longer in a more natural environment. The directors met to discuss what course they would take in the event of his death. The US favoured handing his body over to his next-of-kin, his wife.

Neurath spoke with difficulty, and when he did, had an impediment in his speech. A bedside rug had been laid beside his cell bunk and on 9 September 1953 a truck arrived at the prison bearing an adjustable hospital bed for him. Orders were given that his night inspection light should not be used, but that warders use a flashlight instead.

If he died suddenly, telegrams, already prepared, would have to be immediately sent and the news would be out. It would be difficult to prevent demonstrators gathering at the prison. If cremation was decided upon it would take approximately three hours to take the body to the Wilmersdorf crematorium, hold a short service and return with the ashes. It would be best, the directors decided, to make the journey at night. Police would be notified and road-blocks set up to keep demonstrators from the front of the prison. The prison chaplain was to accompany the cortège of military governors, directors, warders and 20 guard soldiers, and conduct the service. The cortège was to go in trucks and not in cars, to avoid outside knowledge of what was being carried. In order to attract as little attention as possible the directors would also consider sending a decoy cortège. On the return to the prison the ashes would be put in the guarded prison safe while attempts would be made to persuade the Soviet authorities to agree to them being handed over to the family.

If flowers were to be received in the prison they would be allowed to be placed in the chapel so long as they were searched for explosives and their cards censored. At an all-night meeting which argued every angle of the funeral down to the choice of funeral music (to be left to the pastor) the Soviets suggested that the same workers who dug the grave should be the pall-bearers at the crematorium.

Neurath became seriously ill again on the night of 2 September 1954. The British doctor asked for an immediate visit by his relatives. The prisoner had expressly asked to remain in his cell and not be removed to the sick-bay or a hospital. The pastor was told he could administer the last rites, and a telegram was sent to von Neurath's daughter to come to the prison. His wife was too ill to travel.

The doctor told the directors' meeting: 'I have seen von Neurath many times during the last month, and today when I saw him, I considered him to be more seriously ill than he has ever been before. He has had an attack of pulmonary oedema; it is very serious and he could have died from it. At the moment he seems to have rallied very well and I would not say that he was in any imminent danger. However his condition is such that he could have a further heart attack at any time, and die.'

The funeral arrangements were finalized. A cell at the end of the corridor was to be used as a special chapel and the organ placed in the corner. A table with cloth covering it would serve as an altar and chairs would be provided. The casket was to be placed before the altar on two supports and an oak cross bearing in black lettering the name of the deceased should be leaned against the casket.

There would be no cremation. Instead, the prisoner would be buried in Spandau. The coffin that had been made years before would be used and the grave dug behind a wall which could only be reached through a locked door. The corpse would be dressed in clothes obtained from his personal property in the store-room.

Unaware that hours had been spent in the preparation for his death, von Neurath once more rallied and was able to sit up in his bed and talk. But his days in Spandau Prison were drawing to a close. On 5 November 1954 his relatives were called suddenly to the prison and were told: 'Von Neurath is to be freed.'

His release had been decided by the Powers and the details drawn up at a directors' meeting. 'In accordance with an agreement reached by the governors of the Four Powers on the release from prison before the completion of the sentence of Constantin von Neurath, sentenced on 1 October 1946 by the International Military Tribunal to 15 years' imprisonment, the governors of the Allied Prison, Spandau, have agreed as follows: to release Neurath from prison on 6 November 1954 in the care of his relatives. Personal belongings of the prisoner kept in the prison are to be handed over to him and a receipt obtained.'

It had been no easy decision for the Powers. The Allies had tried several times during von Neurath's years of illness to have him set free, but the Russians had refused. Quite suddenly, without preamble, the Russians had sent a letter to the British, French and United States embassies in Bonn saying – without reference to any previous negotiation – that *they* had decided he should be released. It was a 'humanitarian act from the hearts of the Soviet leaders . . .'

Von Neurath lived for two years with his family, and died after an asthma attack at Inzweihingen. 'He was mistaken, as many of us were,' said the obituary in the newspaper *Tagespiegel*, 'and he had to pay for it much more than many of the others. He carried his fate with dignity in his old age.'

Erich Raeder, despite his walking-stick, was still very much the erect 'grand admiral'. He had once told his wife:* 'After my life sentence I requested mercy. I preferred to die as a soldier – to be shot. This was as much for your good as for mine. You would have suffered only for one moment, whereas life imprisonment means endless suffering for me.' But, like the others who had asked for the firing-squad, he had been turned down.

Now, suffering from a serious circulatory disease, he hobbled about the prison, careful not to jar his hip or leg. He had been ill with a high fever the day before his wife made one of her regular visits and Frau Raeder alleged that despite this, he had been forced to get up out of his bed to go to the washroom and to fetch his own meal. She wrote to the director of the Berlin Element,† Mr Cecil Lyon, on 12 January 1954, just after her visit, that Raeder had not been informed of her visit until 15 minutes before it took place. Further, she added, Mr Winston Churchill had recently told Admiral Tirpitz's son that her husband was 'innocent and should be released'.

Dr Adenauer was also endeavouring to obtain release of all prisoners over 75. He wanted the time they had spent in prison before judgement taken off their sentences and remittance of the last third of the sentence or the conditional suspension of it.

Suddenly, on 24 September 1955, came another 'out of the blue' decision from the Soviet Union that they would allow Raeder to be set free, 'taking into account the advanced age and serious illness' of the prisoner. The next day the Spandau directors met and Frau Raeder was alerted.

On 26 September 1955, at 11.35 am, the plump-faced, rather baggy-eyed Raeder was delivered into his wife's arms. They remained for an emotional moment inside Spandau and then Raeder, stepping carefully through the door, turned his back on the prison forever.

He settled down at home in Uhlandstrasse, Lippstadt, in Westphalia whence he wrote to the directors asking for various belongings which he said were still in the jail. He was still missing two note-books 'where he used to enter addresses, dates, dates of birthdays, drafts of letters, reading notes, etc.' One note book had been kept behind by the British director who wished to retain it for its list of documents,

* During a visit on 29 September 1950.
† The overall Allied political controlling body for Berlin.

he said. The other, lined, had been in the bookshelf on the wall of his cell. 'In it were the four photographs which were not hanging on the wall and which were specially dear to me – two of my parents, one of my dead son and one of my son's grave. I had looked on these photographs each morning, and also on 26 September 1955.' He wanted all filled-up note books (about four), some other photographs and some letters. There were also a tool for threading, a saucer made for him by a little girl, his memoirs and copies of his Nuremberg defence. He threatened that if he did not get property back he would 'be forced to take other steps, since by retaining for instance the note-books with the photographs which are dear to me, this has to be doubtless considered as an act of inhumanity'.

He wrote his memoirs, which were, said a critic, dull and pragmatic. 'I always believed it would come to a controversy with Great Britain,' wrote Raeder. 'It is the tragedy of my life that the development took on a different course.' He was able to enjoy a quiet contented life in the mountains before he died.

A year later, it was Grand Admiral Karl Doenitz's turn to go. However, unlike the sudden, unexpected freeing of the sick von Neurath and Raeder, Doenitz's release was to be at the end of his 10-year sentence, and was known to the minute. Both inside and outside the prison an uneasy atmosphere was building up. What would happen when this man, who had briefly stood at the helm of Germany, walked out of jail?

Two months before release, Doenitz's lawyer, Herr Otto Kranz-bueller, visited him to work out the final arrangements. Doenitz agreed with the lawyer that there should be as little publicity as possible at the time of his release. He intended to write a short book, but it would not cover the aspects of World War II or Nuremberg which had been written about. Asked about finances, his lawyer assured him that 'block funds' would be released to him. He asked too about a coat of arms and a painting which had been given to him by the Government on his birthday.

Doenitz asked if the lawyer felt the people of West Germany thought he was guilty. The lawyer replied that only a handful were of this opinion, whereas the great majority considered his conviction a political one. Many journalists, said Herr Kranzbueller, wanted to write about him – but not *against* him. Doenitz, sitting at the opposite side of the interview table, said that what he had in mind for the future was to rest, write, sail and spend a lot of time with his wife. He was grateful to her for her optimistic attitude in the difficult years.

The Allies' plan for a smooth operation of the release was for Doenitz to be moved the day before from his cell to the sick-bay, adjacent to the chief warder's room, where he would receive his personal clothing and belongings from Chief Warder Chisholm and give a receipt for them. But the Soviets put up an obstacle. The sentence, they said, did not expire until *midnight* on 30 September and he should not be given his own clothing until then. He must be held in his cell in his prison uniform until midnight and then his clothes would be handed over. No, replied the Allies, if this was done Doenitz would not be able to get out of the prison at midnight and technically he would be, for some minutes at least, held in prison illegally. The Russians relented a little. 'He can have his clothes at five minutes before midnight,' said the Soviet director.

It was a tense moment for Doenitz as he changed in his cell for the last time. He had been told that there was a crowd outside, including some 200 Press and television men, waiting for the gates to swing open.

Doenitz's daughter had arrived. To elude the Press, she and Doenitz climbed into an ordinary Berlin Mercedes taxi in the yard of the prison, behind the big green gates. In a second car, an Opel limousine belonging to the British Army, was a French interpreter and an Englishman. The Opel swung through the gates first and the Press raced after it. A few seconds later, the taxi emerged, turned left past the directors' mess-hall, right through the gateway and away into Berlin. Realizing they had been duped, the Press tried to get through the police cordon to chase it. Cameras were broken and a truncheon was swung. But Karl Doenitz had gone.

Later that day he posed for photographers and made a short statement. He had been 11 years in prison and was taking his time about forming opinions, he said. He contemplated no political activity. Then he caught the five o'clock British European Airways flight to Dusseldorf, where his wife waited. And that night he had dinner at home.

Left behind in their cells, wondering how he was enjoying his freedom, were Speer, von Schirach, Funk and Hess.

The Joker would be the next to go, said the warders knowingly. Walter Funk, story-teller, organ player, raconteur of scenes from some of the wildest parties Nazi Germany had seen, was a sick man.

On his wife's last visit Funk had quite suddenly begun shouting: 'I can't stand any more operations!' Later, taken down to the garden for exercise, Funk had begun crying again. 'What's the matter?' asked the US chief warder. Funk could only wipe his eyes and shake his head, 'I don't know. I don't know.'

He had been operated on three months before for gallstones, entering the British Military Hospital under the pseudonym 'John Begonia, aged 67'. He had recovered well, but by October 1956 his diabetic condition was causing the doctors some concern. He went on practising the organ on Wednesdays, Thursdays and Fridays for the Saturday concerts he gave, but his heart was not in it any more. He was moving slowly and weakly, suffered from chronic constipation, was easily fatigued and experienced giddiness when he got up in the morning. He wept again on Christmas Day and the medical book recorded: 'There is no response to encouragement. In short it is the examiner's diagnostic impression that there are changes consistent with senile decline . . .'

The French chief warder reported* that Funk staggered constantly and was not in a condition to 'do anything'. Wasn't it time for his release, he asked? The rumour in the prison was that the Powers were considering a 'solution' for all the prisoners: Funk – medical release; Hess – insane asylum; Speer – unconditional release; Schirach – parole with restriction to a 50-mile area.

Mentally Funk was deteriorating, said a report to the State Department in Washington. He was depressed, cried frequently and stared fixedly at the wall for long periods. He was not even conscious of people entering his cell. His interest in reading was declining and in conversation his voice trailed off. His former conversations with the others during exercise periods had been replaced by a simple nodding of the head. He complained of dizziness and weakness and told everyone he expected to die in prison. In several outbursts he had said he was 'sick of pills and operations' and could not stand any more.

On 17 January 1957 when General Rome, a senior American medical officer, came to the prison for an inspection, Funk described to him

* On 28 December 1956.

all his ailments, operations and his current state of health. During the interview with the General he was allowed to sit on the end of his bed in his cell. He asked General Rome to do everything he could to get him released. 'I want to die at home,' wept Funk. 'I don't want to die here in the prison.' The Soviet director shook his head over Funk's 'performance'. 'He is a great actor,' he told the General. 'He is as well as any other 66-year-old.'

Funk's wife, Louise, made a plea for her husband's release a fortnight later: 'I have shared with him good and evil for over 30 years,' she wrote, 'and my conjugal affection towards him has never ceased.

'We have been separated for nearly 12 years now. At my visits, which have been frequent lately owing to the kindness of the Allied authorities, I have noted that my husband's physical and mental condition has been reduced to such a low level as appears to me to confirm what I have feared for years. I have again witnessed a nervous collapse on my last visit, on 30 November 1956, he seems to be unable, in view of his desperate and hopeless situation, to gather sufficient mental and physical strength to live through his confinement. If my husband is not released from prison in the very near future, I have no hope that he will ever return alive to my care.

'I wish to withdraw my husband to a quiet place and spend the short time we can still hope to live, in peace and freedom. I trust that . . . the Great Powers will reduce his sentence.'

Despite the medical reports, the Soviet warders and their director were constantly telling Funk: 'You are looking well. You are feeling well.' Funk would become infuriated and start shouting. Twice he was reported for having shouted at the Soviets. 'Shoot me down – but do not continue to torment me!' he screamed.

His mouth was inspected and the remaining upper teeth were found to be all decayed or infected. His upper denture no longer fitted. The dentist recommended clearing of the upper roots and bridge, and the construction of a new upper denture in acrylic.

Meanwhile secret talks between the Powers gave the hint that release was soon on the way. First news came on 14 May when the directors were told to telephone and ask Frau Funk to come to Berlin. She was not to be told the reason. While she was on her way, the decision was made: he could be set free on 16 May. Because of his age and ill-health, the Press was told, Funk had been shown clemency and would not have to serve his life sentence.

It was first decided to put him in an ambulance. But the doctors assured the directors that the prisoner was able to walk and could leave the prison on the arm of his wife. Frau Funk arrived at the prison in a state of excitement, and within half an hour, was leaving with her husband.

Before he turned his back on Cell 19 and the grim, brick walls that had closed him in for 10 years, Walter Funk was handed 225 private letters and 13 postcards, 14 photographs (10 from his cell walls), 26 books, 26 music books and a sheaf of legal papers relating to the de-Nazification proceedings against him. Funk made a last-minute call on Hess, Speer and von Schirach and shook their hands. His eyes were moist as he took his wife's arm, and at 2.23 pm the doors closed behind him.

Then Spandau's sad little clown was gone.

13

Just Three Left...

AND NOW THE complex of Spandau Prison held just three men. Baldur von Schirach, 50, arrogant, knowledgeable, and superior. Albert Speer, 52, hard-working, pleasant, resigned to his remaining time in prison. Rudolf Hess, 63, cantankerous, difficult to manage, a 'problem-child'.

Alone together in the garden they presented a strange sight. Hess striding along the garden path, leaning forward, almost running; his hands behind his back, overcoat flowing behind him, Groucho Marx style. Speer was as usual hard at work fighting back the weeds among the vegetables, sawing limbs off trees, planting new seeds. Von Schirach: walking slowly, leisurely, thinking.

Von Schirach confessed to me once: 'I have never yet met the man who I could look up to. And that includes Adolf Hitler.' Hitler's former youth leader had a flair about him, even in the faded prison uniform he wore with his number on the back and on the knees. He wore a scarf that was swung back over his shoulder in a jaunty style. His fingernails were always clean, his grey hair always neat. A man of medium height, he was trim for his age, still handsome.

He took a great pride in speaking English, and spoke it with hardly an accent. When we had met for the first time he gave me the feeling that it was *he* who was interviewing *me*. The director I was taking over from introduced us in the garden and the prisoner cocked an eye at me. 'Very nice to meet you, Colonel. I had heard that you were going to take over as US director. We prisoners are happy that you are a Lieutenant-Colonel and not a captain or major bucking for the next rank.' He drawled, in a loud voice: 'We have had our experiences, here in this prison, with young junior officers, and it hasn't been pleasant. So welcome to the team!'

He was not trying to be funny. He *meant* it. Herr Baldur von Schirach was welcoming me aboard! It happened to be the anniversary

of the 20 July* attempt on Hitler's life. And von Schirach went on:
'Today is the anniversary of the attempted assassination of Hitler. Just
leave it to the Army to bungle things. Typical Army! Putting down a
satchel of explosive was as cowardly a trick as ever I heard. As a result
of this cowardly act several thousand people were put to death. The
most courageous thing would have been to put a pistol to Hitler's
head.'

He was smoking his pipe, and his hands waved, emphasizing points.
There was no stopping von Schirach now. While we stood patiently
he went on: 'I can tell you one thing. I was on the trusted list of the
Führer. Everyone was searched on entry and I was one who was not
searched. I could have taken a pistol in myself and I could have done it!'

Speer, his No. 5 on each knee of his corduroy pants, got to his feet
from weeding the garden. His coat was off, his shirt-sleeves rolled up,
soil on his hands. A tall, rather gangling figure, his head seemed
slightly large on his shoulders. He had a habit of tugging at his trousers,
straightening them. He stood to attention, bowing almost impercep-
tibly from the waist. He looked me straight in the eye. His bushy
eye-brows were still luxuriant and black, warts stood out on several
parts of his face. 'I am very glad to meet you,' he said. And he went
back to his work.

Now Hess – the enigma. He was brought to a halt from his rapid,
coat-flapping walk and he stood stiffly to attention, heels together,
head slightly bowed. The eyes were sunk so far back into his head
beneath the beetled eyebrows that it was difficult to see that they were
blue. He did not smile. He had almost a puzzled frown. His whole
presence showed withdrawal, suspicion, subservience. I asked after his
health. 'Bad,' said Hess. 'Very bad,' shaking his head sadly.

He was dismissed. Once more he clicked his heels, bowing. And off
he went again, striding purposely ahead, leaning forward, hands behind
his back, deep in thought.

'I wonder what goes on in that strange man's mind?' I said.

Hess was in trouble with the British director for not standing up
when he entered his cell, and he had been punished. The Soviet warders

* The attempt on 20 July 1944, by Lieutenant-Colonel Klaus Stauffenberg and other
plotters, to assassinate Hitler with a time-bomb.

then adopted the attitude that he should be made to stand up when the aide-man came around dispensing pills. They would shout at Hess to stand up and he would get grumpily to his feet. He decided that he would get even. He scrawled the word '*Aufstehen*' on a piece of toilet paper, in large letters, and hung it in his cell. It was an insult, said the Soviet warder. No, said Hess. It was merely a reminder to himself that he must stand.

When he refused to get out of bed a few days later the warder pulled the sheets from under him. 'Hess got up in a rush,' claimed chief Soviet warder Kasakov, 'had his fists clenched, and was crying and gesticulating with his fists in my direction. He showed great discontent and threatened me. After this he went for a wash and returned to his bed. He refused breakfast. I ask the directors, if possible at an extra-ordinary meeting, to take against Hess measures of most severe punishment.'

A week later Hess was still troublesome. He was groaning and complaining for an hour after his evening meal and lying naked in front of the open window, saying it helped his pains. A doctor arrived and gave him an injection of distilled water, the usual method of con-vincing Hess he was being given 'strong sedation' to calm him. Next day Hess complained to the British and Soviet directors that the warders had dragged him out of bed in the morning by the ankles.

At this stage the directors were worried. It was becoming difficult to draw the line between persuasion and unnecessary force used on Hess. The threat of a warder losing his temper with the man was a very real one. He was punished by five days in the sparsely furnished punishment cell and deprived of the four daily newspapers the prisoners were now allowed to have, as well as his books.

The doctors were worried enough about Hess's mental state to suggest that he might have to be sent to a mental institution. A psychiatrist at the US Army hospital told the directors that there were now reasonable grounds to suspect a chronic deteriorating condition which would warrant his being placed in a mental hospital, rather than a normal hospital. If he were freed there was little danger of him becoming any sort of Nazi leader, said the doctor. 'As a free member of the community, Hess would be a burned-out ember. He would be the type who is argumentative in his neighbourhood; but politically and socially, Hess would not be active. He would not cooperate with any group. Even the family would have a difficult time dealing with him.'

For years the US warders had been assessing Hess and his actions. Now they were ready to present a composite report on him in the light of any pending decision to have him moved. 'Hess has made no adjustment to his confinement and poses the same problems today as he did 10 years ago. He abhors exercise, studiously avoids work, and at times accepts punishment rather than going out into the garden. He occasionally refuses to get up in the morning and for periods refuses many of his meals. He tends to ignore his whole environment and asks if every phase of the routine can be put off to another time. Typical comments are:

' "I don't want to have a shave now . . . Can't I eat later? . . . Bring the soap later, I don't want it now . . . I'll take my bath later . . . Do I have to have my hair cut today?"

'Hess speaks excellent French and speaks English fairly well. He has always refused to have visits from his family or relatives. His wife, in her book *Prisoner of Peace*, explains that a visit under such circumstances would be degrading. Hess writes his weekly letter, although on occasions he has written "No news – will write again next week". He reads all four newspapers. He keeps the *Frankfurter Allgemeine* the longest. Over the years he has attended chapel service only once; he has asked to sit outside the chapel and listen to the music. When Funk played the organ, Hess could hear fairly well from his own cell. Several times a year Hess is invited to the church by the French chaplain, but he has always refused except for the one time, several months ago. Hess talks very rarely, but once asked a US warder if he was of Scandinavian descent. Almost nothing is known of Hess's views. He dislikes Schirach and does not extend to him the normal German courtesies. However, this attitude very likely originated with Schirach. Hess occasionally says a few words to Speer, these are comments on interesting books or newspaper articles. Hess sometimes mumbles or comments aloud, or smiles, when reading the newspaper.

'The attitude of the Soviet warders towards Hess is simply that he is a faker. The attitude of the French warders is quite neutral, except for the warder who proclaims that one day somebody is going to lose his temper and beat up Hess. The attitude of the British warders is that there is nothing wrong a kick in the pants won't cure. The attitude of the US warders is mixed. "Eccentric," some say. "Some of his act has become very real over the years." Or "approaching senility".'

One warder was worried about Hess enough to urge a complete examination. Wally Chisholm, British chief warder, acting as British director on 25 November 1959, declared: 'I feel it is my duty to once again express my grave concern and also that of several warders on duty about the health of prisoner Hess. He has lost over 10 kg (22 lb) in a little over three weeks, and his weight is down to 45.5 kg, which in my opinion is dangerously low. He is now very weak. The health and welfare of a prisoner is very much our responsibility . . . and it is quite obvious Hess is in urgent need of medical attention and care. I therefore request that when the medical officers meet next Friday, 27 November, that they see and examine Hess.' The directors decided to take Chisholm's advice and refer Hess to the medical officers at their meeting.

When the French warder, Morrell, entered Hess's cell at 12.15 pm the following day, he found Hess curled up in bed, blood seeping through his blanket and sheet from a cut left arm. He had tried to take his own life by smashing a lens out of his spectacles and dragging the broken glass across a large vein in his wrist.

The Soviet doctor on duty was called and came running. While he examined the wound Hess said he fully intended to commit suicide. He had taken advantage of the situation when Schirach and Speer, accompanied by a warder, were working in the garden. It was his condition which had finally caused him to take such a step. 'It is based on the nerves,' said Hess. 'The deprivation of every possibility of activity and the prohibition of reading is an unfavourable influence on the nerves.'

The doctor immediately, and without anaesthetic, stitched the wound in his arm and Hess promised he would start eating again. 'Hess was perfectly calm all the time,' said Boon. 'In fact he remained in a much calmer state for a long time after the attempt. Whenever he had any outburst his attitude afterwards was like the calm after a storm.' Morrell's view was that Hess's self-inflicted wound was not a genuine suicide attempt, but merely one of his childish ways of drawing attention to himself.

All sharp objects such as spectacles, nibs and even his dentures were taken away when not in supervised use. His door was to be kept open and a 24-hour watch was placed on him. The dispenser, Boon, was ordered to be in the cell-block at all meal-times and the chief warder was to watch over Hess while the other two prisoners were in the garden. Hess had written his 'last will and testament' in his black notebook. It was ordered to be destroyed.

Just as quickly as he had stopped eating, Hess began eating again. He asked for large amounts of food and his weight in December shot up to 60 kg. His physical examination showed his stomach to be normal, and there was no indication for an X-ray of his gastrointestinal tract. An electro-cardiogram was also normal.

Hess was worrying the warders with his petty complaints and his refusal to cooperate. But his psychiatric condition had not been deteriorating to any marked extent. At his most recent psychiatric examination he had been found by Dr Robbins to be 'in a fair state of order'. 'On the very morning of the examination,' wrote the doctor, 'the prisoner refused his breakfast, having his usual hypochondriacal complaints.

'He . . . rarely talks to his fellow prisoners. He sometimes laughs or chuckles for no apparent reason. He is prone to clench his fists at certain individuals. He sometimes makes noises in bed, but does not talk to himself. There is no true deterioration of his personal habits.

'The examiner approached the prisoner in a cell which was found to be in a fair state of order, and walked with him to the examination-room. The prisoner walked in a bent-over fashion, clutching his outer garments and using a slow, measured, almost manneristic gait, suggesting a slow religious procession.

'He showed a striking, rather gaunt appearance and signs of the beginning of old age. However . . . his responses were brisk, clear and to the point. His eyes were bright and active and his emotional state relatively stable. He showed no evidence of hallucinations. He was able to add two-digit figures rapidly. His past memory could not be accurately evaluated because he refused to answer any questions about the past.

'Hess was asked to draw a person on a sheet of blank paper and he produced, very rapidly, and in correct proportions a figure of a man with a totally blank face. When questioned about the blank face he added features . . .

'At the conclusion of the interview he was led back to the cell. Several minutes later I looked through the cell door and saw him laying on his bed with his fists clenched, staring up at the ceiling. I feel that the prisoner does know what is happening to him and why he is in prison; and that he is not at the present time in such a state of insanity or mental disease as to require a mental institution.'

While the Hess drama was going on a letter arrived for Baldur von Schirach.

His young son wrote from Munich: 'To the directorate. Dear Sirs, I have a very great request. Please would you be good enough to grant my father, Baldur von Schirach, may keep a little dog with him in the Spandau fortress?

'It is my Tibetan terrier, Nylon, who is clean, healthy and cheerful. It would get accustomed to everything and my father would be very happy if he could have a dog.

'Please do authorize it now so I could bring with me the dog at my next visit in April or May. I request it cordially, with kind regards, Richard von Schirach.'

Spandau did not take in animals, and a letter to the young Schirach was sent explaining the rule. The only outsiders to enter the prison were the birds which descended in flocks when a prisoner surreptitiously scattered a cache of crumbs from his pocket. There was no place for Nylon the dog.

14

A Spandau Diary
1961-1963

THE DIRECTORS' TABLE has seen dramas over the years, though nobody has ever come to blows. Long arguments have sometimes gone on all afternoon and all night, only breaking up wearily as dawn was breaking. During periods when the US and Russia seemed poised on the brink of war – as in the Berlin blockade and the Cuban missile crisis episode – Spandau's directors' table was the only verbal meeting place between Russian and American. While summits were being planned to prevent a third world war, we were busy arguing about Hess's new denture or von Schirach's knee bandage. For months on end the operation of Spandau carried on uneventfully. Meetings were short, agendas predictable and quickly disposed of.

The directors' diary from January 1961 and December 1963 records, *inter alia*:

'Von Schirach had all his teeth out and has been given dentures.'

'On 10 May von Schirach complained of pain in the right upper calf, after resting and particularly on getting up. There was no history of previous injury. An elastic stocking was given to him and the pain settled down.'

'The Soviet director was opposed to giving Speer the spirit level for his garden and it was decided to return it to his wife on her next visit.'

'This morning von Schirach slipped on the freshly waxed corridor floor, and fell, striking his right supra-orbital region (above the eye-socket) and both hands. There was no unconsciousness and a neurological examination three hours later was normal.'

'Prisoners are to air their blankets once a week on Thursday or Friday if the weather is clement. They are to clean their cells and the warders' toilet daily and the polishing of the floors of the cell-block corridors is to be done on Thursdays. Washing of underwear and cleaning of the laundry room the same day.'

'Von Schirach fell down the stairs and received abrasions to the hips and legs. He has slight muscular pain and rest was advised. Hess has behaved well during the month.'

'Speer writes: "I beg that the following fundamental wishes be considered. At present my closest relatives consist of my wife, six children, and son-in-law. On these eight persons are to be distributed the annual 13 visits of half an hour each, so that each member of the family can only see me for about 50 minutes per year. Since numerous questions regarding the family are to be discussed with my wife, I provide for her, three times per year, visits of half an hour each. It means I only can see my six children and my son-in-law once a year, for half an hour. The children's visits take place under an unnatural tension on both sides, since they mean at the same time a leave-taking for another year . . . I beg in my case for the number of visits to be fixed in accordance with the number of members of my family." '

'At about 8 pm two youths approached the sentry of Tower No. 1 and started to pelt him with stones from a catapult. Although warned by the sentry, they did not stop until the chief of the Soviet military guard and the chief warder went out to meet them. They ran away. According to instructions, the sentry could have used his weapon to end "this dangerous vagrancy" (said the Soviet military director) and the help of the Spandau police was sought.'

'The Soviet director reported that Speer shook hands with his son at the termination of his visit. As Speer had already been warned after a similar violation of the rules, it was agreed to remove Speer's letter-writing and letter-receiving privileges for a week and to warn him that a similar occurrence in the future will result in the loss of one, two or maybe three monthly visits.'

'Replacements of the prisoners' old and worn-out wearing apparel were made.'

'Hess had dental attention but refused to have the remaining upper teeth extracted so a full denture could be fitted. He writes: "I have a strong natural objection to pulling teeth which are not giving me any problems whatsoever, and to have false ones put in their place. If I had a plate continuously in my mouth – not just at meal-times – this would cause an abnormal saliva flow. If my front teeth are pulled and

I had a plate I could not talk in a correct way and would not have my front teeth for my tongue to press against." '

'The French dentist saw Hess today and told him he was of the same opinion as the British dentist – the old teeth should be pulled.'

'Hess had been fitted with a partial denture and his abdominal complaints have, at the same time, been less frequent . . .'

'Hess's usual complaints. He has not worn his denture because "it makes the gum sore". The US dentist has visited him.'

'We are going to give the prisoners new overcoats. After 16 years the present ones have become useless. Three used uniform coats belonging to the warders have been chosen and will be dyed dark brown.'

'Prisoners will now be authorized to be shaved with electric razors which will be provided for them.'

'The doctors say Schirach has been well and uncomplaining during the month, and that he is always cheerful and cooperative. His blood-pressure and weight remain substantially unchanged. Speer is fit and appears completely adapted to the routine of his environment. Hess's complaints about his physical condition have not altered. He tends to depression, but can be temporarily relieved of this by conversation. Then he is occasionally quite animated.'

'A Dr L. Schmitt has called at the prison. He wanted to give us some facts about Hess, who was once his patient. The doctor says that several times before 1941 he was taken out of Sachsenhausen concentration camp, where he was an inmate, to treat Hess and other high Nazis. Today he treats more than 200 patients a day in Munich, he says. Until now he has been silent about Hess because of the doctor-patient relationship. Now he wants to talk because, he says, Hess's sanity may be in the balance. He wants the authorities to know that Hess flew to Scotland because of pacifist beliefs which he had accepted after joining a religious sect. The doctor said that for several years prior to 1941, Hess had been rendered politically ineffective by Bormann and Hitler and that he had been *forbidden to see Hitler* for about two years prior to his flight. Because of Hess's extremely introvert personality he will become incurably insane unless he is soon released from confinement. Dr Schmitt went on during his 80-minute discussion, about Hitler's grandfather being a gypsy, about Nazi activities in Bavaria, etc. He was of course not allowed to see prisoner Hess.'

'Hess has remained in better spirits this month, and appears to have had fewer abdominal cramps. It has been recommended that he is provided with longer blankets and sheets. His slight constipation has been treated with nightly glycerine suppositories. He has lost $2\frac{1}{2}$ lb in weight.'

'The medical team informed us today that early this morning it was discovered that von Schirach had a blood clot. His condition was serious enough to warrant immediate removal to hospital. The Soviet director agreed on a personal basis with his removal but said he would have to seek higher authority. The British are standing by to remove von Schirach as soon as the Soviets agree. Six days ago he had complained of pain in the right calf aggravated by standing and walking. By 3 December there was swelling, local heat and extreme tenderness of the right calf. Today the prisoner was examined by the medical representatives of all Four Powers. The most feared complication, they say, is that the blood clot would block the artery carrying blood to the heart or lung, which could kill him. Von Schirach was later taken to hospital and by 9 December his condition had passed the danger point and was considered to be "good".'

'Christmas presents have come for the prisoners. Von Schirach was allowed to be given an embroidered table cloth, a finely made shirt and silk scarf. Hess was handed a package of 4711 soap. However other gifts to von Schirach of cashmere underwear, fur-lined slippers and an expensive sweater and other items were disallowed.'

'Hess today dropped and broke his dentures.'

'A note came from von Schirach: "I wish to express to the directors, as representatives of the four occupying Powers, my heart-felt thanks for the measures taken by them to restore my health. In addition to the superior medical treatment and care, the attention shown me by the directorate gave me such a mental boost that I was able to recover as quickly as I did." '

With the other four prisoners gone from the jail there were new pressures on the remaining three to make an effort to get along together. Adjustments in personality had to be made. Where von Schirach had got along particularly well with Funk and had little to do with Speer and Hess, he now had to turn to them for friendship. His wife had divorced him early in his confinement which had for a long while left him withdrawn.

Warders often found von Schirach's observations tiresome and his personality overbearing. With little encouragement he would converse on most subjects. 'He does not feel at a disadvantage', said a former director who reported on the man in 1957, 'in science, nature, gardening or politics. Or indeed on any subject.'

Von Schirach claimed he had collected Hitler's original notes and sketches to Dr Porsche on the Volkswagen, the People's Car, but 'some low person' had stolen them from him. Schirach had often upbraided Funk for telling dirty stories. 'You should remember your position as a former German Government minister,' he told the Joker. 'Schirach plainly dislikes Hess,' wrote the director, 'and has even pointed out to the warders that Hess was not taking his turn with the housekeeping work.'

Now, with only Hess and Speer to live with, von Schirach had swallowed his dislike and was prepared to help Hess. His attitude towards Speer had been cool until recently when Speer made friendly gestures to him and they were accepted. 'They walk together and converse on non-controversial subjects,' said one of the chief warders.

Von Schirach had observed that a former British Prime Minister had difficulties which resulted from his drinking. When he had visited Berlin he had 'stayed drunk in his railway car and then became peeved at the lack of ceremony. An ambitious man with nothing to back up his ambition,' was von Schirach's summing-up.

He had christened a former director 'Colonel Blimp' and had been punished for it. He had little time for Chisholm. 'He doesn't procure enough books for the library and sometimes we get the same books on new issues. Chisholm is a typical Scotsman – when he issues aspirin or even garden seeds he counts them into our hands.'

15

'I Am Going Blind'

BALDUR VON SCHIRACH was taking his exercise in the garden on the afternoon of 25 January 1965. As he strode around the path with snow all around him, he noticed a peculiar flashing of light about his right eye. Every time his right foot hit the ground the light flashed again. He stopped and rubbed his eye. Almost immediately black spots began floating in front of it. Then everything went completely black.

A warder hurried over to him as soon as he saw something was wrong. He called aide-man Boon and together they took the prisoner back to his cell and put him to bed. A doctor arrived a few minutes later and examined the eye. He straightened up, face serious; then he came back with an eye-patch and put it over the eye, ordering that the cell be darkened. Von Schirach lay fearfully awake in his bunk most of the night. Was he going blind?

Under a closer examination next morning with an ophthalmoscope the reason for the flashing lights and the darkness was revealed: he had suffered an almost complete detachment of the retina, the layer of nerve fibres sensitive to light forming the lining of the eye-ball. All he could see was a tiny chink of light.

He was taken across to the aide-room and put to bed, with Boon sitting close by, watching over him. The shades were drawn and the room was almost dark. Eye-patches covered both von Schirach's eyes now, and he lay with his body elevated, his head lowered, turned slightly to the right. He remained still, only carefully sitting up for meals, while an angry debate went on in the directors' room about moving him to hospital. He was seen by a British doctor and an American eye specialist who urged his transfer to a hospital where his eye could be properly treated. But the Russians said no. There was no question of allowing him out of the prison. He could be operated on just as well in Spandau.

134

The Allies said they would not allow an operation to take place in a room which only a year before had been declared unfit for surgery. It had been inspected and the surgeons had reported it too small for necessary equipment and personnel. It was inadequately heated for nine months of the year and inadequately ventilated. The non-conductive floor was seen as an explosion hazard and so was the operating light, which was also immovable. It would take 'many hours', they said, properly to scrub the floor, walls and ceiling, and the dust in the air, because of the absence of any filtration system, would mean recontamination of the room, the personnel and the operating wound.

The argument dragged on in the directors' room, and it was only at an emergency meeting that the Russians gave in: von Schirach could go to the British Military Hospital. The 58-year-old prisoner quickly dictated a telegram to his son Klaus: 'Being transferred to British Military Hospital where an eye operation will eventually be performed for a detached retina of the eye. Visits will take place as usual. There is no cause for alarm.' Then at 7 pm he was placed on a stretcher and carried carefully to an ambulance waiting in the freezing cold of the courtyard. Heavily escorted, it headed for the old* hospital where the eye specialist had been alerted to meet the prisoner. They examined him and took him away to the operating theatre where they tried immediately to stitch the retina back in place. The prognosis was poor, said the surgeon afterwards. We had to face the problem that at von Schirach's age the retina in the *left* eye might soon detach itself as well. Then he would be quite blind.

Von Schirach, his eyes bandaged, lay still in his second-floor bedroom. One night his guards outside saw something stir in a tree that grew by the hospital wall near his ward. They went to investigate and found a woman climbing up its branches. When they got her down she said her name was Karin Stein and that she had always been desperately in love with von Schirach, though it seemed unlikely that she had ever met him. She had been sending him cards, letters and flowers for years she said. (The prisoner of course got none of them, he was allowed only approved correspondence from relatives.) She was quietly escorted away from the hospital grounds and von Schirach went on sleeping.

* There is now a new British Military Hospital.

His bandages were removed but von Schirach shook his head. He could still only see a chink of light out of the side of the bad eye. The retina was too far gone. He lay for days recuperating and thinking, and always an American guard in steel helmet, rifle at the parade-rest position, stood at his door. 'For God's sake,' Schirach asked me. 'Let me be guarded by the Russians. I cannot stand this fellow staring at me.' We withdrew the guard from his sight and he settled down.

He was taken back to the prison and given a low chair in his cell so he could sit with his feet up on the bunk. Speer was allowed to go in and read to him for 30 minutes in the morning and Hess went in for 30 minutes in the afternoon. He was excused all work and allowed to take longer exercise periods in the garden.

Every day, while he walked along the garden path, the white-haired von Schirach closed his eyes and stepped carefully, learning the layout of the prison. When he got back into his cell he closed his eyes again and felt his way about, touching bed and table, feeling the objects on it. *He was practising being blind.* 'I know they fear the other eye will go as well,' he said. 'I want to be prepared for it.'

Carefully he was investigating all that had been written about eyes and detached retinas. Speer and Hess went through text-books and medical papers for him. Soon he knew as well as any eye doctor what he might expect.

Then came a ray of hope. His lawyer son, Klaus, wrote of a Professor Meyer-Schwickerath of Essen who was successfully using light-coagulation – the laser-beam – to heal eyes. He had used it to weld detached retinas and, said Schirach Jnr, it would be particularly appropriate to cases like his father's where there was a threat of thrombosis which made conventional operations impossible. He had written to the doctor. The system had already been used on the Duke of Windsor's eye.

The American eye specialist examined von Schirach's left eye on 22 April when the prisoner gave the alarm that it had been 'flashing' like the damaged right one. His diagnosis was read to a meeting of the directors: 'The degeneration process has started . . .'

I urged the other directors to approve a decision calling Professor Meyer-Schwickerath to examine von Schirach immediately. We already had a cable from Klaus Schirach saying that the professor was willing to come to Berlin and that the necessary equipment to perform the operation was available here. But the Soviet director said such an important decision would have to be made at ambassadorial level; it was out of our hands. The British explained that their expert advice was that without laser-beam treatment von Schirach stood a 50 per cent chance of going blind; with it the threat was reduced to only three per cent. No, said the Russian. The decision was not up to us. 'We must be humanitarian,' protested the French director from across the table. 'We must not think in terms of the doctor's nationality.' 'Nyet!' said the Soviet director. Only a doctor from one of the Four Powers was allowed to examine a Nazi war criminal.

The US eye surgeon was brought in. He said: 'Every day lost reduces his chances. It might already be too late.' In Berlin only the Germans had the equipment and the skill to perform such an operation. The Soviets stood firm. They were not going to agree. And they left the meeting. Back in his cell von Schirach was pacing up and down, nervous and tense. I told him the news. 'I can only hope that my sight will remain until I get home and can familiarize myself with my surroundings. I'll need three weeks to get used to my bedroom, to the steps and the furniture. I will be released in a year,' he said wearily. 'And all I want is to see my grandchildren before I go blind.'

I was in the directors' mess adjacent to the prison on 28 April when I had a call to the telephone. 'Von Schirach,' said the warder, 'is seeing spots with his good eye.' I immediately called an informal meeting of the directors. 'The man could be going *blind*,' I said. 'If he is not allowed out of this prison we will force him out under guard.' The Soviet director refused to listen further and broke away from the meeting table. I got up and followed him into the corner. 'I mean what I am saying,' I said. 'We are not going to bear the responsibility that through lack of guts or character we allowed this man to go blind.'

Colonel Lazarev, the Soviet director, turned on his heel and said he was going to his headquarters. He would return with an answer. He never came back. He too had developed a thrombosis and his chief warder returned in his place. The Russians had agreed, he said, to allow von Schirach to leave the prison and be examined by the professor in a Berlin hospital.

I hurried to a phone to try and contact Professor Meyer-Schwickerath in Essen but was told he was away on an island off the coast of Holland. Several hours later I talked to him and he said he would come to Berlin. He came just after we had taken von Schirach by ambulance to the West End hospital in Spandauerdamm. He examined him and said he could operate. He would perform the operation on 22 May.

The day of the operation von Schirach was stepping from the ambulance in front of the hospital when a woman in a white coat and a stethoscope round her neck came forward; without a word she thrust a note and a small transistor radio towards him. She was hustled away and we read the note. It was Karen Stein again, and she was offering von Schirach her eyes.

Professor Meyer-Schwickerath, a crew-cut young man in glasses, explained to von Schirach and the four directors, who were to attend the operation, that he was going to 'shoot' a beam of light through the eye-ball to weld the retina so it could not tear away, as the right eye's retina had done. Von Schirach nodded and smiled bravely. Looking at his blind eye only the dilation of the pupil showed anything wrong with it; the left eye showed nothing obviously abnormal, but under magnification small holes were already visible.

He was strapped down on the table and his head fixed so it could not move. Clamps were placed on his eye-lid to hold it back and local anaesthetic injected into the nerves around the eye. Professor Meyer-Schwickerath then moved across to the coagulation machine and aimed it carefully into the eye. Squeezing a small trigger he shot into it between 70 and 80 powerful beams of light. The operation took 45 minutes. 'I felt no pain at all,' said von Schirach when it was over, 'only the eye clamps were uncomfortable.' He was examined the next day by the doctor who said he was 'satisfied with the results'. When he came again three weeks later to examine him he said the operation had been a success. The retina was safely welded and von Schirach could go back to prison.

He had regular attention from a Berlin eye specialist and six months after the operation, Professor Meyer-Schwickerath was allowed into Spandau to see his patient. After the examination von Schirach took the doctor's hand. 'I want to thank you for saving my eye,' he said. Von Schirach was immediately chastised. It was against the rules for a prisoner to shake hands with anyone. 'I cannot even thank a man for saving my sight,' retorted Prisoner No. 1 angrily. He was sent back to his cell and punished by the withdrawal of permission to write letters for a week.

16

Cell-Block Tyrant

EVEN THOUGH VON SCHIRACH was over his eye drama, he could not forgive the directors for his punishment. He complained about it to the warders, directors and official prison visitors. At the same time, he was humble enough to write me a private note, expressing his gratitude for all that had been done for him. He signed it 'your worst prisoner'.

He was given a light brown cane to help him get about the jail and it added even more to his style and swagger. He was a complex man. 'A highly intelligent, deeply hostile individual,' said one of the doctors. The same doctor found Speer just as intelligent, and it was odd to hear the Soviet director, Colonel Lazarev, insisting that both prisoners were *dominated* by Rudolf Hess. 'He terrorizes them,' said the Russian. They did exactly what Hess – 'a mean and sneaky person' wanted them to do. Hess made a practice of 'devouring all the garden strawberries while his companions did the work', said Colonel Lazarev, 'swallowed them without even washing them.* He generally eats like a pig and even though he is over 70, can out-walk and out-run the other two younger prisoners. But the moment he sees the Soviet director at a distance, he slows down and simulates weakness and bad health.'

Von Schirach regularly did his best to help Hess retain his mental equilibrium by urging him to have a visit. Since his lawyer, Dr Seidl, had visited him in Nuremberg just before he left for Spandau, Hess had requested that no one should come and see him. And that had been 18 years ago. 'Why not ask to see your son?' said von Schirach. Hess shook his head. He was seeing nobody. Speer tried. They were both due to be released in 13 months and there might possibly be a chance of Hess being released if he began to act normally, they reasoned.

* The Russian ban on the prisoners eating strawberries had been lifted.

If he stopped his loud groaning, which was heard all over the prison, and his petty obstinacy with the warders, he might be considered for release too. If he did not, he might find himself in a mental asylum. Hess said finally: 'All right. I'll have my son come to visit me.' It was a breakthrough, we all felt, and now we waited for him to write his request for the visit. When it did not come, von Schirach asked him why. 'Oh, I've changed my mind,' said Rudolf Hess. 'My son did not get a high enough grade in his State examinations.'

To his credit, von Schirach, who must have been as exasperated as anybody with Hess, never gave up. He tried again. 'Hess, why don't you ask your lawyer to come?'

'I don't have a reason.'

'Then make one up!'

A day later Hess wrote officially to the directors: 'I request a visit by the lawyer Seidl on 10, 11 or 12 August to talk about private matters. I need longer than half an hour, or a second visit of half an hour.'

Now Seidl had arrived.* The Soviet director and myself waited in the interview room to monitor the visit, and watched Hess come in to talk to the man he had last laid eyes on in 1947. There had been a large, square wire screen separating visitor from prisoner, but that had been removed. Now only the frame was left and a table about four feet wide stood between them. Seidl was sitting in the visitor's chair as Hess walked in. The prisoner came stiffly to attention, his hands by his sides, and he bowed from the waist. He was told to be seated. 'How are you?' asked Seidl.

Hess replied that though he felt well today, he really was not well at all. He was getting 'pretty old' and confinement was 'slowly doing him under'. He immediately launched into complaints about his family's tardiness in buying books he had requested, and his mother-in-law's failure to thank him for a birthday card.

Dr Seidl patiently went over the Nuremberg charges with Hess. He had been found guilty of the common plan of conspiracy, said the lawyer, and crimes against peace. Seidl said, in his opinion, this had been a miscarriage of justice and it should be rescinded. If Hess was guilty of this charge, then so were de Gaulle of France and former Prime Minister Eden of Britain for the part they had played in the recent Suez affair. Hess nodded. But at this stage the Soviet director

* On 11 August 1965.

moved forward and the visit, which had lasted 30 minutes, was over. Seidl left his client, promising he would write to the Heads of State of the Four Powers on the subject they had been discussing.

Next visitor to the Spandau interview room was Klaus von Schirach, the prisoner's lawyer son; a bright, handsome young man who had been fighting hard for his father's release. His father always made it a point, before visits, to read all he could about interesting places he knew his sons had been to. Then, when they arrived, he could carry out a learned discussion. 'Oh Paps, all the things you know!' they would say, and von Schirach would smile proudly. When he lay with his eyes bandaged his mind was never still. 'I counted up,' he said, 'and found I knew 10,000 people by name, face and voice. And that, my boy, after being in prison for nineteen years.'

Klaus sat down opposite his father. 'I phoned Professor Meyer-Schwickerath and talked to him about your eye. As you know, father, the long-range outlook is not good, as your eye is the type that shows slow degeneration over a long period. He said that an examination by himself or Kleeberger was extremely important and should be done soon. He stated that with his experience he would be able to detect any danger signs and would then be in a position to recommend further treatment of a type necessary.'

'I agree,' said von Schirach, 'with regard to Meyer-Schwickerath and Kleeberger. Dr Milne is a very competent eye specialist and I am sure that he does his best. He doesn't have certain desirable instruments however, in order to see into the eye with the best advantage.'

'Father, listen carefully and answer this question. Are you allowed to eat with a knife, fork and spoon?'

'That is a very odd question! It has really no bearing on my eye. I have eaten only with a spoon for the last 19 years. You know that . . . Since my last examination by Dr Milne I have not got any worse. I do have the light flickers from time to time, but aside from that, nothing new. I believe the worsening of my left eye will develop slowly and not as dramatically as my right eye. It can take a long period of time, or, what we do not hope for, the worsening could develop in a short period of time. The eye must be followed closely by the same expert. For many years prior to the detachment of the retina of the right eye, my eyes were never examined. Perhaps if they had been, the detachment could have been averted.'

With less than a year of his 20-year sentence left to serve even the model prisoner Albert Speer was getting edgy. The man who was a source of calm in the cell-block in the worst periods of crisis was now being punished for misbehaviour. The latest incident was reported by the deputy British chief warder, Whittaker. 'I respectfully have to report an incident which took place,' he said, 'during the serving of the prisoners' meal at about 0650 hours on 28 January 1966, in the cell section. When proceeding to open the cell doors to allow the prisoners to collect their meal, I had just opened Hess's door and was about to open the next in line, Speer, when Speer suddenly pressed his indicator* down. On inquiring why, he demanded: "Open the door!" I asked the reason for this unusual behaviour and he replied: "Shut up! And you can tell that to Chisholm and Banfield."†

'On further questioning,' the warder went on, 'he said: "You will never change," and repeated, "Shut up!" "And," he added, in commanding tones, "go and open the other prisoner's door." I informed Mr Chisholm of the incident, as there was no cause or justification for his insolent attitude, and he asks me to place the matter in writing before you.' Puzzled, I asked Speer why he had acted this way. 'It helps me let off steam,' he shrugged.

A few weeks later he did it again. Chisholm reported: 'When Speer came to collect his food he was very rude and insulting to me in the presence of von Schirach and Hess and Warder Kyle of the US. As usual I say "Good day" to all the prisoners. I could see he looked unpleasant and with a loud voice he said: "What? Goulash again? It is not good enough. You cannot do that to me. I won't have it. Are you so poor you cannot buy better food? If you cannot do better I am going to complain to Mr Banfield." I pointed out to him that he had had fish, chicken, pork, etc., but he said: "Only once chicken and fish." He was bent on showing off in a very rude manner and did so. No complaints from Hess and von Schirach. Von Schirach was having a good laugh and indicated that he disagreed with Speer's actions.' Speer had to be punished. He was refused permission to have newspapers or books for four days, though he was allowed to keep his Bible and note-book.

* The small tin flap that falls down when a prisoner presses a button.
† The British director, Colonel Ralph Banfield.

Speer deserved his punishment, and, as usual, took it philosophically. The most straightforward of the prisoners, whatever Speer said you could believe. He refused to lie or cover up when he knew the blame was his. He was not talkative; he only spoke when he had something worthwhile to say.

I talked with him in his cell for many hours. Over his bed he had hung a calendar with the days crossed off, one by one. His cell was never as tidy as von Schirach's, it had a haphazard air about it. 'I knew at the end of the war,' mused Speer, 'that I was working for something that wasn't right. But I had become completely infatuated with Adolf Hitler himself. What 28-year-old chosen by a country's leader as his architect, would not have been?' He would go on talking about the Nazi days . . . about his position and his power. Then he would shrug his shoulders: 'How is it possible that this happened to me?' When the life of the Third Reich – and its leader – could be counted in hours Speer had flown to Berlin to see Hitler. Why? 'Just to say goodbye,' he smiled.

Now that release was only a few months away he had pulled his calendar down from his green-painted wall. 'The pressure of waiting for the days to pass is too great,' he said. So he busied himself with the plans for his new house and his sketches of mountain scenes drawn from memory. He was averaging 17 km a day on his 'world walk' and was on his way to Alaska. 'A Russian guard is keeping me informed about the freezing of the water so I can get into Alaska and head down to Mexico.'

Speer also had his books. He had read some 5,000 since his capture, almost rivalling the print consumption of Hess. 'You know the worst thing about being here?' Speer asked me one day. 'It is the expectation of the visits. I can't eat or sleep for two or three weeks before someone from my family is coming. I dread those agonizing silences in the talks when they do come; I have nothing to say. They know of the monotony of the life here . . . they know my health situation . . . and they know my schedule. I can sometimes understand Hess not wanting to see anyone. Perhaps what he dreads more than anything is facing up to the fact that even after twenty-five years he has nothing much to say . . .'

A hundred yards away as we talked in the garden, striding along side by side, came Hess and von Schirach. Von Schirach, scarf flowing from his shoulder, pipe in mouth, cane swinging, expounding on some subject to Hess. It was almost always a one-sided conversation between these two, von Schirach enjoying the sound of his own opinions, but at the same time trying hard to probe the mind of the difficult man walking, shoulders hunched and bent forward, beside him.

Hess was becoming more and more introverted and grumbling. He was withdrawn to the extent that it took a great effort to try and strike up a conversation. After visiting the other two in their cells all the directors found it easier to walk past Cell 23 and forget him. But Speer said to me as I was getting up to leave him one day: 'Please go in and see Hess. Please don't just walk past. He really hasn't said anything to me about being ignored, but I do know it bothers him. It would certainly bother me. Even if he does have these silly complaints, Colonel, please make an effort to go in and talk to him.'

'What will you do when you get out?' I asked von Schirach.

'I will live for my grandchildren. Anyway, the main thing is that I will be free. I am going to build my grandchildren a miniature play-house. It will have antique furniture of a certain period. I will carve out little chairs and beds and cabinets and even have tiny Persian rugs for the floors. My house will have a library and tiny books. In each of these books I will write a poem or a proverb or a wise saying for the children to learn.'

He mused about his future. He had his memoirs to write, and that would take time. 'It is my responsibility to write, for the sake of history. I actually have a rather important request to make concerning my freedom, Colonel,' he said. He patted the bunk he was sitting on. 'I have slept on this bed for twenty years. I want to request that when I leave this prison, it is crated up and sent to me so I can have it made into a couch and I can have it in our home so that it will be in my family forever. My grandchildren can look at it and say this is where our grandfather slept for twenty years . . . I've had many thoughts on this bed, read hundreds of books on it, and spent a great deal of my lifetime with it. I would not like to part with it.'

Blind in one eye, and fearful that one day soon he might also be blind in the other, the white-haired prisoner went on: 'I have some suggestions which you might bear in mind about the future treatment of Hess. I feel he should be given a dog. It would mean companionship for him at a time when he will be extremely lonely. I feel it would help if he also had his own facilities for making coffee and tea, and that he should have a clock in his cell. It hurts me, it really does, to leave this old man behind.'

I got up and left the cell and waited for the warder to unlock the steel door behind which Rudolf Hess sat. He got up, stood to attention and bowed stiffly. 'Please sit down,' I said. He looked at me warily. He had been reading and he had his spectacles on. He sat on his bunk, on his inflatable rubber ring, which gave him comfort, and asked if he might put his feet up. 'If I let them hang down my ankles swell,' he said worriedly. His fingernails were properly trimmed and clean and as he folded his hands I could see the blue veins protruding. 'They will be gone soon,' he said, nodding towards the cells farther up the corridor. 'Who knows?' I said. 'There might even be a chance of your release. Only you should stop this terrible moaning at night and try to behave normally.

'I met a young lady recently,' I told him, 'who had worked for your wife in her guest-house at Hindelang. She says there is a little house in the grounds all ready for you if you are ever released.' Hess's eyes brightened. 'How are things at Hindelang? How is business? What does she say about the guest-house – is it nice?' Then he became suspicious again, 'How did you come to meet this lady? How did she know about your position here at the prison?'

'Every time I mention I am at Spandau, Hess, they all want to know about you.'

'What? That I am crazy? That I am insane?'

'No. They say: "How is he? Do you ever get to see him? Do you ever talk to him?"'

'Are you sure,' asked Hess, looking directly at me, 'that they do not ask if I am crazy, the way it gets reported in the papers?'

'No. I haven't heard much about that.' He dropped his interest in the conversation as suddenly as it had begun. 'I have these pains,' he said. 'I don't think I am getting the proper medicines . . .'

It was time to go. 'Now you think about that, Hess,' I repeated. 'If you behave in a crazy way, groaning all night you cannot expect people to take a normal attitude towards you as a man, or to your release.' He stood once more to attention and bowed stiffly from the waist. As the warder locked the door behind me I looked in through the small window in the door. Hess had gone back to his reading.

17

'Let Bygones Be Bygones...'

IN A FEW days Albert Speer and Baldur von Schirach would be free to drive out of Spandau Prison. The world's Press was already flying in reporters and photographers; television crews were building platforms on the other side of the road opposite the gates.

We tried to persuade the Russians that the prisoners be released a day or two early to avoid the worst of the Press build-up but they refused. The two men could walk out at midnight on 30 September 1966 when they had completed their 20 years' sentence. Not a minute before. The Western Powers favoured bringing the prisoners new clothes so they could look presentable for their relatives. 'They will wear exactly what they came in with,' said the Soviet director. 'They shall not leave dressed like ministers.' Speer had arrived at the prison in a worn ski-jacket, ski trousers and ski boots. Von Schirach had on a faded jacket which he used for fishing. Finally, however, after we had inspected the clothes, it was agreed by everyone except the Soviets that they be brought normal street clothes with shirts and ties. Overcoats would also be purchased for them.

Speer had been booked to fly out to Heidelberg on the Pan American jet he had watched fly over the prison garden for years. 'I have planned every moment of that flight,' he said. He would stay the night before in a hotel in a quiet Berlin suburb. Von Schirach wasn't sure of his arrangements. And anyway, he saw no reason for disclosing them. He would be a free man and what he did with his time was his own business.

The Berlin police had warned, however, that being a Friday night – 'drunks' night' – there could be an ugly crowd situation and they wanted to take every precaution. A British general came on an official inspection in the last week and with an entourage of about twelve dignitaries and officials, waited for the warder to unlock the door of von Schirach's cell.

'No. 1,' said the General, as the prisoner in the worn brown corduroys got to his feet. 'We want to know where you are staying on the night of September 30th.'

Von Schirach looked at him. 'General, as of midnight on 30 September I am a free man. It is then up to me where I stay.' The General reddened, and tapped von Schirach on the chest with his swagger-stick. 'Mister, as of right now you are still a prisoner. And when you leave this prison you will be in my sector of an occupied Berlin. So it *is* my business – whether or not you are a free man. I am responsible for your safety until you fly out of Berlin; I want to know. And I *expect* to know.'

He glared at the prisoner with No. 1 on his knees. 'Am I understood?' 'Yes, General. My son Klaus is arranging my accommodation. I will have him let the directors know.'

When the party had gone I asked von Schirach why he had spoken like that to the General. 'It is a weakness of mine,' he said. 'I've *always* got to tell myself: "Now Baldur, calm down." You see, it's this way. I have never yet seen the man who I looked up to, and that included Hitler or anybody else. I just always feel superior, in my own estimation, to everyone I meet.'

With only hours remaining of their 20-year sentence, the tension in the cells of Speer and von Schirach was electric. They knew there was a great crowd gathering outside the prison. People had been arriving since early morning and could be heard shouting and calling to the sentries in their posts above the wall. Von Schirach and Speer went with a warder to the storeroom to collect their belongings, and from dozens of books he had been sent von Schirach selected five to be left behind for Hess.

He was handed, and signed a receipt for 1,860 Reichsmarks he had brought with him when he was captured, a single US dollar, a cigarette case, a monocle, and a small travelling clock. As the warder passed the clock to von Schirach it began to ring shrilly. The prisoner smiled: 'That is good German craftsmanship! After twenty years the alarm goes off!'

Speer was given his 2,778 Reichsmarks and his collection of books and records, drawings, letters and photographs. They were also given their shirts, ties and raincoats which I had purchased for them, and they returned to their cells to wait. Speer asked Boon for two sleeping tablets so he could get to sleep and reserve his energy for the excitement of the midnight release.

Von Schirach had a final request. 'Colonel, you have told me of this woman, Karen Stein. It is just possible that she will be outside with flowers or something and might make a scene. Is there anything that can be done to prevent this?' His request was passed on to the giant British security man 'Tiny' Miles, and an ambulance arrived to take away an early 'fainting fit'. The British never explained how he had talked her into fainting.

It was 8 pm and the crowd outside had swelled to 2,000. Many of them had placards urging Hess's release, and the front of the prison was lit up by television arc-lamps. Reporters and photographers were jostling for better positions, and, as expected, the Berliners were pouring out of the bars and arriving by taxi to see the spectacle of their former Nazi masters emerging from confinement.

At 10.30 pm I walked down the corridor, past Hess's darkened cell, to get them ready. Von Schirach was dressed and was pacing up and down. His crumpled brown corduroys, which he would wear no more, lay on the bunk, the number 1 showing on the upturned jacket. Speer, sleepy-eyed, and fingers trembling, was having difficulty with his tie. 'I haven't tied one for more than 20 years,' he said. 'Could you give me a hand?' I tied the tie around my own neck and then put it over Speer's head. I felt a small coin in the bottom of the tie. 'That is my lucky coin!' said Speer. 'I found it in the garden today.' He was freshly shaven and one of the warders had brought him some hair-cream. A few days before he had asked the US surgeon to take off the warts on his face with diathermy. 'Are you nervous?' someone asked the pacing von Schirach. 'Me nervous? No. I never get nervous,' he said. Clearly now we could hear the jeers and the cat-calls of the crowd. 'I wonder if Hess is awake listening?' said Speer glancing towards Cell 23.

At 11.45 pm the green gates swung open to allow in two Mercedes saloons; one containing the von Schirach sons, the other Speer's wife and lawyer. 'It's all so unreal,' muttered Speer. 'I probably won't come to my senses until tomorrow.' We stood – the four directors, warders, and chief warders with the prisoners – watching the minutes tick by.

Von Schirach, white hair neatly combed, had on his dark-coloured nylon overcoat with his monocle dangling from his neck outside it.

Out in the yard, Chisholm reported, the prisoners' belongings were being loaded into the waiting cars. At the last moment it was found that the man booked by the von Schirachs to drive the car to take their father away was in fact a *Stern* magazine reporter. We refused permission for him to take the position.

At 11.55 pm I glanced at my watch and the others looked at me. I took von Schirach by the left arm and Speer by the right. 'Come on! Let's go.' We walked past Hess's cell down the corridor to the steel door. While it was being opened von Schirach suddenly stopped and looked across me at Speer. 'Herr Speer,' he said. 'Let bygones be bygones. Let's stay in touch.' He extended his hand. Speer smiled and took it. 'Yes, I agree.' And across me, they shook hands.

We started again through the door and down the 22 steps to the yard where their families waited. The von Schirach sons ran forward. 'Papa!' He embraced them, handsome, neatly dressed boys in smart suits. 'Klaus, my boy! Robert! Richard!' Then he got into the car.

Frau Speer had walked forward to her husband shyly. She took his hand, but they did not embrace. It was their first physical contact in more than 20 years. 'Come, Albert,' she said. Speer got into the right side of the car, and she the left. There was not a dry eye in the courtyard.

Now, at two minutes to midnight, the motors roared into life and Speer's car drove forward towards the gates. A warder, looking at his watch, gave the signal and they were opened. Flash-bulbs went off and the crowd rushed forward. 'Free Rudolf Hess!' someone shouted. The two black cars turned and sped off towards the Hilton hotel with von Schirach, and a smaller hotel in Dahlem with Speer. We had sent Speer out first. None of the directors wanted von Schirach's ego further inflated by leaving the jail first.

We went back into the prison and once more the gates slammed shut. They now enclosed one man. Rudolf Hess, aged 72, sentenced to remain there for life.

18

The Lone Prisoner

AT SIX O'CLOCK the next morning Hess was awakened and handed his spectacles. He made his bed, went across to the washroom with hardly a glance at the now empty cells of his friends, and returned to eat his breakfast.

Had he heard anything the night before? 'Oh yes,' he said. 'I was awake. I was lying with my eyes open and I heard everything that was going on in the hallway; also the noise outside. But I am happy for them. They have their freedom.'

At the following directors' meeting I urged that extra attention be paid to Hess, particularly at night. The coming weeks and months would be a strain on him and there was always the possibility that he might try again to kill himself. Ten days after his comrades had left, his lawyer, Dr Seidl, came to see him. He told Hess about his long letter to the four Heads of State asking for a review of his case. 'I do not want,' said Hess sharply, 'any plea for mercy based on any sort of mental condition. There is nothing wrong with me mentally.' Indeed, said a doctor after Hess's regular check-up, he was mentally relaxed and often smiling.

'What about giving him a clock, a radio and some alarm-bell system in his cell?' I asked my fellow directors. The Russian said he would talk to his superiors. He did so and came back. 'Already things are easy in Spandau, we see no reason to make them any more easy.' Hess had a kitchen with a Chinese and a Spanish chef (one on and one off duty) preparing his meals and ate basically the same menu as the directors.

Within a fortnight he went into a deep depression, despite our efforts to go and talk with him daily. He began to lose his appetite and did not want to get up in the mornings. He hung a notice on his cell door one night: 'DO NOT DISTURB'. When he walked in the garden by himself, head and shoulders bowed, he was a pathetic sight. As quickly as he had been depressed, however, he began eating again. He consumed enormous meals and often asked for four helpings of dessert – though a warder suspected some of it was being flushed down his toilet. He would have soup, hors d'oeuvres, cold cuts, salad, a main course of chicken, or pork or duckling, and then his desserts. The Chinese cook could hardly believe it.

But predictably, at Christmas, his depression returned. I took him in a typical German delicacy, a Bismarck doughnut, which he said he enjoyed. But Hess could not be cheered. 'I am an innocent man,' he said sadly on Christmas Day. 'I see no reason why I should not be turned loose. Even if I were guilty – which I am not – no other prisoner who has been sentenced to life or even death for their war crimes still remains in jail. I am the only one I know of who has not been freed. It is all wrong.'

Behind the scenes the Allies were trying hard to free him. But the Russians would not consider it. It had been the Russian judge at Nuremberg who had called for the death of Hess and the Soviets' deep hatred for the Germans was undiminished. We were faced with the fact that for many years yet we still might have to keep a single old prisoner in a jail built for 600, at a cost, which had to be borne by the German Federal Republic, of about 850,000 DM a year. To keep the prison operative each of the Four Powers had to provide an officer and 37 soldiers as guards during their respective turn, a director and a team of warders throughout the entire year. On top of that a team comprising in all 22 cooks, waitresses and cleaners had to be kept employed. All for the incarceration of one man: Rudolf Hess, now in his 73rd year.

With this brigade watching over him, Hess slowly and disgruntledly went about his daily chores. He washed his underclothes and sheets, but he would not polish the cell-block corridor or clean the warders' toilet. He did nothing in the garden, which was already being swallowed by weeds. He said he found it difficult to sleep without his injection – as always, distilled water administered by Boon, but described to Hess as a powerful narcotic.

One surprised doctor reported that Hess had suddenly brightened again. 'A remarkable occasion arose,' he said, 'when Hess actually asked for his medical examination to be cut short so he could get out to do his exercise!' But Hess's interest in the garden was not just as a place to walk. He had made some new friends and he wanted to hurry out to see them. Twice a day, his pockets crammed with paperbags of crumbs from the kitchen, he went out and looked for his birds. The moment they saw his thin figure appear, pigeons, seagulls, crows and songbirds fluttered down from the trees where they had been waiting. Hess would scatter his crumbs, then stamp slowly about watching the birds feed. He would not stand still in one place because he claimed it affected his circulation. He also had a garden project. He was measuring the tall poplar, planted years before by Doenitz, and now the grandest tree of the 14 in the garden. Reading instructions in a book, Hess first measured his shadow, then the shadow of the tree, and staked them both out. He checked them at regular times during the week and then made his calculation: the tree was 23 metres high.

One day he noticed a duck fly down from one of the trees into a corner of the prison garden. The duck was seen flying in and out several times and then Hess saw that she had laid seven eggs in a spot sheltered by a bush. It was not long before he saw, to his delight, that the eggs had produced seven little ducklings which he immediately made it his business to feed.

Hess lovingly tended the ducks until it was felt they needed a pond. They would have to leave. He watched as Warder Banham and a Russian warder herded the mother and her ducklings out of the garden. They shooed them out of the yard and through the huge green gates of the prison while another warder held up the traffic so that they could cross the road. They had almost made it to the other side when the last duckling toppled down beneath a steel trap over a storm-drain. The warders removed the cover but could not extract the duckling. A call went out to the Berlin Fire Brigade, which sent an engine, and the procession of warders and ducks set off once more. The warders returned to report to Hess that his friends were safely settled on a pond a kilometre away from the prison. Each year the mother duck, or one of its offspring, returned to Spandau and laid and hatched its eggs. And oddly, there were always four or seven ducks to take part in the annual procession through the gates.

Hess's 'difficult periods' began again in August 1967, manifesting themselves first in a refusal to shave. He became more unkempt-looking and bristly, but he could not, under the regulations, be forced to take off his whiskers. To make matters worse, it was time for a top US general to officially inspect the prison and its prisoner. What could we do about Hess? Pleading by Chisholm fell on deaf ears. Then, just 20 minutes before the scheduled visit, Boon heard the whirring sound of an electric razor in the bathroom. Hess had out his Philips razor and was taking off his beard.

He had unlimited books and he could listen for hours to records played in the chapel on the Dual record-player; or tapes of classical music on the prison tape-recorder. He had been given permission to abstain from heavy work and as much as possible had been done, within the prison regulations, to help him.

But he still had 'severe' abdominal pains at night which caused him to howl loudly through the empty prison. Repeatedly the doctors urged him to have a barium test which would determine once and for all if he had an ulcer, a remediable organic complaint or even a malignancy. He refused. On 20 June, after he had complained again about his cramps and pains, he tried to put a stop to the doctors' pleas. He wrote an official letter which was his 'formal refusal' to take any such test. 'An X-ray should have been done three months ago,' wrote Hess, 'and such delay is inexcusable.'

Some more of his upper teeth were pulled and a new denture made,* which, said the doctor who examined him, were working well. 'His attitude to the barium test is, however, "What difference would it make?"' His hair was now grey and receding slightly at the temples, his deep-set, serious blue eyes still half-hidden by the bushiness of his eyebrows. But he still walked with a brisk and purposeful gait.

For the next two years Hess existed alone in the prison, his dream of release faded and gone. He was well aware of the Allies' efforts to have him set free: but he also knew of the Soviets' refusal to agree. 'I will die in prison,' said Hess. 'That is now certain.'

25 October 1969: I walked down the cell-block corridor to visit Prisoner Hess. Cells on the left and right were closed and dark and

---

* One of the impressions was used later, I believe, as a rather macabre ash-tray.

there was a sense of stillness in the block. Suddenly it was broken by the strains of music coming from the chapel. I entered and saw the French chaplain sitting on a chair listening to the record-player. Hess sat on another hard chair on his left, with his feet up on a chair in front of him, his way of preventing his ankles swelling. He had on a pair of grey denim trousers with a matching jacket, both rumpled from wear. His glasses were on and his head slightly bowed as the two of them concentrated on the Haydn record.

The moment I entered the double-cell chapel Hess got to his feet. 'Guten Tag, Herr Direktor,' he said, bowing slightly. I asked them to sit down and continue listening to the music. He did and when he put his feet up again I saw he had on a pair of striped blue socks with a pair of American walking shoes. I watched him as he quickly lost himself again in the music. The man who had been deputy to Hitler has a simple, even gentle face. It is not a face that shows great intellect, yet it belies the man himself – a man with a tremendous thirst for knowledge, a man with a sharp, alert mind. When the record had come to an end he turned and said almost to himself: 'That is the most beautiful music in the world.'*

He stood up. 'May we go out into the garden?' He noticed I had no overcoat and said: 'I know it is raining outside. I have a spare coat in the coat-room. Perhaps you will wear that?' I put on one of his shapeless, ex-Army raincoats and followed Hess out into the garden. As I reached into the pockets I found two walnuts in each pocket. 'Oh yes,' said Hess, 'they're mine. I use them to play with – like marbles – as I walk around. They help me think.'

Immediately he started into step and asked: 'How does the new revaluation of the mark affect you? It seemed certain to come, but I didn't think it would come so fast.' I had just come from having lunch in the directors' mess and asked Hess if he had been given what we had – *paella*. 'No. I have never heard of it. What is it?' I explained that it was a Spanish dish and told him of the ingredients. 'And it was authentic because it was cooked by the Spanish cook.' 'You mean we have a Spanish cook here?' asked the prisoner. 'Yes. He has been cooking for you for two years, didn't you know?'

'Oh no,' replied Hess. 'Those things are always kept secret from

* This was the theme on which the German National Anthem, 'Deutschland über Alles', was based.

me.' Then he said: 'Do you know they are painting my cell? One of the painters is a young blond man with very long, feminine hair. He is very pale. I expect that is because he works inside so much. I suppose there are people who always paint inside and those who always paint outside.'

We walked around the narrow path for half an hour and Hess told me about his birds. 'They always know when I come out,' he laughed. Then as we turned to go back inside the cell-block I motioned for him to go ahead. He laughed and shook his head. 'No. You must go in first, Herr Direktor. I am at home here and you are my guest.'

29 October: I went to the cell-block again, past Hess's cell which was open, past the chapel and out to the back of the prison and into the garden. Hess was taking his daily walk, in his old dyed brown overcoat with the number 7 printed large on the back. As we met and fell into step I told him of an elderly woman who had approached me a day or two before, representing the 'Freedom for Rudolf Hess Movement'. 'Have you ever heard of it?' I asked. 'No,' he said. 'Never. But my son *may* have mentioned it in a letter.'

'It exists,' I told him. 'About 800 prominent people in Europe have signed a petition for your freedom. Among them are lawyers, judges – even Nobel Prize winners.'

'That *is* interesting,' he said in a voice that gets high when he is excited. 'I would love to know who they all are.'

'Not only that, Hess, there was recently a movement in the United States Congress to have you set free. Shall I read you what they said?'

'Yes please. I would very much like to hear that.'

'I must warn you,' I told him, 'that there are some embarrassing paragraphs in it and it is not my intention to make you uneasy or cause you worry or frustration. There are references to your alleged insanity . . .'

'Oh don't worry about that!' he chuckled. 'I've heard this word so many times and I know what people think of me – please read it.'

I read the report to him and he listened intently. 'That *is* interesting,' he said. 'Very interesting.'

When I got back into the prison the US chief warder came to see me. 'The old man is giving us a bit of trouble with food,' he said. 'He keeps asking for more. He takes three or four desserts and then flips a button like a coin to see which one he will eat. He flushes the rest down the toilet.'

19

'Kidnap Me!'

MIDWAY THROUGH NOVEMBER 1969 Hess had stopped eating, and his weight was dropping. He refused to shave and just stayed in his bed, groaning, his noise so loud that it could be heard by the sentries on the guard-posts at the wall. It was an eerie moan, as loud as a human being could groan without actually screaming.

On Wednesday, 19 November, the Soviet surgeon called the chief British doctor, Lieutenant-Colonel D. D. O'Brien, to the cell-block where they both examined Hess and found him in a serious condition. His stomach was distended and sore to touch and they diagnosed a blockage of the intestines. The only way to find the cause of the blockage was to examine Hess in hospital. The directors were hurriedly called to the prison and decided that the prisoner should be moved immediately to the new British Military Hospital, two kilometres away; it would be Hess's first time outside the prison in 23 years.

'No,' said Hess, between groans. 'I refuse categorically to go to hospital. Treat me in prison.' The directors tried hard to persuade him but succeeded only in having him refuse medical treatment altogether. 'There is no doubt,' said the Russian doctor. 'He is in a very serious condition.'

The doctors wanted to give him a saline infusion and to extract the large gas bubble in his stomach with a tube. 'Nein!' he shouted. But he did agree to an enema and that seemed to ease his pain. On the Friday, after sedation with drugs the night before, his condition improved, and he was taking a light diet with copious liquids, which he was managing to keep down. But the doctors warned that if he was not properly X-rayed and the trouble found and treated it could suddenly flare up again.

Patiently, the directors argued with Hess in his cell. It was for his own good that he went to hospital, they insisted. Hess looked thin,
158

pale and haggard. He wore striped pyjamas and he sat up in bed with his knees drawn up to his chin, his hands clasped around them, shaking. I had, minutes before, arrived home from leave. My warder, Donham, was on the phone: 'Colonel Bird, you must come quickly. The prisoner is very, very ill and he is calling for you. He refuses to leave without seeing you.' I hurried to the prison and quickly motioned all the others out of the cell. 'Leave me alone with him,' I said.

Hess was weeping. 'I don't want to go, Colonel. I am afraid.' I assured him: 'If you agree to go, Hess, I can guarantee you will have the best treatment. You must go. It is urgent for you to go.' He looked up at me, clasping my hand: 'Will you go with me? Will you visit me every day at the hospital if I agree?' I said I would. He nodded, and I quickly wrote out an agreement and, shakily, he signed it. It read: 'I hereby certify that I agree to be transferred into the British Military Hospital in order to have a medical examination – Rudolf Hess.' I promised to walk alongside the stretcher to the ambulance and to go on with him to the hospital. Before I left the cell he reached out his right hand and caught hold of my sleeve, pulling me down towards him. In a low voice, he said: 'I'm afraid. I have only a few days to live on this earth. I'm going to die . . . I'm at my end now.'

Then he began sobbing. 'Why don't they release me?' he cried. '*Why* must I suffer so? I alone tried to bring about peace in the world and for this I must stay here the longest. It is not right. It is not just! All I want is to go home and die in peace and be buried in the garden.'

He had his hands together in the prayer position and tears were streaming down his cheeks. I took one of his hands. 'Hess you are sick now, for sure. But you must not be afraid. We are going to get you well again. We will take you from the cell and put you on a stretcher and into a British ambulance which is coming for you. In the hospital they have all the special equipment to look after you.'

'Listen,' he said, his sobbing suddenly stopped. He glanced around to see that nobody could hear. 'Colonel, I want you to do something. *I want you to kidnap me.* You can arrange it. There would be of course a scream of protest from the Russians. But once I am free and out of Berlin in the West they could do nothing. It is not a decision they could make at the White House. But you could make it. Of course there would be trouble – but not for long. It would soon be forgotten.'

Already the ambulance had arrived and the crew brought a stretcher into the cell. Hess was carefully lifted on to it and carried down the 22 steps to the courtyard and into the back. We went off; the directors in a car, German police escorting behind and in front. Hess took with him a small portable urinal, his spectacles, a novel* and his bedroom slippers.

At the hospital British soldiers with machine-guns were covering the first trip into the outside world Hess had made since 1947 and more armed troops were up on the second floor outside the security suite that had been prepared for him. There was a small ante-room between the passage and Hess's own room and the warders took that over.

Hess was wheeled along to the X-ray department and it was revealed that an accumulation of gas was present under both sides of his diaphragm and in the beginning of the duodenum and stomach; there was a partial organic blockage. The radiologist's diagnosis: a chronic ulcer condition. 'One can assume,' said his report, 'that the severe pains in Hess's abdomen are evidence of a perforated ulcer, localized in the duodenum with subsequent organic peritonitis.'

Lieutenant-Colonel O'Brien was of the opinion that the perforated ulcer, having broken open, had closed itself. Owing to the prisoner's extreme weakness it was impossible to do a barium X-ray. He had already collapsed once during examination. In the past month he had lost over 15 lb. He was given intravenous glucose-saline and the gas was removed from his stomach. His wife had been informed of his condition and she and her 32-year-old son, Wolf-Rudiger, now living in Hamburg, were ready to fly to Berlin if needed. But Hess had passed the danger mark ('I really believed he was going to die,' the Russian doctor told me), and was improving. The barium X-ray, which might have shown an ulcer years before, would be performed in a few days.

However, on the night of 29 November – eight days after arriving in hospital – Hess was sure he was going to die. He called through the adjoining door of his suite to Warder C. R. Belson and the US warder, Kyle, and he wanted the four directors alerted immediately by phone. He dictated the statement in English and Belson took it down with his ball-point pen on an Army memorandum form. 'During the night,' dictated Hess, 'the heart of the prisoner No. 7 stopped beating suddenly. It also happened several times during the day, each time it was difficult to start again – that is to say there is a

* Me – Poor Child with Three Fathers, by Vera Hartegg.

great danger to the life of No. 7. I request that the four directors hold a meeting of the following persons. Firstly, a British heart specialist, a German heart specialist, Dr Seidl, my lawyer, and a German notary so that I can make a statement that can be signed by me. My son shall be informed, he is either at Hamburg or Hindelang. The pastor has his number and he can be reached by telephone, also the number of my wife.'

When the statement was made one of the warders went off to deliver it. Then an hour later Hess called again. 'It is now 2330 hours, neither the British nor the German specialists have been to see me. If the heart specialists can come and find a way to improve the heart I would not need the notary or my lawyer or son. Until now I have not had an answer that the heart specialists will come. I am now preparing to write my weekly letter and I do not intend to go to sleep tonight. It is a case of life and death.'

Belson reported: 'I allowed the prisoner to make these statements. It was a way of getting him to talk and give us an idea of what is going on in his mind. That could be helpful for his treatment. During the evening he spoke of the splendid room he was in and that he has not had anything like it for so many years. "Only walls and bars," he said, "and nobody can know what only I know – what it is like to be alone with no help at all." '

The first day of December 1969 was wet and miserable in Berlin. Snow covered the small garden in front of the British Military Hospital and bored German police wearing pistols and carrying walkie-talkie radios tramped along the frozen pavement. More armed police chatted in the gatehouse, and outside Hess's door sat a British soldier with a sub-machine-gun at his feet.

Hess lay with a tube running into his left nostril through which dripped citrated milk en route to his ulcerated stomach. After initial refusals he had finally consented to a barium test which showed a chronic duodenal ulcer complicated by perforation which had sealed spontaneously. After his barium meal – an uncomfortable experience for an elderly man – he had been given his cardio-vascular system: a treat. It was his first taste of alcohol since 1941. 'Very good!' he told the doctors. 'Very good!'

Hess had made a remarkable recovery. He was now free from pain and had put on three kilos in weight. 'There were occasions when the patient claimed his pulse had disappeared,' reported the doctors wryly, 'but this was not confirmed by the nursing orderly.' The future? 'We will continue conservative treatment and then repeat the barium studies in six weeks to see if the ulcer has healed.' His blood pressure had given some concern and he had fainted twice while on the toilet adjoining his room, but now the blood pressure too was improving.

I walked into his room, a Russian warder following me, and with some difficulty Hess slightly turned his head to see me. 'Good evening, Colonel.' How was he? 'Well you will be surprised to hear this thing does not hurt me at all.' The man who had for most of his life shunned modern medicine in favour of homeopathic and natural remedies added: 'There is something to be said for modern medicine after all!'

He had some colour in his cheeks and as he sat up in bed in his blue-and-white striped hospital pyjamas he looked quite perky. Not the man who a short time before had been sure he was dying.

'I would like to get my hair cut,' he said. 'And perhaps some olive-oil to put on it?' Then he pointed to a small electric clock on the wall opposite him – the same clock which we had finally put up for him in the cell-block after long argument with the Soviets. 'I would like that thing removed. It makes a slight ticking noise for a start. And every time I open my eyes I see its hand sweeping away the time. When I close my eyes I dream of it in a huge tower, ticking my life away. Do you think it could be removed?' I said I thought it could.

That night, just five kilometres away in Spandau, the sentries were still rigidly pacing their towers in the bitter cold, guarding a prison without a prisoner. We on the US side thought it was ridiculous and told the other three Powers. Britain and France agreed it would be far more sensible – particularly to avoid the humiliating TV publicity that had already begun – if the sentries patrolled inside the wall until Hess was returned. The Soviets said no. They would not agree with any alteration in the regulations governing the security of the prison unless it came from a highest political level. It was agreed to submit the question to that level and meanwhile the fruitless patrolling went on.

Strangely, the Russians were working behind the scenes to have a decision made on Hess's burial. The US preferred that his body, when he passed on, should be turned over to his next-of-kin for burial outside

Berlin. The Russians agreed that his remains should not be buried in the prison grounds, but should be cremated and interred somewhere outside Berlin. This was a relief: we had feared that even with Hess dead, Russia, intent on keeping its toehold in West Berlin, would insist on burial in Spandau and the consequent 'ceremonial' guarding of the grave by the Soviet Union.

Hess meanwhile, very much alive, was being pressed to ask for a visit from his wife or son. 'Nein!' he said. There was little point in arguing. He stubbornly refused to discuss the matter further. He had pulled his mental blind down on the chink of light that we were struggling to make larger. If he could be persuaded to have normal family visits, it was believed, a lot of normality would return to Hess. But it was always the same when anyone brought up Hitler, his past or his flight. The shutters would come down and Hess's eyes would take on a pained look and there would be stubborn silence. Colonel Banfield, the British director, looked in on him in hospital and said outright: 'Hess, now that you are out of prison wouldn't you like to see your wife and son?'

'No,' came the answer. 'So long as those guards are outside, I am still a prisoner.'

I went in to see him the same night. Drawing up a chair I sat close to his bed and talked to him in a calm, low voice. 'Hess, I know what your feelings are about what I am going to ask you, but I want you to consider now what I have to say. I want you to see some member of your family. Now I know this is a very painful thing for you, even just the thought of it. But at this time it could help in many ways. It could help influence world opinion, help influence the Russians. I remember, you know, how Speer had this build-up of anxiety before his family visits. The long, awkward silences after he had asked after their health or their school work . . .'

He was listening. His eyes were downcast under the thick eyebrows. 'Yes,' he said quietly, almost to himself. 'Speer used to tell me about it.' Then he looked at me directly, his face sad and resigned. 'Do you really think it would be a good idea to ask for my wife? There is still time . . . I might just do it. I will have to think about it.'

I left him. There had been enough said. When I returned the following night Hess was expecting me. He was nervous. But he was determined to face the problem that had been hanging over him.

'I have been giving serious thought to what you have asked me. I have, however, one worry that frightens me. It is the Russians. They are trying to destroy me. I fear that if my son flies in from Hamburg they may try to kidnap him. They know that this would break my spirit. My nerves would snap. I could not stand it, Colonel. *I would go stark, raving mad.*'

I said: 'What do you mean, your son would be kidnapped? He could fly in. He doesn't have to come in by car, through the Soviet checkpoint.'

'Oh, something would happen. The plane might have to land in the DDR [East Germany] and when it lands in an emergency the Russians will capture my son. I can't afford to take that risk.'

'But Frau Speer goes into East Berlin! She goes through the checkpoint and travels in and out.'

'Oh you can't compare the Speers with Rudolf Hess. I was deputy to the Führer. The Russians hate me. They want to destroy me.'

He was annoyed that some years before his son *had* made a trip to Berlin. Hess had immediately written to chastise him, warning him of his fears of kidnapping. 'You must not come back to Berlin ever again,' he wrote to Wolf.

Hess had apparently decided to discontinue the conversation about the visit. 'How are my birds?' he asked. 'Are they being fed? Are they hungry?' I assured him they were missing him but that one of the staff was giving them crumbs. His face relaxed. 'Ah, that is good.'

I glanced up at his clock. 'I see it has been moved.' 'Yes. I could not stand watching that second-hand moving on – just like the destiny of man, always moving on, moving on.' Then he asked: 'How are things at the prison? Is it still there?' We both laughed. I did not tell him that we had made another routine search of his cell and found the usual hidden aspirins, small paper bags of salt and rotting potato salad. Chisholm had made the inspection and found even pieces of bread wrapped up with numbered tags on them.

That day he had again been contrary. Warder Denham, a keen amateur barber, had made a special trip to bring his clippers to cut Hess's hair. Half-way through the job Hess had said: 'Stop. I can't stand it any more. I'm going to faint. My neck is paining me. Anyway,' he shrugged, 'nobody is going to see me here. Nobody is going to visit me.'

20

'I Have a Request...'

SPARKLING SUNSHINE BATHED Berlin today. After weeks of darkness and cold, it brought a glitter to the snow and the fir-trees dripping their icicles. Up in his room Hess padded over in his slippers to the barred window to gaze out on the Berlin he had last seen in 1941. There was the Olympic Stadium where he had spoken to the crowds at huge Nazi rallies; the buildings in which he had worked and dreamed. He was savouring it all, when the Russian warder walked in and tugged the aluminium venetian blind louvres closed. Suspicious that a TV cameraman with a long-range lens might be mounted on a near-by building, the warder's superiors had given orders to block any possible view of the prisoner.

Hess was white with anger. 'Why are you doing this?' he demanded of the warder. 'I am a 76-year-old man, deathly ill! I only have several weeks to live on this earth – a dying man! And you Russians even deny me the privilege of seeing the tops of the trees and having the sun shining into my room.'

By the time I arrived that night he had calmed down, but the deprivation still rankled. I called in the Russian and the US warder and together we adjusted the slats to two-thirds open, giving Hess his view and still preventing anybody seeing him from outside. He was satisfied. 'It was such a beautiful sight. I saw the trees, and the snow with the sun reflecting off it. It was something I had not seen in so many years; something so different from a prison wall.'

He wanted us to see his new hospital pyjamas made in blue and white flannel. 'They are so nice and wide at the arms and legs and,' he added, pulling his sheet and pink cellulose blanket down for us to see, 'look at the waist-band, it is a cord and I can adjust it if I wish. Everything in the prison has this crazy elastic and I can't stand tightness round the waist. I have to cut it open and sew on buttons instead.'

When the warders had gone back to their room he motioned to me that he wanted me to come closer to his bed so he could speak confidentially. His face tensed a little. 'You asked me about a visit from my wife and son. I have something to say. But I want it to be kept for the moment between the two of us. I have brought myself to a decision . . . I will see them – on Christmas Day. I want to see my wife and son.'

His lip quivered and tears came into his eyes. He could not talk any more. He tried again to speak and his voice choked. But he finally got control of himself and said: 'I will see them under the following conditions . . . For the first 15 minutes I want to be alone with them. The Russians will have to understand that. They will have to understand what a shaking thing it is for a man who has not seen his family in 28 years to confront them again. You can have a listening apparatus and even cut a hole in the wall if you wish, so everything that is said between us can be noted down. But I do not want to be stared at by anybody when my wife and son come into the room and see me for the first time.

'I know,' he went on, more confident now, 'that the regulations mean only a 30-minute visit from one member of a prisoner's family once a month. But I hope that in view of the fact that I have never had a visit from them before, that they might be allowed to come in together. It all hinges,' said Hess, 'on the permission to be at first alone with them.'

I stood up and said that if he would make out an official request for a visit I would put his conditions to the other directors when he wished. He lay back in his bed staring out at the night. His thoughts were probably miles away.

That night he took pen and paper and wrote:
'*December 8th, 1969.*

Request to the directors:

I request the visit of my wife and son if possible in the early part of 24 December. It is the first visit for 28 years, so I beg that at the beginning there should be no witnesses in the room. The talk that I will have with my wife could be recorded on a tape-recorder or a hole could be cut into the wall so that anybody could see that I will not put any writing or anything like that into the hands of my family. Also I will promise that I will not stretch out my hand to them. My family will promise the same thing.

'I beg you to realize that von Schirach and Speer within 20 years had a great number of family visits, but for me it will be the first one. It will lessen the psychological tension with my family very much if I can get this permission. I ask you, realizing it is my first visit, and that it will only last for half an hour, to please let us eat a Christmas dinner together.

'It will not matter at all to me if direct witnesses are there at this dinner. I intend to be silent about all these privileges so far as my family are concerned. I won't tell them. – Rudolf Hess.'

No. 7 had just taken an historic step. None of us would have ever believed he would do it. He was even writing cheerfully about it to his wife asking her 'not to be disturbed that my cheeks have not filled out . . . and I am sure to look a little drawn'.

He was still in a happy mood when I called to see him. 'I have done it,' he said. 'I have written. You know what the doctors told me today? They said I talked too much! I ask too many questions. So they tell me: "Leave these questions up to us. Just take the treatment and be quiet." But I know now what doctors are. I tell them they can't shut my mouth and I will keep on asking questions. "If you don't want to answer them that's up to you," I told the doctor! Now that I have made my decision I am feeling so much better.

'I am still rather tired you know. Through lack of solid diet and exercise. I am still only being drip-fed. I can read for about a quarter of an hour and then I get tired and cannot concentrate any more. I have to stop halfway through any letter I am writing. Tomorrow I start on a diet of protein and the juice of fish, followed by some chicken bouillon, so it will be different then. I am really so terribly happy,' he laughed. 'I can't tell you how happy I am that I won't be in prison for Christmas. It is the loneliest time of the year. I did not even allow a piece of Christmas tree in my cell because it reminded me of it.'

He was in an unusually talkative mood. 'It was my fault that I got so ill in prison. I was crazy not to have agreed to go to hospital long before.' He was propped up by three pillows, his cheeks were a good colour and he looked amazingly fit. 'I must say I admire the way you have looked after yourself physically with your exercises,' I told him.

'Yes, it is something I have always done. The knee-bends, the arching the back exercises. I do them here,' he said. ('You've got to admire the old devil,' the British warder had told me as I went into his room. 'Yesterday the Russian warder and I were in his room holding him steady while he tried to use the bottle. He was sitting on the edge of his bed with his feet on the little steps provided for him. While he was trying to urinate he was raising himself up and down, doing his knee-bends.')

'I have now been a prisoner for 28 years,' said Hess, his face now serious. 'At the most I only have a couple more years to live. Surely there is no earthly reason why the Russians cannot agree to me being let loose. Maybe it would help their reasoning if the Western doctors here would say that my ulcer might pop out again when I go back into prison . . .'

I told him Boon, who had done so much for him in the drama of his sudden illness, had himself had a heart attack and was now at home. 'Please give him my best wishes,' said Hess. 'He is a good man.'

As I left, the warders were helping him set up the Dual record-player brought from the prison chapel so he could enjoy his classical music. 'I have already asked for the Schubert Octet,' he had told his wife, 'and here you are writing that I should listen to it!'*

A few kilometres away from Hess's hospital bed, the prison aide-man Johannes Boon was convalescing. He was sitting in his lounge-room with his wife when I called to see him. He chuckled as he told me about the Hess *he* knew . . .

'I have served at Spandau as a medical orderly with only one short break since 1946,' said the 54-year-old Dutchman. 'I had been a POW in Germany and stayed on, marrying a Berlin girl. I had a small grocery store and bar a few yards from the prison. Without a doubt Mr Hess has been my most difficult prisoner. And also the most interesting.

'The least difficult was von Neurath, who had great distinction. Von Schirach was an "I" person. Very proud. But always talking about himself first. Funk was the joker, he loved to joke and clown. I felt Raeder was always the solitary type, always the Grand Admiral. Doenitz was very friendly and nice; but he and Raeder often had words together. Speer? Industrious and hard-working, a loyal sort of person.

'I think Hess, you know, took a great deal of pleasure in causing

* Both Hess and his wife have given instances of mental telepathy between them during his years in prison.

other people work and frustration.' Boon turned to his wife. 'How many times have I gone over to administer some medicine to Hess and returned home and then at 12 midnight the phone would ring? I would have to rush back because Hess was calling for me. He wanted another type of medicine or a shot of something that had to be specially administered by myself.

'I would go back and see that was taken care of, only to be called back four and five times during the night. They were specially rough periods.

'I don't believe Hess is insane at all, and I have studied him for years. He just thinks differently to other people. He thinks oddly. He has a way of cutting off bad memories. Anything unpleasant to him, he cuts off. He pulls down a shutter in his brain.

'On the other hand, he talks perfectly intelligently about his medical condition, about the medication he is taking. He follows the doctors' explanations and asks brilliant questions. He is a very intelligent man who thinks and acts differently to other people.

'Many times he has refused to take a particular medicine. But if you explain the reason it has been prescribed and what it will do for him, he will probably take it. He does tend to hide things,' mused Boon. 'Several years ago we found several hundred pills in tiny packages hidden behind the radiator in his cell and along the window ledge. These were pills he was supposed to swallow and the chief warder should have supervised him swallowing. He is medically checked three times a week. He is probably the most "doctored" man in the world.'

What Hess hated more than anything else, said Boon, was for anybody to be insistent with him. Instead Boon would take up to half an hour gently persuading Hess to take a particular medicine, going through its properties with him and explaining its effects. 'Small things tend to upset him . . . like one of his letters being sent back by the censor for alteration, or a news-item being cut from his newspaper before he gets it. Then the shell around him suddenly breaks and he gets angry and upset. He then falls into a deep depression and will not eat. More than once he has had to be threatened with forcible feeding with a hose and funnel. I would tell him: "OK Hess. You had better lie down because we are going to feed you forcibly now." He would say: "Wait a minute, Boon. Let's make an agreement. Put that thing away and I'll eat a little bit." '

In his prison cell, an angry Hess presented a rather weird sight to the uninitiated. Unkempt hair, bony forehead and thick, bushy eyebrows above staring eyes, he presented, standing with his arms hanging by his sides, an almost ape-like appearance. 'After some years I took over the shaving with the safety-razors and the cutting of the hair,' remembered Boon. 'Then Hess was given a Philips electric razor which has since been replaced with a small Braun. Hess had always been hardest to shave because of his thick growth of beard. Speer, with his facial hairs growing in many different directions, and the warts on his face, was almost as difficult. It took about 15 minutes to shave Hess and now he does it himself in the washroom mirror, he takes almost as long.

'Of course he has often claimed that I am trying to poison him. When the food cart was wheeled into the cell-block he would take Speer's coffee and von Schirach's dessert to avoid poisons meant for him. He was always brave about injections and would ask for them when he couldn't sleep. I would give him sterilized water or sugar pills instead of sleeping pills and he would sleep like a baby.'

Back in the now empty prison we talked about its absent inmate. 'When I went to see him a couple of days after the crisis,' said Colonel Banfield, 'he asked me to "do away" with him. He said: "I want you to take my life." He may have meant it, but he was in a very weakened state.'

A young US captain who had done guard duty in tower No. 3 asked how Hess was. 'I'll never forget one day when I was on duty,' he said. 'I saw Hess deliberately trampling in Speer's vegetable garden and Speer take the hose and chase him off with it!'

Stamping about their towers* in the cold the sentries looked boredly out on to the snow-covered roofs and streets of Spandau. They were soon to hand over their responsibilities to the British and they were warned to clean up the untidiness of crushed Coke cans and wrappings from candy lying about on their catwalks.

High above them, on overhead wires sat lines of birds overlooking the snow-covered garden. One of the kitchen-maids who was feeding

---

* One of them had scrawled on a tower wall: 'Men may come and men may go, but this damned place goes on forever!'

them their crumbs in Hess's absence said: 'He might be fond of them now, but it was Speer who really started to feed them. Hess refused for the first year he was alone, to have anything to do with them whatsoever.'

Back in his hospital room, Hess was lying in bed undergoing a blood transfusion. His extreme fatigue led the doctors to suspect he had probably lost a lot of blood when his ulcer had burst. The blood was coming from a plastic bag suspended from a metal stand, fed into his right arm by a needle inserted intravenously. 'Don't be alarmed,' Hess told me. 'It is quite usual. Anyway,' he smiled, 'I'm told it is good British blood from British soldiers. Can you imagine that!'

He had been reading the *Frankfurter Allgemeine*, one of the four papers from each of the zones he was allowed daily, his favourite paper.

Outside, the night-shift had taken over and four new military guards, armed with their sub-machine-guns, were on duty in the passage. Between Hess's room and them were the warders. And outside the patrolling, radio-equipped police. It was snowing on them heavily. 'On a night like this' (it was minus 22 degrees centigrade, the coldest in Berlin for 130 years) 'I would rather be in here,' said the former deputy Führer.

I sat for many evenings by Hess's bedside, sometimes for hours. His thoughts flowed calmly and as he gained confidence in his surroundings he ranged over many subjects. He chatted about the American moon-shot which he had listened to on the radio. About permissiveness. About flying. About his past life.

Much of what he said was not of any world-shattering importance, but for the first time in 30 years it helped construct a true picture of the man who had been shut away and largely forgotten by the outside world. I have recorded* as accurately as possible, some of his random thoughts so they may remain as part of the Hess picture . . .

On newspapers: 'My first love in reading is the newspaper. I read it from cover to cover. I take notes from it every day in my note-

---

* As soon as I left the hospital I recorded our conversations on tape.

book. Then I write to my son making references to certain papers and certain articles and he files everything away for me so I will be able to refer to it when I get home. The part of the newspaper that interests me most is the Letters to the Editor section. After that I read politics and book reviews. Newspapers give me a connection with the free world. They have done a great deal towards keeping me going over the years.'

On dialect: 'I find the Saxons are not so popular with the other parts of Germany. Maybe it is because of their dialect. In my younger days I could see the most beautiful girl under the sun, but when she opened her mouth and spoke Saxon dialect everything was over from that moment on. This doesn't mean they are not good people. I just can't stand their dialect!'

On flying: 'I took to flying like a fish takes to water. It was never any problem. I am rather technically minded – that is why the space programme and the landing of a man on the moon was not such a great surprise to me.'

On the Russians: 'I cannot understand, for the life of me, why the Russians will not agree to my release. They must know I have only a short time to live. Even if it is several years it is only a short time. I'm an old man and I'm certainly politically harmless in my state. They must harbour some hatred towards me. Only if I was sick with a very short time to live and the world was screaming for my release would they let me go.'

On his 'kidnapping': 'By the way – I've dropped the idea about the kidnapping. You will remember when I first came into hospital I asked you to kidnap me. Perhaps at the time I was weak and feverish, then one says funny things like that. There was a possibility that you could have kidnapped me, but that was only possible for a short time. That time has passed now and I realize it was pure fantasy.'

On Fate: 'I have reckoned on my destiny. It seems that it is to stay in prison. I am a great believer in Fate; there is nothing one can do to alter it. Fate is as realistic to me as the seconds ticking away on that clock.'

On youth: 'I hear the music of youth on the warder's radio. Somehow I cannot reconcile this with good music. However it is one form of protest. The youth of today are protesting for many reasons and they want to be heard. One way of being heard is through their music. I do enjoy the Beatles however; their music has a definite beat and in many ways their music is good music.'

On Playboy *magazine:* 'I do not read magazines like that.' (A warder who showed him a copy, which he rejected, said: 'I have taken them into him at Spandau and he has always pushed them aside. He will never tell or listen to a dirty joke.')

On lawyers: 'It is not a good profession for anybody to take up. They are the most inflexible people. They go by the paragraph of the law and they are so tied up in it that as a result, they cannot think clearly.'

On chess: 'I love to play it. I was always a chess player and won competitions. To play chess is a good exercise for the mind.'

On fresh air: 'I like the cold. In Spandau I always have my cell window open with the heat turned off if I can. It is far healthier to sleep in a cold room.'*

On mountains: 'I love the mountains and remember the mountain walking-tours I made with my wife. We used to belong to the German-Austrian foot-touring club and we would go on hikes for up to three days, trekking from hut to hut. It is healthier to live in the mountains.'

On medicine: 'The doctors tell me I have *angina pectoris*. I'm convinced I should have a homeopathic doctor, as I have never been a great believer in modern medicine. I have been mostly treated by homeopathic doctors, and with great success. I don't believe in chemical medicines. I think it is all overdone. I believe in Nature's medicines, from roots for example. Even though they tell me my heart condition is incurable I'm going to ask for a good homeopathic doctor. I'm sure one could do something for me.'

On mental telepathy: 'It is a very rare phenomenon. In fact the Russians are studying it right now. The closer you are to someone the more you can communicate in this way. Hundreds of years ago it was not uncommon for people to correspond through telepathy. I have often been on the same wave-length as my wife; telepathy has taken place. It happens between animals – why not between humans?'

On beds: 'I sleep in the prison with a board under my mattress because it is far healthier that way; it helps the posture and the spine. You should never sleep on too soft a mattress.'

* In the coldest of weather he would sleep with only a sheet covering him and with his feet elevated and *exposed* at the end of the bed.

On excesses: 'People these days drink and eat too much. They then sit in their cars and go to work, eat some more, then come home in their cars and eat and drink and go to bed. Their bodies then have to carry a load of extra fat, the heart works overtime and the man loses intelligence. Yesterday I saw a heating mechanic who had fat jowels and this great belly sticking out. The sort of person who has nothing on his mind but plodding from one day to the next to make a living for eating, drinking and sleeping. Only pleasures . . .'

21

'It's So Mixed Up...'

WE HAMMERED OUT the details of Hess's visit at our directors' meeting. We agreed that like all other visits, it had to be witnessed. It would take place in the warders' ante-room adjacent to his bedroom and a table would be placed between the prisoner and his family. They could go in together and the visit would last 30 minutes. We could not agree to the Hesses having Christmas dinner together.

Hess smiled anxiously as I walked in to see him. 'Please pull up a chair and tell me all the news.' 'Your request for a visit has been accepted, Hess.' 'Oh thanks to God!' he exclaimed. 'And I can see them both at the same time?' I nodded. 'But I cannot have dinner with them, can I?' 'No. I'm afraid not.'

He lay back on his pillows. He looked weary, but contented. We chatted about the details of travel for his wife from Hindeland in Bavaria and his son from Hamburg. Then Hess said: 'After you leave tonight, I am going to get up and do some walking in my room and in the corridor. It is good for my blood-circulation and my muscles and it helps me sleep.' I glanced down at the worn, brown slippers under his bed, the same pair which had been hurriedly brought from his cell as he was carried off to hospital. Their backs had been squashed down by Hess's habit of stepping straight into them without putting them on properly.

I walked into the warders' room and as we talked I saw Hess through the glass partition walking up and down in his blue-and-white check hospital bathrobe, his hands behind his back, head forward, deep in thought. The warders had a touch of Christmas in their room to share with their prisoner – four large Advent candles, four small pine-cones and a red ribbon.

'He listened on our radio to the recent football match between Scotland and Germany,' said a warder, nodding towards the pacing figure. 'He followed every minute of it and got very excited.' The

US warder butted in. 'When I was on duty on the night of the German elections he wanted to listen to every minute of that. He took down a lot of notes and the number of votes that had been gained by each party.'

I talked with Chaplain de Luze, who had brought in the decorations. 'We often philosophize,' he smiled. 'We discuss certain passages in the modern version of the Bible and argue them back and forth. Could they be true? How did they fit into the overall picture of how God was? At Christmas in the prison every year Hess recites the Lord's Prayer aloud with me. Otherwise he has never attended any chapel services.'

The following night, when I arrived at Hess's room 204, he was sitting upright in bed, propped up by four pillows. His hair was neatly combed and he looked trim and well. On his bedside table stood the extension speaker of the record-player and by it his supper of fish and milk soup. He was eating an egg and some bread and butter. 'It is the first time I have been allowed butter with my bread, and it is delicious.' He had on his brown-framed, plastic-lens spectacles which he had been made to use instead of glass lenses ever since his suicide attempt. A German–English dictionary lay on the bed near his newspaper.

'You look positively handsome tonight,' I told him.

'Ah, yes, dangerously so, Colonel! I have been enjoying my meal and some Schubert as well. Now that I have taken this step of asking for my wife and son, can I see them once a month?' I assured him that he could. 'I won't let a month slip by without asking for them,' he vowed.

He glanced at the clock. 'Are you too tired to talk?' I asked him. 'Oh no, I just look at the time, watching it move away.' He looked over his spectacles. 'You know, being out of prison like this has done an enormous lot for me psychologically. To be in such pleasant surroundings and looking forward to my family coming to see me has done much for my psychological recovery. But do you know what they have given me? A jigsaw puzzle and a painting-by-numbers kit! For occupational therapy, I am told. But really it is too primitive, it is surely just for children. I can't possibly be seen *painting by numbers*!

'Once I used to paint a little in water colours, but never in oils. I have never really been any good at drawing, I am more technically minded.

'By the way, look at that picture they have brought in for me. It is of the old market square in Dresden, how Dresden used to be before it was bombed. I think it is terrible. I know they meant well by bringing it in, but when I think of what happened to Dresden, my heart breaks. It brings back memories for me – the whole city crushed by British and American bombs . . . They must take it away.'

He stayed silent for a moment, staring at the picture. 'What I am going to ask for is a canvas and paints so I can copy the picture in the warders' room. It is a pleasing oil of a boat on a lake surrounded by trees. I would much rather copy that.'

Now he had a request. 'I have a good grey suit jacket, Colonel, which I would like to wear to look presentable when my wife comes. But the trousers are old and worn. Do you think it would be possible for the authorities to provide me with a new pair of trousers to go with the coat?' He climbed out of bed, pushed his feet into the slippers and shuffled to the cupboard. He pulled out a pair of grey trousers on a hanger: they were neatly but heavily darned on the fly and crotch, and they were shabby. He stepped out of his slippers and pulled on the trousers over his pyjama pants. 'You see, they are also too small.'

We measured his waist with a pyjama cord and knotted it on the exact circumference. 'I believe I will need a size fifty-two.' A chart by his bed showed he had weighed 117 lb on 3 December, and now he was 139 lb. I promised to get a pair that were 'good and loose' about the waist.

In the corridor a Scots Guard corporal armed with a sub-machine-gun said as I was leaving: 'Do you know, sir, when that old man jumped from his plane, he landed only a mile from where I live.' A younger soldier said: 'It's a pity to keep the old fellow in prison, particularly now that he is completely helpless.' Another, who had probably not even been born when Hess made his flight, said: 'Oh no, that man's not helpless. Not Rudolf Hess . . .'

Hess sat up in bed to read a three-page letter from his wife. He lay on one side on his elbow, holding the letter with both hands. His heavy eyebrows twitched, particularly the left one, as he concentrated. 'They will fly in at 2.10 pm on a BEA flight to Tempelhof,' he said.

'Yes. I am having my chief warder pick them up in a car. They will be driven straight from the plane to the hospital.'

I showed him a second letter from a researcher asking if Hess could help him at all in reference to Dr Fritz Todt. Hess took the letter and frowned as he read it through. He finally removed his glasses. 'Excuse me,' he said quietly. 'I cannot comment on this. You see, I do not remember any more. You will understand that a lot of things have gone through my mind in the past years. There are certain periods in my life that are blocked out to me. I cannot remember . . . I would rather not give any information to the writer of this letter which might not be factual. You see many things are so mixed up in my mind . . .'

'But you must have known Todt well? Didn't you in fact introduce him to Hitler?'

'That may be so. That may be so, I can't remember.'

I prepared to leave, and noticed a canvas and paints by his bed. He had already painted in some blue clouds in his scene on the lake. 'Oh that is terrible!' he said. 'A complete catastrophe. I am no artist.'

Hess, smartly dressed, reading in his cell at Spandau shortly
before he became ill and was taken to hospital

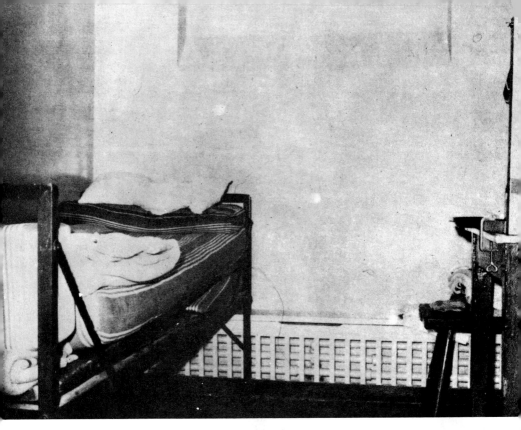

Rudolf Hess's cell, before he was moved to Cell 17 after his 1969 illness

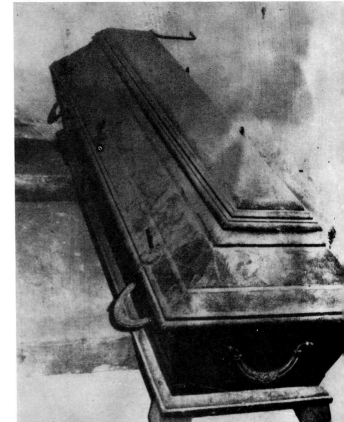

The coffin built when Funk was dangerously ill, and kept in readiness for any other prisoner's death

Hess's table and reading 'lectern' in his prison cell

Some of Rudolf Hess's books in the prison library

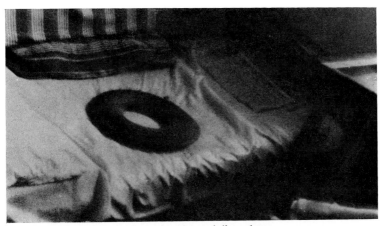

Hess's bed with invalid's cushion

'Gesuch' from Hess to the prison Directors: note the Spandau stamp which is on every piece of paper handed to a prisoner so its issue can be recorded, a problem Speer got around by writing his memoirs on scrap paper left by painters

An die Direktion

The letter Rudolf Hess wrote as he was waiting to be taken to hospital – he was seriously ill and his writing had deteriorated

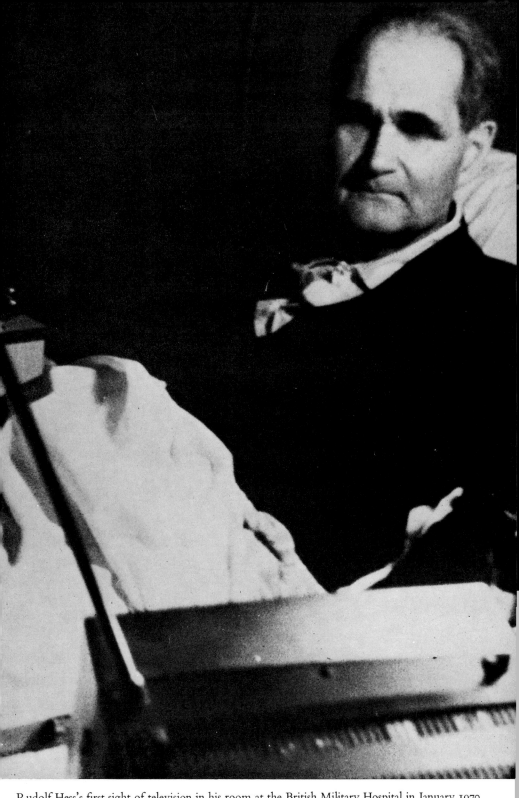

Rudolf Hess's first sight of television in his room at the British Military Hospital in January 1970

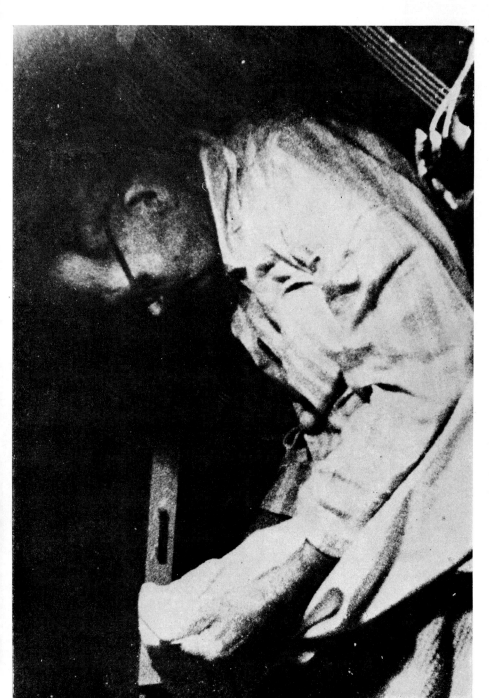

Hess reads a letter from his wife, overjoyed that he has asked for her to come and see him after 28 years

The captain's uniform jacket, the flying-helmet, leather flying suit and boots worn by Hess on his historic flight from Augsburg to Scotland in 1941 to secure peace with Britain

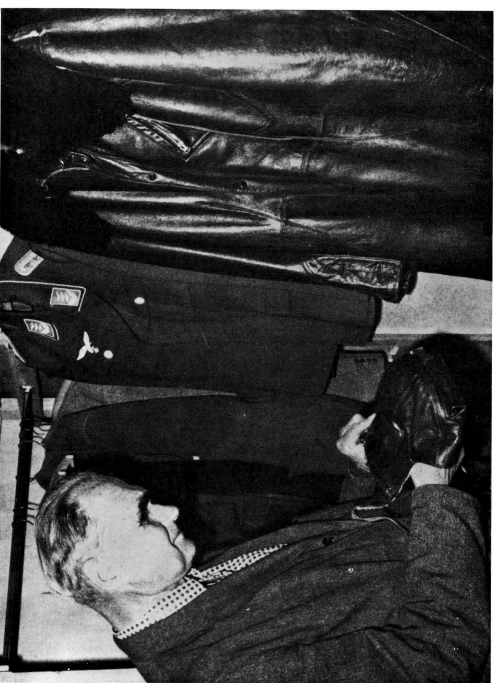

Hess looking at his old flight uniform, 11 September 1971

22

Twenty-Eight Years, Six Months, Twenty-Five Days

WHEN I ARRIVED at the hospital on the night of 23 December Hess had the small transistor radio on, listening to classical music. Beside it on the table stood a jug of milk and a jug of orange juice.

'Well, tomorrow will be an historic day for you, Hess.'

'I'm a little nervous about it,' he smiled. 'You can understand that.' We went over the details. The drive from Tempelhof to the hospital would take about 25 minutes. Taking into account the various formalities, it would be about 3 pm before they entered the room where he would be waiting.

'Will there be much Press interest, do you think?' I said it was already building up. (In fact I had noticed in four British newspapers the kilted guardsman outside was reading, that they had it on the front page.) 'This cannot hurt,' said Hess. 'Not that I need the publicity. But any Press statement whatsoever will help my cause through world opinion.' I told him that once the visit was over, he would have built a great bridge between himself and his family. 'Yes, I know it,' he said.

On 24 December – 28 years, 6 months, and 25 days since Hess had taken off from Augsburg – a BEA jet landed at Tempelhof, Berlin, bearing the Hesses. Frau Ilse Hess, a greying woman with a determined face, and her bachelor son, Wolf-Rudiger, a designer of airports, stepped out into a waiting cream Mercedes-Benz. Escorted by German secret police cars, they swept through the wide, slushy streets of the city, arriving at the hospital's main gate at 2.45 pm.

Frau Hess, neatly dressed in a brown fur coat, with a scarf about her head, stepped out. Her son, 32, a serious-faced young man, in dark overcoat and dark suit with a red tie, joined her. He had been $3\frac{1}{2}$ years old when he had last seen the father waiting for him now on the hospital's second floor.

I took them up in the elevator, where I introduced them to the three other directors. The Russian stepped forward, bowed, but did not offer his hand. Nor was a hand offered by the Hesses. We took them past the guard to a small ante-room where they removed their coats. On the other side of the wall, in the warders' room, waited Rudolf Hess. Frau Hess had on a two-piece suit with a white collar and a blouse. Her hair had obviously been freshly set and was swept back with a slight wave. She had on a wrist-watch and, on her other wrist, a plain golden chain. I handed them the book of rules for prison visits and they both read it, until Wolf Hess got to Rule 8 which forbade disclosure to the Press of details of the visit. 'No,' he said, 'I cannot sign this.' The Soviet director said bluntly: 'If you do not sign there will be no visit.' It was now 3 pm. I asked the Hesses and the interpreters to leave the room while we discussed the matter. When they returned I told Wolf Hess: 'If you use your head with regard to the Press and don't hold a Press conference then everything will be all right.' 'How can I say "No comment" to them?' argued Wolf. 'They know where I have been.'

At this point Dr O'Brien entered the room. 'The patient is getting nervous and excited,' he said. After a short deliberation mother and son took the ball-point pen and signed the book. We left the room to go next-door and I warned them as we walked: there could be no embrace, no handshakes.

As we got to the glass-panelled door it was 3.15 pm. Warder Fowler stepped forward on the other side, unlocked the door and opened it. Hess was sitting at a 4-ft square table in his blue-and-white striped pyjamas* and red, white and blue dressing-gown; his feet were resting on a pillow on his bed steps and his hair had been freshly combed. His face was excited, aglow with anticipation.

The moment he saw his wife and son enter the room he shot up from his chair. He saluted, his hand to his brow, palm inwards. 'Hello! I kiss your hand, Ilse!' Hurriedly Wolf Hess, smiling but cautious, put his hand on his mother's arm. 'Mutti, don't give him your hand.'

Frau Hess, staring unbelievingly at the husband she had last seen on

* He had decided at the last moment not to wear his new jacket and trousers, feeling it might offend the Russians.

10 May 1941 said: 'I kiss your hand, Father.' Wolf Hess smiled across the table at his father who was still on his feet. 'We don't dare shake hands, but how are you?'

Hess sat down, as they did, at the opposite side of the table, not taking his eyes off them. 'How was your flight?' he asked happily. 'Did you enjoy it?' 'But Father, your health . . .?' Hess spoke confidently, brightly. 'I want to make it clear that I am receiving excellent treatment. Absolutely overwhelming treatment and excellent medical care. And I am responding well.'

None of the directors took their eyes off Hess as he went on. There was no sign of emotion. His wife was obviously shaken; but the son, a big, strapping fellow showed signs of moisture on his cheeks. 'How did it all happen, Papi?' he asked.

'The day just came when I could not swallow, or take any food whatsoever. The pains continued and got worse and that is probably when the ulcer broke open.' He explained about the tests to come in the middle of January which would determine if an operation was necessary. 'I can now eat anything, but I stick mainly to chicken and fish,' he said. 'I have had a three-litre blood transfusion. It came from English soldiers so this makes me half-English now! As a result,' he chuckled, 'I now speak much better English.'

His son, studying Hess's face as he spoke, said: 'Then there is something to modern medicine after all?' 'Oh I have never completely pushed modern medicine to one side,' said his father, his eyes twinkling under his brow.

Frau Hess changed the subject. 'It is a long time since I have flown – the last time was with you.'

'Yes. Times have changed. And you have changed.'

'And you too!' she smiled. 'You have changed. Your voice is much different now to how I remember it.'

'How do you mean?' asked Hess, puzzled.

'Your voice is deeper, much deeper than before.'

'Oh you mean it is more *manly*?' They both laughed.

'Father,' said Wolf Hess. 'This is not just a getting-together meeting. It is a getting-to-know-you meeting. I hardly remember you. I'll look forward to other visits when we can prepare subjects we wish to talk about.'

Hess gazed across at his big son, four feet away. 'It is such a long time since I saw you last,' he said slowly. 'You were a little, tiny boy. Now you are a grown man.'

They talked about relatives. About his son's engineering work which had just won him an international prize for airport design. And Hess Jnr promised to bring his father the plans of a house he was building. There were seven minutes left. Then three . . . Hess saw me looking at my watch and got to his feet, straightening his dressing-gown. 'I'm afraid it is time. The visit is over.'

His son asked quickly: 'Who do you want to see in January?' Hess replied: 'It is up to you entirely.' He bowed to say his goodbyes. Together, mother and son stood up and remained looking at him. As Frau Hess finally turned to leave her son put his arm around her. 'Now be brave . . .'

They walked out of the room, Frau Hess's head still turned, taking in the last seconds of the sight of her husband. Then the door closed behind them, and only then did Hess slump into his chair. It was 3.49 pm. He had been with them for 34 minutes.

Outside, the Hesses were in conference with the medical super-intendent, the matron and the directors. 'Tell me,' Frau Hess immediately asked Dr O'Brien. 'Why did he request this visit? *Has he got cancer?*' 'I do not think he has cancer,' said the doctor. 'I would say it is almost certain that he has not. Everything will depend on his next X-ray.' He drew a sketch of the ulcer, showing where it was and how it had burst. 'I can assure you he is getting the best medical attention the Four Powers can provide.'

As they were about to leave, Frau Hess handed me some parcels for her husband. 'They are his Christmas presents.' There was a sandalwood box of Mousson Lavender soap, a pair of pale-blue fine cotton pyjamas and a record of Schubert.

Back in his room when they had gone, Rudolf Hess was lying with a contented smile on his face. 'I'm so happy I have seen them,' he said. 'I'm just sorry that I waited so long. What a big man my son is! Of course he was a complete stranger to me. Like somebody I have never seen before.'

23

Sparkling Christmas

RUDOLF HESS WAS given his Christmas presents early on Christmas Day. Chaplain de Luze arrived and said a short service for Hess after which they turned on the record-player so that Hess could hear his new Schubert record. On the bars inside his hospital-room window the chaplain had hung a coloured transparency of a mountain scene that enlivened the grey of the weather outside. At the end of the prisoner's bed four yellow candles, surrounded by an Advent wreath tied with a red ribbon, burned on a small table.

There was a tap on the door and to Hess's surprise in walked Father Christmas himself – in red costume, full beard and red cap. The twinkling eyes above the whispers were Dr O'Brien's; and his costumed helper Hess's medical orderly. They presented their patient with a Red Cross package of soap and after-shave lotion, and hardly had they gone when Christmas dinner was brought in. Hess had turkey, dressing, mashed potatoes, asparagus, broccoli and carrots. And a bottle of 1965 German sparkling wine to go with it. He drank all the wine, finished the meal with some ice-cream and then dozed off happily.

On the way in to see him I chatted with the orderly, now out of costume. 'I have,' he said, 'been an orderly for a long time. And I have never had a patient more difficult than Hess was when he first came in. He had us running day and night, and he was rude. But now I could not have a better patient. He is gaining confidence and trusting us, and we are able to trust him. We now have a fine contact.'

Hess sat up in bed in his black cashmere cardigan and pyjamas. 'I will never forget my visit from my family for the rest of my life,' he said. 'There were a few tense moments when there could have been tears shed. I tried to get over this by being extra-exuberant. Perhaps, in my enthusiasm, I might have overdone it. You see, I thought for a long time about how I should react, about how I should greet them when they came into the room.'

Hess was interrupted by an orderly coming in with two small medicine glasses on a tray. They were filled with a brown liquid and Hess took one, passing me the other. The Russian warder watched curiously as Hess said: 'Colonel Bird, this is something to take as a preventative against the influenza which is raging in Germany at the moment.' I smelled the liquid and immediately realized what it was. I thanked Hess and said seriously: 'I do have a slight cold. It is a good idea for me to take this.' '*Prosit!*' said Hess. 'Good luck!' And we swallowed our medicine glasses full of sherry.

Hess said his diet had been gradually increased and he felt no signs of pain. His weight had gone up to 152 lb. He had gone through his second barium test ('they turned me into some strange positions') and it had confirmed the doctor's diagnosis that the ulcer had healed by itself. There was no sign of cancer.

At the end of December he developed a slight cough which rapidly became pneumonia. He was treated with antibiotics and soon got over it. 'It's the first time in my life I have ever had it,' he said. 'It could have been rather serious if it had not been for the exercises I take every day – jumping up and down on my bed, doing my push-ups and walking in the corridor. Unless I had been fit, it would have been a hard struggle for a man of my age to shrug it off.'

He had his spectacles pushed up on his forehead as usual and lay back on his pillows recalling the past. He chatted about von Schirach and Speer and about his son's effort in London to initiate political pressure for his release. 'The Russians are stubborn, however. It is doubtful that they will ever agree to my release. I have reconciled myself to this. My destiny,' he said, 'is to go back to prison and stay there. There is nothing I can do about it. There is nothing my son can do about it. There is nothing you can do about it. There is nothing even your President can do about it. I will die in prison. I simply must accept it.'

I asked: 'If you were released, Hess, would you write your memoirs? Do you think it is your responsibility to history to write them?' He nodded. 'Yes, I suppose it is. I was the one who tried to get freedom for the world.'

'Did Hitler *know* you were going to fly to England?'

He shook his head. 'No. He didn't.'

'And yet you did this, knowing it might not succeed. And knowing you could be shot if you returned?'

'Yes,' he smiled a little ruefully. '*And* be called "crazy"!'

'Why did you do it then?'

He seemed surprised at the question. 'To secure peace of course.' And he went on: 'Because I did it, I am the one who has to stay longest in prison.'

He had never before allowed me to probe the past. I asked one last question. 'Did you know before you left about Barbarossa – the intended German attack on Russia?'

His eyes quickly turned away. He did not answer.

Then he had a request. 'I would like permission to take my walks, on sunny days, up on the hospital roof.' I knew there was no security on the roof, nothing to prevent him suddenly breaking away from his guard and jumping.

'You think I might commit suicide?' he said, almost reading my thoughts.

'Well, would you?'

He laughed. 'Oh you don't ever have to worry about that. I will give you my word of honour that I will never try to take my life. I will sign a statement to that effect. However I know I might be seen and photographed from near-by high buildings so I have worked it out that they could put up a screen to hide me.'

The following week I decided to allow him – for the first time in his life – to see television. I brought in a small Sony portable set and told Hess what it was. His eyes lit up. He had been listening to Beethoven on the record-player and hurried over to exchange the plugs. 'Oh this is wonderful!' he said, waiting for the picture to come on. When it did it was a beautiful girl modelling a brassière in a commercial. 'Fantastic!' said the man who had not seen a good-looking model in 28 years. He watched commercials selling salad, soap and hair-cream. Then the Berlin news came on and soon the subject was the Reichstag, now being re-built and soon to be the venue for an important political conference. Hess's eyes narrowed and his fist clenched as he saw the building. I wondered if he was thinking of his own Reichstag speech, prepared in his Nuremberg cell but never delivered. He watched for two hours and I then switched off the set. 'That little thing is just fantastic,' said Hess. 'I never believed it could be like that.'

I then had unhappy news for him. It had been finally decided that he was well enough to return to prison, but the date had not yet been set. 'It is not good news,' he said quietly. 'But it is something I have to face up to. I am destined to die in prison. It is the Russians . . . they are terrible people.'

He sighed. 'I have been completely examined and all is in order. My prostate is said to be enlarged but in no need of an operation.'* He looked down at his fingers. 'Therefore there is now no reason to keep me here.'

I changed the subject to talk about East Germany which had just been discussed on the television programme. 'They have been successful economically,' said Hess. 'But it is a police state and there is no freedom of movement. In one way, I suppose, that's not bad. They have nationalism. West Germany, for example, *lacks* nationalism, lacks a pride in itself as a nation.'

'How could they have a pride in their nation after having gone through two world wars and been beaten badly?' I argued. 'It is a divided country and pride has been taken from them. It will take another generation or two for pride to be instilled back in the people.'

Hess answered: 'So far as I am concerned the Versailles Treaty started it all. That was the seed that was planted for World War II. Under the conditions of the Versailles *Diktat* it wasn't possible for a nation to exist. It robbed Germany of national pride. No army, no merchant fleet, trade restrictions . . . all those things started World War II.'

* On 23 January 1970 a top British neurologist flew from London, and examined him, returning the same day.

24

Back to Prison

RUDOLF HESS SAT in bed, propped up by three pillows and looking puzzled. 'Something terrible has happened! Do you know – I am losing my *mind*!' He shook his head. 'It is just like it was at Nuremberg. And before that, in England. I just can't remember anything. I'm looking at you now,' he told me, 'and I don't even know your name. After about fifteen minutes of reading or writing I am completely mentally exhausted. I stretch out my hand for a glass of water to have a drink and before I've grasped it, I've forgotten what I wanted.'

I looked at the old man. What was he up to this time? Was his fear genuine? Or was this another of his deliberate 'losses of memory' in the hope that it would delay his return to prison. I decided it was best to ignore what he had said, and chatted to him about other things. He interrupted. 'I have been thinking about my return to prison. I do not think it is a good idea for me to have my new cell in the aide-room. It is too clinical. It reminds me too much of examinations. I would prefer the chapel. It is large, it has a tree hanging in front of a window and I would have a little greenery to look at. Nature, Colonel,' he said (he knew who he was talking to again), 'gives me a lot of strength.

'The worst thing about being in prison is the loneliness. Not being able to talk to anyone. Oh, I know I can talk to the warders. They are good fellows. But I cannot find much in common with them. Their ability to converse along the lines I would like is limited. I really am very much alone . . .' Then he brightened a little, taking off his glasses and smiling. 'Are all the arrangements made for the visit of my wife and sister tomorrow?' I assured him that all the arrangements had been made.

'I have told my wife that she must not be emotional about our visits together. I hate tears and undue emotionalism. Before her first visit I wrote to her and told her I would try and not be emotional myself when she arrived. She assured me that she would not cry during the visit . . . that she would do all her crying before – "with the joy of seeing me".'

He settled back into his bed and I bade him goodnight.

Frau Gretl Rauch had not seen her brother for 30 years. Aged over 70, wearing a brown coat and with a maroon scarf on her swept-back grey hair, she arrived next morning with Ilse Hess. She went in first to see Hess while Ilse talked to Dr O'Brien. Immediately Hess's wife asked the doctor: 'How is his heart?'

'It shows a little weakness,' said Dr O'Brien, 'but for a man of his age, it is in good shape. His ulcer has healed but he will have to be careful with his diet for the rest of his life. He must eat the proper foods.' 'Do you think,' asked the ruddy-faced Frau Hess, 'that the ulcer is something that he might have had for a long time?'

'I believe so.'

'How long?'

'Maybe for the last twenty years or so.'

'Well,' said Frau Hess, 'I remember that over twenty-eight years ago whenever he became excited he got pains in his stomach. He would come home from the office worried about something and he would have these pains. Do you think it could have been an ulcer even then?'

'It would be entirely possible.'

'My husband, Doctor, is an extreme introvert. He keeps all bothers and cares within himself. That is probably the trouble with him. He doesn't let go, blow off steam so to speak. What is your opinion of his bladder?'

'We have had the best man in this field come and examine your husband,' replied Dr O'Brien. 'He flew over specially from England to do this. He said no operation should be conducted at this time and that your husband is as well – having regard to his age – as most people.'

Ilse Hess seemed satisfied and thanked the doctor. She was ready to go in and see her husband. I offered her the use of a mirror to touch up her hair, which looked a bit wind-blown. '*Nein!*' she laughed, running her fingers through it. 'I was never too conscious of my looks. I am not a vain person!' And in she went to see her waiting Rudolf.

Half an hour later she emerged.

Now they were gone. And a relaxed, contented, former Deputy Führer shuffled back into his bedroom in his slippers. Within minutes, he was asleep.

In Spandau Prison the atmosphere was ruffled. Directors' meetings were going on for hour after hour as we tried to hammer out the date Hess should be returned to prison and the new conditions he would enjoy. The doctors were adamant that he must have a new cell, a consistent new diet and more relaxed conditions. The Russians were all for an immediate return to prison. The Allies did not believe he was yet well enough. The newspapers of the world were talking of 'an old man, no longer a danger to anyone, being used as a pathetic political football'. Pressure from each individual director's government was showing on all of us.

Eventually we reached agreement. He would be returned to Spandau on 13 March; he would move into the chapel, have a new schedule, and an approved diet that would not vary as each nation took its monthly duty. He would use the same hospital bed he was using now, with its adjustable controls for raising his head and feet. Hess would be allowed an hour's exercise in the garden each morning and another hour in the afternoon. If he agreed to do some light work – like raking leaves or weeding – he could stay in the garden longer.

His cell door was to remain permanently unlocked. As there would be no toilet in the old chapel he would need, with his bladder ailment, quick access to a near-by cell toilet without the necessity of warders unlocking and locking the cell several times a night. He was to be provided with a urine flask to use when his bladder bothered him excessively. He would, we agreed, be able to switch his own cell light on and off, though not off before 6.45 pm.

When I told Hess of the new conditions he grunted; 'I won't be doing any work in the garden. I have put up with that theatre for the last twenty-eight years and I am not going to continue it into the twenty-ninth year.' I smiled to myself. In all the years I have known

Hess I had never seen him work. He went on: 'I consider it beneath my dignity to work in the garden just to get two hours' more exercise. I don't care if it is just raking leaves or pulling weeds, I won't do it. My leg condition won't allow it anyway. If I stand in one spot too long my ankles swell.'

On the morning of 13 March he was told that he was to leave the British Military Hospital for Spandau. He reluctantly gathered up his papers and books, put his gramophone records together and at 3.45 pm climbed into the same ambulance that he had arrived in 14 weeks before, when he was sure he was dying. He said goodbye to the nursing aide who helped him; the porter in the gatehouse withdrew the long admission barrier leading to the street and the ambulance sped off towards the prison.

His new cell was ready for him. The old harmonium that Funk had played so often had been taken away. So had the Dürer pictures, the altar and the wooden cross; though there was still an imprint of unfaded paint where it had been. All the walls had been scrubbed and the paintwork gleamed freshly; green to half-way up the wall, then cream, and on the ceiling, white. The composition floor of the cell was black and newly waxed.

Hess's hospital bed came in a lorry and within an hour he was lying in it in his new surroundings. I walked down the end of the cell-block passage to where a cardboard notice on the chapel door said 'KIRCHE', the number 17 printed above it. I pushed the steel door open. Hess was sitting up, his spectacles on, reading, 'Well, Colonel, what did the Press say about my return to prison?' 'They did not even know you had gone. They have been taken by surprise. Nobody saw the transfer at all,' I told him.

Near the foot of Hess's hospital bed was his old brown table, brought from Cell 23. On it stood a jar of Nescafé, a spoon and a mug. Just inside the door was an AEG electric water-heater he had been given to make his own coffee. Two round neon tubes lit the cell and through the two barred windows (it had been two cells before the common wall had been knocked out) Hess could see the trees. Masking tape had been stuck around the edges of the windows to keep out draughts and a hot-water radiator warmed the room. His worn cupboard shelving had been brought from his old cell and his coat, jacket and two towels were slung from it on hooks. On

the shelves stood an enamel plate, two enamel cups, a spoon, salt
and pepper, two hair-brushes, a roll of pink toilet paper and a
comb.

'It is so much better for me here than it would have been in my
old cell,' he said. 'I think of the hundreds of hours I have spent listening
to Funk playing the harmonium, and the sessions of classical music
with the chaplain. I prefer not to have my own toilet in the cell.
It is not nice to see it when visitors come. I use the toilet two cells
away and that is adequate.'

He could also tell the time. The electric clock was back in its place
in the passage after its removal with Hess to hospital. Hess's old
straight-back wooden chair had been painted a sparkling white.
His sheets, blankets and pillow-cases from the British Hospital had
BMH printed on them. His hospital table that could be swung over
the bed and adjusted for reading and writing had come with him,
and on it lay five newspapers.

Within a day Hess had a 'complaint'. Chisholm, he said, had been
making his life difficult. Colonel Banfield, the British director, discussed
the matter with his chief warder and the Scot was asked to have regard
to Hess's condition. He must be treated less intolerantly, said Colonel
Banfield.

Hess also asked me if he might have a new coat. 'I want a trench
coat, one that comes down lower than the one I have at the moment.'
I brought three different coats from Berlin stores to Hess, but he found
fault with each of them. Finally he settled on one costing 189 Deutschmarks; it had a belt, high collar and a certain military air about it.
First he had wanted it sent back like the others. Then the next day he
said: 'It is really a beautiful coat. Can I please keep it?'

It was midnight on 5 April that the first alarm went out from Cell
17. Hess was heard moaning loudly and the warder on duty hurried
in to see him. He quickly telephoned Boon to come from his home
and a doctor was alerted. Hess had stomach pains again. 'They are
vicious,' he told Boon when the Dutch aide-man got to his bedside.
'Give me something to stop them.' Boon gave him medicine and
then Dr Burry, the US physician, arrived to examine Hess. The
prisoner ate no breakfast and little lunch. When I called at 3 pm to

see him he was sitting up in bed clutching his stomach, his face pale and twisted in pain. An hour or two later, however, the attack had passed and he was able to eat a light evening meal.

He was brighter next day and began chatting about the past. 'I'm afraid,' he said, pushing his glasses up on to his forehead, 'the historians are going to be disappointed with me. The fact is that I find it difficult to remember things from the past. I have forgotten so much. It is true that I have already written hundreds of pages in Nuremberg, and perhaps as many pages in notes and letters while I have been here. But now when I try, I cannot recall names and dates. I am convinced,' he went on, 'that I will one day leave the prison a free man.' (I looked sharply at him. Here was the man who had been telling me all the time he had been in hospital: 'I will go back to that prison and die. They will never let me go.')

Hess went on: 'Then I will be able to write. I have found peace within myself while I have been here in the solitude of the prison. I lead a very quiet life. No excitement arouses me. I have found an inner strength, the strength that carried me through my illness. I knew I would be well . . . that I could overcome it. I will write about that.

'I am feeling much better today. Do you think that I might have some young calf's meat or some game, like deer or rabbit, cooked for me? It is just what I feel like. I certainly don't eat as much as before, but I have a good appetite.'

His spectacles were down on his nose again and he looked over them at me. 'I know that as far as my ulcer is concerned, it was my own fault. I was stupid to refuse a barium test when I was asked so many times to submit to one. I should have had one long before. The ulcer would have been discovered and I would have saved myself a good deal of pain and torture.'

He turned his head towards the cell windows behind him. 'Listen. Do you hear the birds? They are outside in the tree, waiting for me to come and feed them.' Twice a day the bird-feeding ritual was being resumed in the Spandau garden. As if they knew the time, the birds would fly down from the trees and overhead wires around the prison and settle on the garden trees, waiting for the shuffling figure of Hess to appear, his overcoat pockets crammed with bags of breadcrumbs from the kitchen. He would scatter a handful in one direction, and then, waiting a few seconds, a handful in another, making sure the smallest sparrow got his share. Only the crows annoyed him. He did his best to make sure they missed his handout. 'They are robbers,' Hess said angrily. 'They will take food from any bird that is small and defenceless. I will not give them anything.'

25

One Day in a Life

BY THE WARDER'S watch it is 6 am. He sits yawning at the small table outside Cell 17. Through the half-open door he hears a movement and glances through the small inspection window. Hess is stirring, stretching, awake. He reaches out and turns on his light, rubs his eyes and removes wax ear-plugs he has inserted to blot out the clang of metal on metal in the huge, empty prison.

He lies there, as he must, for another 45 minutes. The new rules for Hess allow him to sleep until 7 am, but habit dies hard, and for many years Hess has been waking, unaided, at 6 am.

At 6.45 am he climbs out of bed in his blue-and-white striped hospital pyjamas and, hands on hips, begins his squatting, jumping exercises. After deep-breathing and more stretching he steps into his slippers, their backs broken down by his constant laziness in putting them on properly, pulls on his dressing-gown and, taking a towel off a hook on his wall-shelf, opens his cell door. '*Morgen*,' grumbles the warder. '*Morgen*,' growls Hess at Lucien Barcanan. The French warder's snoring has kept him awake for hours again and he is annoyed by the man.

He walks two cells up to Cell 19, von Schirach's old cell, and before that, Funk's, and uses the toilet. He flushes it with its strange whirring sound, then plods over to Cell 8, the washroom. Hess removes his dentures and cleans under the basin tap. He takes from a small locker the new Braun electric razor that has replaced his worn-out Philips and switches it on. The noisy hum echoes round the cell walls as he runs it over the dark stubble. Reflected in the mirror are pale, but no longer gaunt, cheeks. The blue eyes are still sunken under thick eyebrows, but no longer quite as hollow as before he went to hospital.

He runs the Braun up under his nostrils, cleaning the wide upper

194

lip. Then over his cheeks, across his chin and finally up past the level of the tips of his ears. No modern side-burns for No. 7.

He finishes, blows out the razor and replaces it. Then, stripped to the waist, he washes. He carefully brushes his greying hair, thinning even at his age only a little from the peak of his forehead, and turns to make his way back to his cell. He walks exactly 28 steps, his slippers flapping on the hard, composition floor. Now it is 7.15 am.

Hess quickly removes his pyjamas and dressing-gown and puts on the long combinations that cover him from his neck down to just below his knees; underpants carefully chosen not to restrict the circulation on the calves of his legs. Then on go his black-and-white check shirt, grey denim trousers and grey socks. Barcanan comes in and wordlessly hands him his spectacles and the prisoner climbs onto his bed again to read and wait for his breakfast.

On cue, at 7.45 am, he hears the crash of the first steel door closing and soon the squeaky 'clonking' sound of the rubber-wheeled trolley bearing his breakfast from the kitchen. Hess takes his tray from the worn, brown top of the trolley that has brought him Spandau meals for more than 20 years and carries it to his cell. He sets it on his table: a jug of black coffee, bread, butter, apricot jam, cereal, a boiled egg, milk and a plate of fruit. Slowly, savouring one of the few remaining joys of his life, Hess eats his breakfast, careful not to hurt his gums with his new dentures. He props up in front of him the book he is reading, *Wallenstein*. A small leather bookmark protrudes from the pages. It was given to him by Dr O'Brien before he left hospital. 'It was given to the doctor by a Catholic priest,' said Hess, 'who, even though I am not a Catholic, prays for me every day.'

Hess is allowed to use a knife to cut slices of his special dietary bread, closely watched by the warder, who then takes it and returns it to a locked cupboard. By now the sun is shining through the cell windows. Shafts of sunlight fall across his bed, where he lies with his feet propped up.

At 8.30 am, breakfast finished, he stacks the plates back on the trolley and pushes it along the corridor, past the empty cells that had once held Doenitz, Funk and Speer, to the first steel door where a warder waits to take it. He returns to tidy his cell or wash out some socks and underclothes in the laundry, and once more to his book. At 10.30 am the warder taps on the barred cell-door window and

Hess gets up and goes to Cell 19 where he takes his beige trench coat from the locker, pulls a grey cap down on his head and over his ears, and plods down to the garden. Head bent forward, hands behind his back, he walks briskly 215 steps one way around the garden path and 215 steps back the other, a lone figure, dwarfed by the leafless garden trees.

He covers the 210 metres 28 times. After scattering the crumbs for the birds Hess settles down on the hard little garden seat that Speer made, props his feet on a shabby garden chair and opens his book. The tall poplar that Doenitz planted so many years ago throws a shadow across the pages that helps his eyes. Boredly a warder stands at the cell-block door kicking a stone away with his boot. At 11.30 am he glances at his watch and calls out to Hess: 'OK No. 7.' The exercise period is over. Up the spiral staircase again, pulling on the worn, shiny handrail for support, Hess plods back into the prison, and along to Cell 19 to return his coat. Systematically the warder runs his hands over the prisoner's clothes and delves into his pockets to see if Hess has brought any sharp instrument from the garden with which he might injure himself. His cell has been thoroughly searched while he was out. As he has done hundreds of times before, the warder makes his entry in the 'occurrence book'. The time. The date. The result of the search: 'Nothing found.'

Sharp on 11.45 am, the squeaking wheels of the trolley herald Hess's lunch. Shrimp cocktail today, with fruit juice, mashed potatoes, broccoli, fruit pie and ice-cream. It is the American month. Though the agreed new constitution for Spandau means a constant diet for Hess that will not lead to malnutrition or affect his ulcer, he enjoys the generosity of the American guardianship. Today it has been the Italian chef's turn to cook for him. The day before it was the Spanish cook.* Each hot dish has an aluminium cover over it, but Hess plugs in his water-heater so he can put his dishes on top of the boiling water for additional warmth. He eats slowly, enjoying each mouthful; his newspaper, the *Frankfurter Allgemeine* propped up in front of him. The meat has been cut into small pieces so he can eat it with his spoon. Though he is allowed a knife under supervision to cut his bread he cannot use it for his meal.

Lunch over, he settles down to write to his wife on the foolscap

* The Chinese cook had long since departed from Spandau.

sheets with the Spandau stamp on them; the paper lying on his adjustable hospital swing-table which he uses as a lectern. At 1.30 he climbs onto the bed to sleep for half an hour. And at 2.30 it is time to go out into the garden again. So long as there is no rules-conscious Russian on duty, and no Russian in the one guard tower that overlooks the garden, Hess is allowed to stay out longer than the regulation hour. When he returns he goes through the search ritual again and then washes before preparing for his 5 pm evening meal. From 5.45 pm until 10 pm he can go to his library cell to choose a book or make notes in his black note-book. He is using a new one because while he was in the hospital his current book containing 2,500 painstakingly made literary references disappeared. It was a bitter blow to Hess. Now he is starting all over again. 'Can you understand that?' asked Hess. 'Because of somebody's carelessness all that work has just been wiped away.'

At 10 pm the warder on duty calls for Hess's plastic-lens spectacles. The prisoner pulls the blankets over him, inserts his wax ear-plugs and goes to sleep. Every 30 minutes during the eight hours the warder on duty outside his cell peers in through the half-open door and listens to his breathing. He no longer uses a flashlight. He can, by flicking on a blue-coloured light, see the prisoner in his bed without disturbing him. Every two hours, on the hour, the cell duty is exchanged with the warder at the main gate. It used to be changed hourly, but after Hess complained in May that he was being unnecessarily disturbed by the clanging of the cell-block door it was altered.

On Saturday the daily schedule changes. Hess has a bath. He changes his bed-linen, and he is given his weekly letter by the Soviet director and the British translator, John Hartman. At the same time he hands them the one he has written. Chaplain de Luze arrives and the prisoner and minister sit together listening to classical music on the prison record-player or tape-recorder.

The day is the highlight of Rudolf Hess's week; the pleasure of closeness to his wife and son with the music he loves as a bonus.

A day of escape, for the loneliest man in the world.

26

Aged Seventy-Six

FOR THE FIRST time, Hess's wife and son were to see him in prison. And now the moment had come for their arrival. Sharp on 10.50 am they drove up to the gates in a rented Opel Rekord and the chief warder opened the small door in the green gates as they got out of the car. Frau Hess was clutching a bouquet of flowers, and in response to a call from the TV and news photographers gathered in front of the prison, she and Wolf-Rudiger turned briefly to face them.

Entering the directors' office and unwrapping the obviously expensive bunch of flowers, Frau Hess asked: 'May I give these to my husband?' The Soviet director stepped forward, shaking his head. 'No. You cannot. It is against regulations.' Frau Hess, in fawn camel-hair coat and two-piece suit, pleaded with her voice and her eyes. 'But in two days it is his birthday. Please give him the flowers when I am gone.' 'No,' repeated the Russian. 'We cannot.' The bouquet of tulips and carnations was left on the directors' table.

When she walked into the visitors' room Hess's wife said she was expecting to have to speak through a wire-mesh grille. 'It went years ago,' I told her. 'Would you like to sit down?' She shook her head. 'No, I prefer to stand for a moment.' She paced slowly up and down the small bare room, which had been freshly painted and cleaned. The floor smelled strongly of a pungent wax. On the other side of the bench partition a door suddenly opened and in walked the chief warder, followed by Hess.

He was clean-shaven and his hair was neatly combed. He raised his hand happily to his wife, palm inwards towards his forehead. 'I greet you, Ilse!' They sat down and immediately began chatting about letters, one in particular she had written to him which had apparently gone astray. Then the conversation turned to Hess's only other outside
198

source of information, the newspapers. 'They are killing the German language,' he said. 'Ja,' said Frau Hess. 'Even my driver says "OK, OK" to me!'

She looked hard at her husband. 'You have got a little thinner since I last saw you?'

'Yes. But not too thin. I weigh about 64 kilos. That is good. I look at it this way – if I carried an extra 5 kilos around it is like a bag of 5 kilos of fat. And it gives my heart more work to do. Anyway, I feel better when I weigh less.'

Hess had taken off his spectacles and laid them on the table in front of him. His legs were resting sideways on a chair to help his circulation. Frau Hess had hers tucked under her chair and crossed.

After a chat about private matters Hess asked his wife to buy and send him a particular book. 'But that is about World War II, Rudolf, you are not allowed to read that.' He smiled. 'All right. Buy it anyway and keep it so I can read it when I get home.'

The half-hour had come to an end and it was time to leave. Frau Hess stood up and Hess got to his feet at the same time. For a moment they said nothing, their eyes looking. Briefly their mutual play-acting to be bright in front of witnesses was suspended and there was a second of great emotion which we all felt. She turned, putting her left hand on the door-knob,then looked once more at her erect, greying husband. He bowed to her from the waist and she opened the door and walked outside. She was close to tears.

Hess's son visited him for half an hour and found the prisoner pale, drawn and suddenly tired. They groped for conversation, and Wolf told his father again about his trip in a jumbo-jet. As he enthused about his own private flying Hess quickly broke in: 'Never be so foolish as to go up in a plane without a parachute. Always remember that.'

Together, son and mother left the prison, she clutching the now withering flowers she had brought in. Frau Hess's eyes were glistening with tears as Wolf-Rudiger told the Press she had been unable to give the flowers to her husband. Then they drove off.

It was Rudolf Hess's 76th birthday. He had put on his corduroy suit and after a walk in the garden enjoyed a lunch of duckling, red cabbage, dessert and a birthday-cake made for him in the prison kitchen.

As he took his afternoon walk in the sun a group of about ten people had gathered in front of the gates demanding his release. They leaned two bunches of flowers against the gate and shouted over a loud-hailer about inhumanity. One bore a placard: 'WHERE IS JUSTICE?'

Hess, continuing his walk at the rear of the prison, told me: 'I heard a loudspeaker and somebody's voice screaming. What were they saying? Were they protesting against me?' I told him they were wishing him a happy birthday. 'They know?' asked Hess. 'Did they remember that?'

Hands behind his back, he walked some more in silence. Then he said: 'I have been thinking about those cosmonauts. What brave men they were. What heroes. They had no guarantee that they would for sure get back to earth.'

'Well when you went on your flight, Hess, you had no guarantee that you were going to make it, either.'

'No. I knew where I was going. I knew I would make it. However, I did not know whether I would be delivered back here or not. If I had been sent back Hitler would have stood me up against a wall.' His eyes, blue and direct, a little frightening in their seriousness, turned to me. 'I did not know, either, that when I went to England nobody was going to listen to me. It was my full desire to bring about peace in the world and yet Churchill was in no position to listen to me. He did not have the *power*, in fact, to change the direction of the rolling stone . . . The most horrible thing they could have done to me was to give me over to the hands of the Russians. And that's what they finally did. That is where I am now.'

'You are saying for certain that Hitler had no idea that you were going to fly off to England?'

'No. He had none. Nobody knew. Not even my wife. I left a letter with Pintsch, my adjutant, for the Führer, to be delivered after I had gone.'

'Yes. Speer was there. He said Hitler was in a rage.'

Hess threw back his head and laughed. 'I can well imagine it!' He looked serious again. 'You can well believe me. My earnest desire was to stop the war, not to continue it. At the same time I wanted to warn about the coming danger of the Bolshevists, of Communism. The world cannot say I did not warn of this, and look where it stands today. There are those who say I wanted to continue the war, against Russia . . .' He broke off, deciding apparently to say no more.

'The reason,' said Hess, striding along the path, 'that the Russians won't let me go is that they think I knew a great deal more than I did; that I had a great deal more influence than I did have. That is why I am still here.'

27

'He Never Knew'

THE DATE WAS 10 May 1970. Twenty-nine years to the day that Hess had made his flight. I found him lying on his cell bunk; he had on a short-sleeved shirt, a pair of braces held up his denims and showed his socks cut off at the ankles so that their elastic would not restrict his circulation.

I had with me the recently published English book: *Hess – The Man and His Mission*, by J. Bernard Hutton. 'I thought you might like to see what they are writing about you.'

Hess sat up and began eagerly thumbing through the pages. He glanced at a picture of himself – thin and haggard-faced – eating lunch during the Nuremberg Trial. Then he came across a photograph of two children, captioned: 'Rudolf Hess as a child, with his sister.' 'But that's not *me*!' he exclaimed. 'Of course it's you,' I said. 'Look at the title.'

'No,' said Hess emphatically. 'I would know if it was me or not. And that certainly isn't my sister. Look, there she is much older than me when in fact Gretl was born in 1908. She is fourteen years *younger* than I am.' He laughed and ruffled through pictures of himself with Hitler; pictures taken before he was to climb into his borrowed Messerschmitt. Then he stopped at page 21 which began: '*Hess's historic flight was made with Hitler's full knowledge and approval.*' He chuckled. 'No. As I've told you, the Führer didn't know anything about it.' We read further: '*The venture was discussed endlessly before Hitler sanctioned it.*'

'Not so,' repeated Hess. 'He knew *nothing* of my plan.'

Tucked in the pages I had left an article which had appeared a few weeks before in the London *Sunday Times*. It was a discussion by a historian about a letter Hess had written from his Nuremberg cell to the London Nazi sympathizer Sir Oswald Mosley. This time he read it in silence, his brow puckered in thought. At last he handed it back

202

to me without a word. He suddenly looked very depressed. The long, rambling letter had made him think back too far on this day of all days. He turned over to have a sleep. He had remembered enough about the past.

Ilse Hess arrived a few days later and after her visit came out smiling. 'I think he looks much better than the last time.' It was the 13th visit Hess had had since the very first from his lawyer, Dr Seidl. Frau Hess went on: 'Albert Speer came down to Hindeland to see me after he had been released and he told me: "I can understand why Rudolf refused to see you for so long. He saved himself the torture we others went through. The very worst thing for me in prison was suffering the excitement – about a fortnight ahead of the visit, and a fortnight after it – of seeing my family. If I had to do it all over again I would not ask for a single visit. It was just mental torture."'

After Frau Hess left we suddenly had another Hess problem: the World Cup. Not content with bringing radios into the cell-block to hear Germany battling in Mexico, a French warder had brought in a portable television set. And together the warders and their prisoner had watched the match. The 72-year-old British warder, Swan, got to hear of it and immediately went to the British director. And it became a matter for discussion at a directors' meeting. The Soviets, already grumbling about the 'soft life' Hess was leading, were furious, and an immediate inquiry began. Afterwards it was decided that no television sets could be brought into the cell-block in future.

Next day I was walking in the garden with Hess – a hot, dry Berlin day. But despite the temperature he still had on his 'Long John' underpants, specially cut off at the knees for his circulation. He had his collar and the top of his denims open and he walked, shoulders slightly slumped, arms behind his back, grasping his left arm just above the wrist with his right hand. He brushed away a fly from his ear now and again as he discussed the British election he had been reading about in the newspapers.

'I just don't understand it,' said Hess. 'Heath seems to have won. Yet here is Wilson, who has done more for the British economy than perhaps any other British Prime Minister, and he is thrown out. Through the lack of support of the unions he has lost the election.

He has stabilized the British economy! I wonder what Heath and his Conservatives think they can do that is better? There you have it again – the people actually destroy their purpose. They want higher wages; but they don't sit down to realize they are out-pricing themselves by their demands. As wages go up so do prices and the cost of living. It is a never-ending spiral. It is the same here in Germany, but perhaps a little more conservative. Recently the members of parliament voted themselves an enormous increase in salary in the face of trying to hold down wages. It is false, what they are doing. They should always set an example.'

He went on: 'I have a very difficult task before me today. I have to give it a lot of thought. You see it is soon my mother-in-law's ninetieth birthday and I am writing her a letter. It is a very difficult letter and I have to concentrate a lot. Here is a lady ninety years of age. What in the world am I going to wish her at that age? She has had a long and happy life.

'Relatives from the four corners of Germany are gathering to celebrate her birthday. Colonel – the biggest thing I could do would *be* to be there . . . Do you suppose – if the Russians and all the other directors agreed – that I might go off to Bremen and celebrate her* birthday with all the other relatives?'

I looked at Hess in astonishment. He was serious! 'Don't smile,' he said. 'I have been a prisoner for almost thirty years. There is no earthly reason why I should not have two days off for good behaviour. I would return to Spandau. Really I would.'

It was getting so hot in the prison that I suggested we might put a small refrigerator in the cell next to Hess's so he could keep his milk and fruit juice cool. Colonel Banfield nodded agreement for the British side, but straight away the Russian, Colonel Tarutta, said: 'No. He has it too good already. We can't do everything this man wants. There has to be a limit *somewhere*.'

I realized the cause of the Russian's abruptness. Already Hess's conditions in the prison were far superior to that of 75 per cent of the Russian people, and Tarutta felt it. 'Then why don't we get a

* Hess's mother-in-law's surname was Horn. When Hess landed in Scotland he had introduced himself as 'Hauptmann [Captain] Horn'.

refrigerator for the chief warder's office in the prison block?' I asked, knowing, as Tarutta did, that Hess was free to wander the cell-block and would still be able to use a refrigerator. 'The warders like to keep their milk cool too.' Tarutta agreed.

I went out into the garden and found Hess sitting in the shade of a tree. He got to his feet and with a glance up at the guard tower, led me furtively to a spot by one of the bushes. 'Look,' he said, pushing some leaves aside. There, poking its head out of the ground was a small mushroom. And by it another. As we looked, a male duck settled on the ground 25 yards from us. 'Isn't that beautiful?' asked Hess. 'Can you imagine anybody shooting a bird like that? It bothers me whenever I eat meat that an animal has to die to feed me.' I told him about the refrigerator arrangement. 'Wonderful,' he said. 'I do know my conditions are better than that of millions of Russians. Millions of Germans, too, for that matter.'

A snag came up the next day. We heard that the French – although they had signed a long-argued agreement with the rest of us – were now saying they could not agree with the cremation of Hess's body when he died, and the handing over of the ashes to the next-of-kin.

It meant they had had second thoughts, changing the decision passed on in the name of France by the French director, Max Farion, the man who had been at Spandau for 15 years, longer than any of us. The convivial Max, with the rather long nose, high forehead and long list of jokes, was as dismayed as anybody. A lover of good food, good French wine and cigars, Max was the typical *bon viveur* and raconteur. What was to happen with Hess's body was now, he knew, something over which he had no control.

I was that day censoring yet another long Hess letter to his wife; marvelling over the choice of words, the prose and the excellence of his intelligence. He wrote beautifully. There was soon to be another visit from his wife, and he was suggesting subjects they might discuss in the short time available to them. 'If we decide on this, we can go right into matters without wasting time,' he wrote. 'We don't lose one moment that way. No hesitations! No long silences! No stopping to think about what we will talk about next!'

Hess had become obsessed, now, with the moon and the moonshots. He was absorbing every piece of information from his news-papers and added a long postscript to his letter to his wife listing 17 questions on the moon to which he wished to know the answers. As well as the moon, he had The Pill on his mind, and wrote a long dissertation on its effect on the population explosion. This was no simple man . . .

He had only one short burst of abdominal pain in April and now it had cleared up. His weight and blood-pressure remained constant and his urinary troubles had cleared up. He looked younger than ever. Only one thing bothered him. He asked the American dentist, Dr Samuel Roy McCuskey Jnr, for another dental plate. The present teeth were not white enough, Hess said, and he needed a plate that would fill out his upper lip. Dr McCuskey said it could be made, but it would not be as satisfactory for eating. No matter, said Hess. So long as it *looked* better. Now he was having visits from his family he wanted to look his best.

On 26 August we had an alert. An anonymous call had come in threatening to bomb the prison, the US Consulate and several official buildings in Berlin, unless Rudolf Hess was released by 1 September. The calls were tape-recorded and were both in English and German. The Berlin police took the matter over and as a precaution we strengthened the Spandau guard. 1 September came and went. And nothing happened.

28

A Decision to Talk

ON 30 AUGUST Rudolf Hess came to an important decision: he would like, he said, to set the historical record straight about his life. He was disturbed by books like *Hess*, by J. Bernard Hutton, and *The Rise and Fall of the Third Reich*, by William Shirer. They contained statements about him which he said were not correct. Hutton's book had a photograph of a letter purporting to have been written by him, but which was a fake. Not only was it not his handwriting, but it used a slang German he had never been guilty of using.

'It will not be easy,' he warned me. 'My memory is not good. However, you already have my papers and diaries. They are accurate and they were written when the facts were vivid in my mind. I will do my best to answer questions not contained in them.'

Hess had given this a great deal of thought. He knew deep down that it was likely that he would die in jail and that the myths about him in newspaper and magazine articles would be repeated by authors writing after his death. Partly because of his anger at seeing things written now which were wrong, and because he had grown to trust me over the years, he had made up his mind. He was basically a wary, mistrustful man and it was no easy decision to come to. What actually swayed him, I believe, was my tape-recorder. I promised him that if we talked on tape we would be able to make a verbatim record of history as he saw it and that it would be kept for posterity. What he said into the microphone would be *his own* version of events, not something set down by guesswork. 'Ah,' said Hess. 'Good. Good. Yes. We will work on that.'

In the afternoon sunshine, sitting on a seat in the garden, we began on our mission. We decided to work as far as possible in English. Then, if he found explanations easier, to use German. Hess sat beside me in his prison corduroys, hunched a little, deep in thought, his voice slow, a little husky, but his choice of words precise.

'People will wish to know about your life here and how you see it. About the books you read for instance?'

'I have,' said Hess, 'read one book in a week; and I have taken two or three weeks on a single technical book. I am of course an avid reader. I read four newspapers a day from cover to cover. I enjoy historical books and scientific books. Books about the economy and modern history interest me. I am at the moment reading all I can in books and in the newspapers about Man's attempts to walk on the moon. I like to know about the moon's surface and the problems of craters. This is gone into in the American, Baldwin's book *The Face of the Moon*.'

'Which writer do you think has given you the most in life – the best guidance?'

'Ah. Without a doubt Schopenhauer. He strengthened my inner convictions that man is guided by Fate. Therefore I am sure that one day I shall be set free,' he laughed, a little nervously. 'Everything,' Hess went on, 'that comes to us . . . that happens in our life, is because of Fate. There are times when we have the power to guide our fate, by doing things ourselves that will determine that fate. But at the end of it all it is man who is guided. And Fate does the guiding.

'Schopenhauer asserted that the fate of man is predetermined. That main idea of his work impressed me strongly. The will can be so strong that it influences a body and spirit. Without a strong will I would not have been able to hold out all these years . . .'

We rose and began walking in the garden, Hess with his hands behind his back, thinking aloud. Now and again he stopped and re-read the questions I had written out for him. 'My own source of real strength is through God, and my philosophy of Life,' he went on. 'I am a great believer – a *strong* believer – in God. Not in the Church, only in God. A faith in God I consider the same as a philosophy of Life. Because, really, isn't our fate in God's hands? I draw strength from both.'

'What about music – does it help you?'

'Oh yes. I have several favourite composers. Schubert, Mozart and Beethoven. I can hear their records once a week and that helps a lot.'

'Hess, it has often been said that when the Führer wrote *Mein Kampf* in Landsberg, where you were in prison together, that you acted as his stenographer. Others say you supplied some of the ideas. Which is true?'

'I don't believe I helped the Führer write his book. I might have done, but I don't think so.'

'What about your learning from Professor Haushofer? They say you passed on his ideas to Hitler about geo-politics.'

'I did study geo-politics under Professor Haushofer. According to my memory I do not believe I passed on his teachings to Hitler. Probably he himself read geo-political works; perhaps some of them by Professor Haushofer.'

'What was your most lasting memory of Hitler?'

'Well. I used to see him striding backwards and forwards in his large room, dictating orders and letters as he went. In this manner he would exercise at the same time as he discussed things. He was warm and friendly to those he chose to be warm and friendly with, but he could also be very cold and distant to those he did not know intimately. Of course, like anybody else, he had great worries and he had moods.'

The birds in the tall poplar were chattering away as we walked by it. In the background a sentry could be heard whistling quietly to himself in the guard tower. 'It will soon be time for you to feed them,' I said, nodding towards the birds. '*Ja*,' replied Hess. 'I have a great love of nature. It is interesting for me to stand and watch the movements of birds. Crows, you know, are friendly in their conduct towards each other. But they are also jealous – screaming hysterically when food appears. Both the seagull and the crow are very human. The crow is the more cowardly. Suddenly, as I am feeding the birds, a flock of seagulls fly down and the crows retreat. The black bird always retreats from the smaller and weaker white bird, even though the white birds are in the minority. The black birds stand at a respectful distance watching the invaders, but not taking any action. People, of course, react differently when they are invaded by another race. They will attack those who try and interfere with their rights.'

I said to Hess: 'You have told me several times over the years about your flight. I am sure it is always vivid in your mind. What was the real story behind it?'

He looked at me for a long time. 'You have what I have written about it. There is little to add,' he shrugged. 'But it is quite true that I flew to England on a mission of humanity. The Führer, you see, did not want to defeat England. He wanted to stop the fighting. But he did not know that I was going to fly there to bring this about.

'I took it on myself to do it. I took the full responsibility,' he went on in his slow, husky voice, choosing his words carefully. 'It was on my own shoulders; I flew on my own initiative. I did not, as some say, fly to England for any personal advantage. It could have actually meant death for me. The Führer wanted to end the war with England with an *understanding*.'

Hess was silent for a moment as we walked. 'I took off in a Messerschmitt from Augsburg two or three times, but I was turned back by the weather. How many times I am not sure. But it doesn't matter now. It is not important. There was no question in my mind of telling Hitler about it first. If he had known of my plan he would have had me arrested. I took a letter to the Duke of Hamilton who I had seen during the Berlin Olympic Games. But I cannot remember what was in it. It must still be on my files somewhere. You can look it up. I also left a letter of explanation to Hitler with my adjutant, Pintsch . . .'

'Yes,' I reminded him. 'Speer was present when it was delivered. Hitler was very mad with you.'

Hess laughed. 'That I can imagine!'

'Hess, the American author, William Shirer, has written [in *The Rise and Fall of the Third Reich*] these words: "[Hess] had come to have an abiding belief in astrology . . . late in 1940 one of his astrologers had read in the stars that he was ordained to bring about peace. He [Hess] also related how . . . Professor Haushofer . . . had seen him in a dream striding through the tapestried halls of English castles, bringing peace between the two great 'Nordic' nations." Is this true?'

Hess stopped and read the page of Shirer's book. 'No. It is not true that I am especially interested in astrology. I never asked an astrologer to read my horoscope; in fact I have never let myself be influenced by an astrologer. I know nothing about any such dream by Haushofer. If this were the truth,' he said, tapping the page, 'I would most certainly have remembered it. I never – at any time – regulated my life, or decided political action, by horoscopes. Even if Haushofer had written or said such a thing it would not have been the decided factor in my decision to fly. I would not have been influenced by that.'

'A lot of writers say you knew before you flew of Barbarossa [Hitler's secret plan to attack Russia]. In fact the Russians still believe this was so. What do you have to say about that?'

Hess's eyes narrowed. This time he took a long time to consider the question. There was silence, except for the soft whistling of the sentry. 'I'm sorry,' he said shortly. 'I don't know. If I knew about this Barbarossa I cannot remember. But in any case I did not fly to England for this reason. I only flew to make peace.'

'Some also say that you went because Hermann Goering was replacing you in your influence with Hitler, and that you flew to do something dramatic to gain favour again. How did you get on with Goering in the end?'

'Oh, I liked him. He was a very colourful person. Very impressive. He was very demonstrative and quite outspoken. He was also a good pilot. No,' said Hess, remembering my question. 'I was never jealous of him.' Then he laughed, almost to himself. 'He was, you know, about as round as he was tall!'

It was time for the exercise period to end and Hess and I walked slowly back to the cell-block, climbing the old spiral staircase with its hand-worn banisters. We walked along the silent corridor leading to his cell, and when we came to the cell-door I noticed that somebody had attached gold-painted wardrobe handles to it, inside and outside.

'On the question of Barbarossa,' I said, as he sat down on his bunk. 'You must have known *something* about Hitler's intention to attack the Soviet Union before you took off. The Russians have always thought so.'

The old man's eyes were serious, and there was a touch of exasperation that I had repeated the question yet again. 'I told you last time that I would think about it,' said Hess. 'I did think, and I wrote down the answer to your question. You may use what I wrote in your book if you wish.' He rummaged amongst his books and took out a piece of paper on which he had written in ink: '*Before I flew to Scotland I did not know of Hitler's intention to attack Russia. I did know, however, that he was no friend of the Soviet Union. Hitler did not know of my flight prior to my making it.*' That was, he said, all he wished to tell me about the matter. In other words, would I kindly drop the subject?

Next day I found him in the garden again, but this time walking close to the wall of the prison itself. 'What on earth are you doing,' I asked, 'hugging that wall in the shadows on such a sunny day?'

'Ah,' smiled Hess, 'you see there are workmen up there repairing the prison roof. I have instructions from the warders that while they are there I must keep out of sight. I dare not show them who it is they have in this prison!'

Hess looked smart in his trench coat and cap and I told him so. 'It's a funny thing you should say that,' he said, falling into step beside me. 'I have always tried to dress neatly, but I have never paid much attention to style. Just the other day my wife wrote to me and said how simple it was to live in the country and not be bothered about fashion. She wrote: "Actually you were never one to worry about styles. I doubt, for instance, that you even notice that every time I come dancing to you in that prison that I am wearing the same outfit."' He smiled. 'I did not realize it, but when I came to think about it, she does. She blames my lack of interest in fashion for her own lack of interest in it.'

He had a good colour in his cheeks and he looked fit for his 76 years. I dared not tell him that at that very moment insistent demands were being made by a group of British Members of Parliament that Hess be thoroughly examined to prove or disprove a rumour that he had a malignant growth. It was of course nonsense. Few men of Hess's age were enjoying such robust health, and few were examined as regularly as he was. Nevertheless, to satisfy the MPs the British authorities in Berlin had asked for a complete medical examination and it was going to be done the next day.

Hess was in the headlines again in Berlin: This time because a dramatized documentary film about his flight was to be shown soon on BBC television in colour. I had received a copy of the BBC's *Radio Times* and showed Hess the preliminary publicity the film was getting. He looked at the photograph of the Nazi-uniformed actor who was to play the Hess part, and exclaimed: 'That man's likeness to me is fantastic. It says here that my son and Albert Speer are both to appear on the programme. I would love to see it. I expect hundreds of thousands of people will be watching this film. I wonder what they will be thinking of me. What will they say, when it is over, of that fellow Rudolf Hess?'

As we walked in the mid-afternoon sunshine he suddenly stopped in his tracks to point up at the full moon shining over the steeple of the church opposite. He pointed out the various seas that were identifiable to the naked eye. 'Isn't it beautiful? I cannot get over it. That man has actually walked on the surface of that moon . . .'

29

The Burning of the Reichstag

WOLF-RUDIGER HESS ARRIVED at the prison promptly at midday to visit his father. He signed the book and the visit was recorded as the nineteenth Hess had had since he entered Spandau.

I carefully went over all the aspects of Hess's medical condition to the son, and detailed the treatment he was being given for his various ailments. Wolf listened intently and then we made our way to the interview room. Almost at the same time the door on the other side opened and a warder led in Rudolf Hess. He hailed his smartly dressed son: 'Guten Tag!' 'How are you?' They sat down and Hess, pulling a second chair up to support his legs, launched immediately into a conversation about his son's work, designing airports of the future.

'You know what I think?' asked the father. 'I believe that within Germany there should be no internal airports such as we have in Berlin, Hamburg, etc., and no internal flights. The only flights from Germany should be overseas, and my idea is that the airports used for these flights should all be located on the coast. That would do away with the noise, the pollution and the confusion air travel causes in the cities. Why spend millions of marks on airports that will only contaminate cities more than they are already contaminated? Rather, they should save that money and build fast trains that will take people from any German city to a coastal port within an hour or two. I am of course talking,' he told his son, 'of trains that will travel at 500 mph.'

Wolf-Rudiger looked surprised. 'Father you will be interested to hear that this is exactly what we are talking about for the future. Such airports are a long way off, but there are already designs on the boards for fast monorail or air-cushion trains that will travel as fast as you say. We are at present engaged in planning airports for Hanover, Hamburg and Frankfurt at a cost of two billion marks. Imagine what we could do with that money if it was to be put into one airport on the coast.'

Obliquely the young man, who was still almost a stranger to the prisoner sitting opposite, changed the subject to Hess's health, and they began discussing blood-pressure. Rudolf Hess felt atmosphere conditions influenced blood-pressure to a marked extent. Then one of the two Russian observers present made a sign and the time was up. Both men got to their feet and Hess told his son: 'This is the last visit we shall have before Christmas. I want,' he said, tilting his chin upwards a little, 'to wish you a Happy Christmas and a Happy New Year. Also the same for your mother. Would you please buy her a nice present for me? I will write about it in our next letter and you can give it to her in my name.'

After his son had gone Hess had a request. 'The doctor has told me that I should have a heating pad in my bed. As you know, the electricity socket in my cell has been disconnected to prevent suicide attempts. But that is silly. I have a glass in my cell and if I wished to commit suicide I could smash it and use that. But I am past that stage now. I would not commit suicide. If I wished I could have thrust some wires into the extension lead I use to operate my coffee- and plate-warmer but I would not think of it.'

I agreed that he should have the bed-warmer and would, I said, make arrangements to have the socket repaired. 'And while the electrician is at it,' said Hess, 'do you think he could also fix the socket near the spiral staircase? If he did, a radiator could be used on a long lead for the warder who has to sit outside watching me take my walks in the garden. Often in the winter, because warders get cold and want to go inside, my walk periods are cut short.'

He had, he said, just one more request. Could he have a watch with an alarm on it? 'Last time the dentist arrived it was 6.35 in the morning and I was still asleep. I should have been up at the time, but the warder outside my cell – *guarding* me – also overslept. If I had an alarm it would be good for the warder and good for me too. Do you know, I haven't had a watch in my hand for thirty years?'

Then he smiled. 'At 9.20 last night I thought of that TV programme starting on the BBC and I wondered what people were saying about me and my flight. I wonder what they think about me.'

I had in my attaché case a book I had been reading called *The Reichstag Fire*, by Fritz Tobias. I asked him directly: 'Did you know anything about the planning behind the burning of the Reichstag? It was officially stated that the Dutchman Van der Lubbe started the fire. But it was proved later that he could not have done it alone. Tobias talked to more than a hundred people and he claims the fire was without doubt ordered by the Nazi Party. It gave Hitler the opportunity to take one of his major steps to power and mastery of the German people.

'Hess,' I said, 'it is believed by many that you are the only living person who really knows the truth behind the burning of the Reichstag. Would you like to glance through this book and tell me later what you remember?'

He was silent for a moment, then his eyes met mine. 'I knew nothing. I know nothing now.' His eyes dropped and his hands clenched tightly together. 'Even if I did know something I don't want to talk about it. I do not want you to leave that book in my cell.'

I got up and left him. I felt he was not telling the truth.

When Boon arrived with his midday meal on 26 April, I gave orders that Hess be given a knife and fork – the first time he had used a knife in 30 years. It was his 77th birthday. 'I had almost forgotten how to use a knife,' chuckled Hess. 'This is far easier than eating with a spoon.'

Two weeks passed and the fateful date 10 May came round again: 30 years since he had flown to Scotland. Colonel Ralph Banfield, the British director, went in to see him first and reminded him of the significance of the date. 'It's the anniversary of your flight.' 'Oh I had forgotten completely,' replied Hess. 'If you hadn't told me about it I would have passed the day without realizing.' When I went to see him in the afternoon he was pacing out in the garden, head down, hands behind his back, obviously deep in thought.

'So it's thirty years, Hess. You know, I have just been reading a book* by James Douglas-Hamilton, the son of the Duke of Hamilton. He tells about his father's connection with your flight. You remember telling me that nobody knew about your plan to go? Well this book gives evidence that you and the Haushofers not only talked about it in detail but exchanged letters about it. Was that true?'

He slowed down in his walk and for a moment there was silence in the garden, save for the shuffling of a guard in one of the towers. Hess stopped: 'Colonel Bird, I told you I flew on my own – in that

* *Motive for a Mission* (St. Martin's Press, 1971).

I took it on my shoulders to do it. Of course I talked about the plan with others before flying. I was in touch with Professor Karl Haushofer and his son, Dr Albrecht Haushofer. I have never denied it. Nobody has ever asked me as much. It is untrue, though, to say that I knew the Duke of Hamilton. I had never met the man, never dined with him. If he was in the same room as I was during the Berlin Olympic Games we never conversed. I of course knew about him and his flying.'

We sat down in the shade of the tall poplar and Hess stretched his legs out, showing under his denims his mesh socks cut off at the ankles. I had brought with me a recording of the BBC television documentary on his flight and his arrest. As I fitted the cassette into my tape-recorder he played nervously with the knot on his white-silk scarf. 'Colonel,' he said, 'whatever they say on this programme, I want you to under-stand for the purposes of history and your book that the mission I undertook was a great mission. I am not ashamed of it. It was a mission for humanity. I wanted to end the war and bring about an under-standing with England; to stop the bloodshed and end the suffering. I took it on myself to go. I made the decision. Little did I know that I would be received the way I was. Little did I know that Churchill did not have the power to change the direction of the rolling stone.

'But I was too late. It was impossible. My mission was a failure.' Then almost to himself, he added: 'It was a great mission . . .' I had the tape ready to play. 'Did you really have high hopes of bringing about a settlement with the British?' 'Of course!' he laughed. 'Other-wise why would I have gone?'

I switched on the tape-recorder 'Play' button. The English com-mentator's voice rang out and Hess put his head down closer to take in every word. His body gave an involuntary shudder at the simulated crash of his plane, and then he smiled when a Scot recalled asking Hess for his name and he replied: 'Alfred Horn.' The Scot said: 'Alfred is not a Germanic name. And AH happen to be the initials of Adolf Hitler, don't they?'

When he heard this Hess threw back his head and laughed. 'I never thought of that – but it's true,isn't it? That fellow knew who I was all the time.' His eyes watched the machine eagerly as the story unfolded . . . his arrest . . . his interrogation . . . his imprisonment in Wales. 'That doctor's voice [Dr Dicks] I remember very well.'

He heard 20 minutes of the tape and then I stopped it. 'We will hear the rest another day. It's time to go inside back to your cell now.' Almost as an afterthought I said casually: 'Did Hitler know you were going?'

Hess's eyes narrowed. 'The Führer,' he said slowly, 'never wanted to fight against England. I knew that from discussions I had in the early days with him in France. I knew it most surely. Hitler actually had a great respect for the English people, for their culture, for their British Empire and for the civilization they had shown the world.'

'But did he *know* you were going to fly?'

He looked embarrassed. 'What does Hamilton's book say?' We were about to walk inside when his eyes turned to me. 'At this point in history I want to tell you one thing, Colonel. I did not realize when I flew, that thirty years later I would be sitting in this prison garden, under a tree planted by Grand-Admiral Doenitz, listening to a BBC documentary about my flight: thirty years ago was a much more exciting time for me than it is today.'

He went on: 'Regarding the Führer's *Mein Kampf*. It is true, as they say, that some of his ideas in the book – Lebensraum for one – came no doubt from the teachings of Professor Haushofer. He used some ideas too from what I told him. Hitler, you see, was not a studious man. He took these geo-political ideas from Haushofer and used them in a sense to suit his own ideas. But Haushofer, although he visited us in Landsberg, did not write a word of Hitler's book.'

'You didn't remember this before?'

'No. But I am an old man who has been in prison for a long time. I have lapses of memory. It is true that at times in earlier years I pretended to lose my memory, but really, I have genuinely lost it sometimes.' He seemed stimulated by what he had heard and went on. 'It is quite untrue that I took the action I did because (as you said once) Bormann and Goering were taking my place in Hitler's eyes. It was never the case.'

We began walking into the prison. 'Do you remember now whether, before you took off, you knew about the planned attack on Russia? Hamilton says in his book that you were on the central planning committee and that you knew.'

This time it was obvious my question had touched what Hess called his 'black memories'. I had, on this day of days, delved too deeply.

His face dropped and noticeably paled. His eyes sank even further under the brows, and he looked drawn and old. He said nothing.

I worried whether the old man had been taken back into the past with too much of a shock. But next day he was cheerful again, obstinate that the sandals he had been given (the fifth attempt to fit him) pinched him and would have to go back. He had been told the newspapers were full of articles about his flight and the 30th anniversary. 'I'm not sure whether the publicity helps me or not,' he told me.

I said there was a British proposal that he be allowed to go home during the British, American and French months, and, if the Russians insisted on keeping him in prison, he could return in their month. '*Never!*' Hess almost shouted. 'A ridiculous idea. Do you know what it would be like to go back, to visit all my old friends, and be with my wife, and then every four months have to return to this place?'

'One of the papers says it is remarkable how you have been able to keep your balance all these years in the prison.'

'It is because I have made an effort to remain mentally active. I have done my serious reading, writing notes about articles and books in my note-book. And now I have my moon hobby. [He had just received four close-up photographs of the moon from NASA in Texas.] I do not just stroll about the prison garden watching the flowers grow.'

Then he said: 'Colonel, referring to your questioning yesterday. I want so much to tell you what I can so you can write it down for the sake of history. It must be the true story. But in reality I have not told you a lot. And that bothers me. You must know that I am searching my memory as deeply as I possibly can.'

He remarked about how happy he was that his cell could now be cooled by an electric fan he had been given, and how much better it was at night with a blue light for inspection. He had been repeatedly awakened by warders turning on his ordinary light to check on him. 'And I am grateful for all the trouble you are taking to fit me with summer shoes. Really though, I ought to go barefoot on the earth. It is good for the body. The earth sends out a magnetism and it re-charges your batteries.'

I was puzzled about my present assessment of the old man. One day, specifically and in writing, he had said Hitler had no idea he would take off on such a mission as he had. A few weeks later he was hinting that his Führer would have been in agreement with what he had done. One day he was adamant that his mission was self-inspired. Now he was admitting there was a connivance with the Haushofers. What should I believe? I decided that if I was to be Hess's historian there was only one course open to me – religiously to write down everything he said, and let time be the judge of his veracity.

30

The Ghost of Nuremberg

IN NEW YORK a legal battle was going on over the rights to publish the Pentagon Papers. In Spandau's garden, Hitler's former deputy was relaxing in the sun discussing Vietnam, the right to kill . . . and the precedent set by Nuremberg. Hess said that though he understood – and agreed with – the American involvement in Vietnam, the world 'was now examining its conscience'.

Albert Speer had just been invited to take part in a mock tribunal in the US where the US would be put on trial before the world for war crimes. He had declined to go. 'He was absolutely right,' said Hess. Then he stretched out his denim-trousered legs under the shade of the tall poplar and said he was prepared to discuss Nuremberg, a subject that had previously sapped his strength, had given him a hunted, blank look the moment it was mentioned.

'Nuremberg did establish a precedent, didn't it?' he mused. 'It is interesting to look at the position in which the United States finds itself today. Look at what happened with the trial of Lieutenant Calley. I don't think it was wise for President Nixon to have set aside his prison sentence. It was an ill-advised step for a President to remove a man from prison; he moved too quickly. Probably in your army, as in most others, all sentences are reviewed at different levels. Calley's Commanding General in that area would have had the prerogative of reviewing the court's finding. He himself could have set aside any portion of the sentence, or lifted it completely, if he felt it was an unfair trial.

'Nuremberg set the stage for the judgements of the future on alleged war crimes. You know, it will not pay for any nation to lose a war in the future. Because if you lose a war you might find yourself tried as a war criminal. There are always crimes that take place in war. How high up the ranks are you going to go in order to prosecute

221

them? Are you going to prosecute the soldier who murders men, women and children in a village? Or are you going to try the Company Commander, the Regimental Commander, the *Army* Commander? Or, in the case of Vietnam, the President of the United States?'

I had brought the recording of the BBC's Hess documentary so he could hear the last 10 minutes. Speer spoke slowly and carefully about Hess, obviously not wishing to harm the old man. Hess's head nodded as he followed the words in English. Frau Hess, speaking in English, said that when she last saw her husband before his take-off he had appeared nervous and tense. She had suspected something. 'He said he was going off to Berlin and would be back on Monday. But I had thought: "No. I do not believe you will be back on Monday." '

Hess, head bent down to hear the recorder, chuckled. 'She was right!' He had his hands on his lap, his feet on the seat before him. 'My wife speaks excellent English. I had no idea she was so fluent.'

A hundred yards away, up in Tower No. 3, the stony-faced Russian sentry had not taken his eyes off us. He had one hand on his rifle butt, and was staring down into the garden. I recalled what one of his high-ranking superiors had said of Hess at dinner the night before: 'The moves the English are making to have Hess released simply will not succeed. He must die in prison. He is the last living symbol of the Nazi Party and the Tribunal at Nuremberg sentenced him to imprisonment for life. Nobody has the right to rescind that sentence. You Americans, Colonel Bird, look on war as a game of "cowboys and Indians". You do not know the horrors of war. Our country was devastated, and that devastation was caused by a Nazi hierarchy of which Hess was a vital part. You cannot tell a Russian that Hess did not know of the pending attack on the Soviet Union when he flew to Scotland. He did not go to arrange peace for the world; he went to make a neutral Britain so Germany would be free to go ahead on a single front and attack Russia. I do not believe my country will ever agree to the release of Rudolf Hess.'

The Russian guard in Tower No. 3 moved as Hess and I got up to walk, leaving the tape-recorder in my brief-case on the bench. Hess said: 'I have been reading today of the deaths of the Soviet cosmonauts. As I have been studying space travel now with the help of NASA for so many months I do have some ideas on this. Perhaps the capsule was not closed tight enough as they came back into the atmosphere. This would have caused too much sudden pressure, driving oxygen out of the capsule. However, it might well have been that weightlessness over such a long period was the problem. Nobody before had remained weightless for 24 days.

'In long periods of weightlessness the muscles tend to go to sleep because they have no work to do. The heart works with less energy; the blood does not flow properly into the extremities of the legs. The heart goes on beating with little effort, then, suddenly, when the body goes into the atmosphere again, the shock of having to go quickly back to normal is too great. It just fails.

'Therefore,' said the prisoner who had through study become one of the great lay experts on space, 'this must be corrected by artificial means. I am writing a letter at this moment to my wife – and you may wish to send copies to NASA with my ideas – telling her of how I would get over the problem.

'What I would do would be to put a revolving platform, some four metres in diameter, into the spacecraft. In the weightless condition, one man could lie strapped on it with his head toward the centre, and the other, turning a hand-crank, would make the disc, with his colleague on it, revolve. As the man revolves, the blood is forced to flow into the legs, thus strengthening the heart and the body's entire blood distribution system. And the man doing the cranking of course gets his exercise at the same time.

'Anyway,' said Hess, striding forward, hands behind his back, 'why not send into space fanatical scientists who are prepared to give their lives to research? They could stay there for an indefinite period and when they have had enough, come back and see if they can live through the situation. It might be suicidal, but they would be giving a great deal to science. There are, on the other hand, people who are ill with cancer: they know they are soon to die. They could volunteer and give what is left of their lives to science and the clarification of what period man can stay weightless in space. The programme must of course go on. And in the pioneering of space men must die.

'It is absolutely necessary to explore space; and don't forget,' he said, nodding towards the guard tower, 'the Soviet Union is doing it. Perhaps when they withdraw from the war in Vietnam the Americans will be able to put even more money into it than they are spending now. A powerful nation *must* keep up with other powerful nations. There is prestige involved; but aside from that there is also a question of military threat.

'If the US does not go on with exploration they might well be threatened with an attack by the Soviets from the platform they have already in space. Is it only for scientific purposes? Or could it be used to launch an atomic war? These things must be considered.

'One thing that already interests me now, aside from the moon and this platform, is whether there really is some form of life on Mars. I believe that will be the next thing that will interest the world. One thing that must be done, however, will be to have some form of filtered ultra-violet light coming into the capsules. At present there is none. And it is essential to the human body.'

Hess quickly dismissed science to point out a denuded raspberry bush. 'Look,' he exclaimed. 'The Russians have come in again like a plague of grasshoppers. They do the same every July. They have taken all the cherries, and, apart from six washbasins full of raspberries that I managed to gather for myself, have stolen the lot. Thank goodness the plums don't ripen in their month or they'd have them too. I suppose it's the only chance in their lives the Russians have to eat fresh fruit. Just like a plague of grasshoppers,' the old man muttered.

Hess's sudden pride in the garden was ironical after all the years he had refused to work in it. Once, when the seven were in residence, he had been asked by a British general why he did not just take a hose and water the flowers and vegetables. 'That,' Hess had replied, 'is a job for the water department in this prison. You have two admirals in here – Doenitz and Raeder – that is their job.'

31

'Hitler' - by Hess

'There was an ultimate coldness about Hitler. I never met anyone else with whom I felt this sense of something missing, this impression that at the core of his being there was just a deadness.' – Albert Speer in an interview with *Playboy*, June 1971.

I HAD WITH me in Hess's cell a clipping of this interview Speer had given and had read the above when Hess stopped me. 'That's exactly right about Hitler. What Speer said is correct. (Though I cannot imagine why he gave an interview in a magazine with all that naked-ness. It is most disturbing!)

'I felt it with the Führer as well,' Hess went on. 'I discussed this once with Speer and we agreed that there was only a certain point of familiarity you could reach with Hitler, and beyond that point you could not go.

'It was just as though you had run into an invisible wall. There were times when I felt close to Hitler, but they were very seldom. He was a man who never revealed much warmth. He kept himself aloof. Hitler felt he was destined for great things and I think he felt superior to the people around him and to the common folk. His inner sense of superiority probably made him the way he was.

'I, for instance, never used the familiar "Du" when addressing him. I always said "Sie". We were always on "Sie" terms. Even in the early days, and during the war when we worked closely together. As Speer said, there were only four people who used "Du" with him – Roehm, Julius Streicher, Christian Weber and Hermann Esser. And of course Eva Braun. Actually it was unwise to become too familiar. Look what happened to Roehm!

'Speer,' said Hess slowly, 'gained the admiration of the Führer for his ability and his genius; but perhaps because of his ability most of all to meet deadlines and even to be ready ahead of them. Of course Hitler was an amateur architect and so he felt he and Speer spoke the same language. In this sphere Hitler did not have much respect for me, because I knew so very little about it. I recall that Speer would come into my office after I had made him an appointment to see the Führer, his arms full of plans and sketches. He would be wanting to see the Führer about some important building that meant very little to me. I had no sense of colour either, and in this respect Hitler considered I was quite ignorant.'

The old man sitting on his bed in crumpled denims, a floppy white shirt half out of his trousers and wearing braces, stopped talking, his eyes, almost lost in their sunken sockets, shadowed by the heavy eyebrows, remembering.

I broke the silence. 'Hess, if you had your time over again would you do the same?'

'What do you mean?'

'Would you have studied geo-politics and become so involved in it – serving a man like Adolf Hitler?'

'Yes I would,' he said quickly. 'I believe I would travel the same route and end up here in Spandau Prison. I would certainly have flown to Scotland. I had great convictions, you know, and there was only one way to work for them. When I realized fully that the war was being lost, and what it would do to Germany, I knew there was only one way. We would have to make peace with England. Hitler wanted it too. Yes, I was always a dedicated person. I believed in what I was working for.'

'Even when it meant war – expanding Germany's borders by force?'

'My sincere desire from the beginning was to bring Germany back to the old heights which it had attained before World War I. Before the Versailles *Diktat*, which was wrong. I wanted to give Germany back its old pride and its old fame. This is what I had in my mind when I became active in politics in 1923 as a young man. I just became involved in the situation . . .

'Tell me,' said Hess rather loudly, 'of a single young person in world politics today who is not interested in bettering the situation of his country – as it stands at the moment?'

'What I really wanted to know, Hess, is whether you would still serve under a man like Hitler if you had your time all over again?'

He looked hard at me over his spectacles, his jaw square and jutting. He had his sleeves rolled up over his elbows and his hands rested on his lap. 'Colonel Bird, of course I would. I would not have wanted to miss the opportunity of serving under Adolf Hitler as his deputy. I was a *dedicated* man.'

'Do you think he is dead?'

'Oh of course. There were stories that he escaped to South America but they were not true. He would never have run away. So far as I am concerned he definitely committed suicide. I haven't the slightest doubt in my mind. It would have been entirely against his nature to escape from Germany and go and live somewhere else. He too was dedicated, and he had his ideals. When he realized all was lost, that the war would soon be over, I believe he would certainly have decided to take his own life. He most certainly would not have wanted to turn himself over to the Russians – that would have been worse than death. Like most of us he feared death. He worried a lot about being assassinated, as there had been several attempts on his life. I have read recently that the Russians have absolute proof of finding his remains outside the bunker, they even have a photograph. I believe them.

'I was not there of course in the final stages but I believe that he could have arranged for many people to have the means of suicide. The Goebbels family for instance, and Himmler, and of course Goering who suicided at Nuremberg. I do believe that Martin Bormann fled in the last hours. Possibly to South America. I believe that – it would be in keeping with his nature.'

'You didn't care for Bormann?'

'I was never *jealous* of him or Goering; that is what people keep on saying or writing. I was never jealous of any person.'

'Was it you who first called Hitler "*der Chef*"?'

'Possibly, but I cannot recall it for certain. It started very early in the Party days. Hitler was chief of the Party – the boss – and so he was called "Leader".'

'A great deal must have been done to build up Hitler's personality in the eyes of the people?'

Hess replied stiffly: 'Yes. That belongs to any great leader.'

'Did you know Hitler's real name in Austria was Schiklgruber?'

We both laughed. 'Yes, well you could hardly call out "Heil Schiklgruber!" That was certainly one of the reasons he changed it.'

Glancing about his cell I noticed open on the bed-table the thick scientific dictionary which had been bought for 106 DM from prison funds at Hess's request. It gave an explanation of space terminology in English and German. Hess, in his thirst for space information, was reading daily long and complicated details of the moon landings and probes. Hanging from the walls were photographs of the moon's surface sent by NASA from Houston. He had brochures and time-tables, interviews with the cosmonauts and piles of cuttings from his newspapers. Hess asked me if I had sent on to NASA his suggestions for a revolving exercise platform. I said I had. 'You know they have been most kind to me,' he said. 'Would it not be a good idea to send off a signed photograph of me? I would autograph it and date it and they could have it as a token of my thanks.' He had already autographed another photograph for an official of the Archives – a stiff, official Nazi portrait in full uniform. I tried to imagine Speer or von Schirach doing the same and could not. Hess was still a vain man.

He picked up a newspaper lying on his bed. 'I wanted to show you this. Here is a doctor who exactly agrees with what I said about cosmonauts needing exercise. He states that if you exercise daily to the point where your heart-beat is increasing rapidly over a three-minute period, you are strengthening your heart muscles. It is just what I was saying. If they build a platform as I suggest it would very much improve their blood circulation.'

I asked him if his clock still kept good time. 'Excellent. Excellent.' He had tampered with it for days, with a special tool made by the prison handyman, so it lost less than six seconds in 24 hours. NASA had sent him a minute-by-minute timetable of space activity for Apollo 15 and Hess wished to follow what was going on. The clock had an alarm and he had it set for the various direct broadcasts coming from Houston. A warder had 'unofficially' brought in a small transistor radio for the occasion and we pretended it wasn't there during the Apollo mission.

Hess's bed had not been slept in the night before. Now the Berlin weather had become so hot he had asked if he could sleep on the cooler side of the cell-block. He had been given access to Cell 13 and his old bed from Cell 23 had been brought in – much to the annoyance of the fat French warder Barcanan who used it to catch up on his sleep at quiet times during the night. Barcanan snored louder than any man I have heard, the noise penetrating through the cell walls and out through the cell block into the yard. Hess requested that when he was on duty outside his cell, his warder's table and chair be moved as far away as possible so that the prisoner himself could get some sleep. Every night he pushed his wax ear-plugs deep into his ears but even they were not enough to keep out Barcanan's trumpeting. 'I even have to wake the fellow in the morning,' Hess complained.

He then began to busy himself in the cell, preparing it for an official visit by Major-General Cobb, the US Commandant in Berlin, later in the day. When the General arrived Hess was smartly dressed in a new light-blue sports jacket which had replaced his frayed denims. He was polite and chatty, as he had been with me a few hours before. He and the General had a 20-minute discussion on food, Hess's health, the Olympic Games and the idea that a Russian and an American cosmonaut might one day fly together in space. When I told General Cobb that Hess's flying suit and Luftwaffe uniform in which he had flown to Scotland were near by in the store-room the old man chuckled with pride. When the General said he saw no reason why the prisoner should not have access to a small television set to watch the next space shot, Hess nodded excitedly. 'That would be excellent.' 'And perhaps you might like to see the Munich Olympics on it,' said General Cobb. Hess agreed. He had watched the 1936 Berlin Olympics, he said. He did not mention that it had been under slightly different circumstances . . .

General Cobb departed and soon after a glossy volume from the United States Information Service called *Das Grosse Projekt* – the story of American space exploration – arrived for Hess with the General's compliments. 'That was very good of him,' said No. 7. 'Do you think I could send him a photograph of me signed, with a letter of thanks?' I told him the letter would be enough.

During the visit nothing had been mentioned of the Four-Power talks on Berlin. They had just reached agreement and many were wondering whether they had discussed Hess. He discounted the idea. 'No. I don't believe they would have discussed me. Although it might be a subject that could come up later when the Russians get their consulate in West Berlin. But whatever happens, even if they discuss it a hundred times it will do no good. The Russians won't let me go.'

We left the cell and made our way down the spiral stairs to the garden. Its trees and shrubs were heavy with leaves, and in the stuffy atmosphere of summer in Berlin it was a green oasis. 'Isn't it beautiful?' my companion remarked. 'If it were not for the circumstances of my being here I could be very happy in this place.' The narrow path we walked had been worn down to a packed, hard surface about $2\frac{1}{2}$ inches deep, pounded by the feet of one old man. Time after time he had made the circuit . . . 215 steps. We passed the sentry high in Tower No. 3; he stood rigidly to attention, watching as we passed.

'If I should by some miracle be released,' mused Hess as we walked, 'I would always be grateful to Speer for the beauty of this garden he worked so hard for. I would go and visit him and tell him.' He said no more for about 20 yards. Then: 'I suppose the old friends I would look up you could count on the fingers of one hand. All dead. I would go and say hello to Schirach. He lives not far from my wife. Of course,' Hess went on, 'I would probably have to go into hiding at first, the Press would hound me for a few weeks. It would be hard, wouldn't it, getting used to being a free man on the outside. But I would have the garden at Hindelang to enjoy with my wife. I would enjoy her simple cooking,' he said, warming to the idea. 'I believe I would not eat too much meat. I would look forward to her noodles and dumplings. And of course a lot of fresh vegetables and fruit. I would have to watch those dumplings – they tend to make you fat! A person of my age just cannot afford to put on too much weight.'

'You enjoyed a bottle of wine with your meal in the hospital,' I said. 'Have you missed alcohol much while you have been in prison?'

'Oh no. I haven't missed it at all. Alcohol is no good for the human system. Beer is different. Beer we call "fluid bread" in Germany. It is healthy when taken in reason, but like dumplings can easily make you fat. I would have to watch it because I put on weight very fast. I would not touch whisky, or schnapps or cognac, though

I would like a glass of good white wine. It would have to be a natural wine however, with no sugar added. And at night,' he smiled, 'perhaps a glass of good champagne. It would relax me. But nothing more than that. I never was one for drinking.'

'Would you like to travel?'

'Not outside Germany. It would not be wise. I would not be well received. Look what happened to Speer in Norway. I read that even though he went in a private capacity the Norwegian Government came out with a statement that he was unwelcome and should leave. He was not a welcome guest in their country. There you are,' said Hess, shaking his head, 'people don't forget, do they?

'I would always have to watch myself on the outside. There are always fanatics who would like to do you in. They could possibly give me a bad time by harassment. I know most of the Press has been sympathetic to me, but there are always those newspapers who are not, and they stir things up. One has to be careful. I should probably have to keep a guard at Hindelang to keep them away for a while.'

We passed Tower No. 3 again and the sentry stood to attention. 'I think I should probably remain at home most of the time in the study my wife has prepared for me. I would read. I would be able to learn more about my scientific interests in space travel – there would be a lot more facilities for research.'

'Would you write your memoirs?'

'No. My memory is far too bad. I simply don't remember the important things I should remember and I don't believe that I could add much to history by writing. My memory is failing me more and more as time goes on. I do my best to answer the questions you ask me, but I'm afraid I'm not much help, am I?'

We sat down in the shade. Hess had rigged up a makeshift air-conditioning system in the garden by playing the spray of a garden hose on to the leaves of the plum-tree, now heavily laden with plums. A fine haze of water blew through the tree and around us and we felt the cool moisture. 'Anything I should write,' Hess went on, 'would be open to a great deal of controversy; I would want to spare myself all this anguish and anxiety for getting facts right by not writing at all. I am not up to it.'

I leaned forward. 'That is exactly why I am asking you these questions about the past. To set the record straight. All these months we have been talking to right the inaccuracies that have been repeated about you – the old Hess legends trotted out by authors because they have no way of finding out anything else. I have dedicated myself with all I have within me to get from you the factual first-hand story of your life. *Now you have to help me.* You must clarify so many things that have been misunderstood until now. Did you know that even Khrushchev has mentioned you in his memoirs?'

'No!' said Hess. 'Really?'

'In his book *Khrushchev Remembers* he has said that Stalin told him the purpose of your flight was to free Hitler's hands from his engagement with the British so that he could concentrate on fighting Russia.'

'Stalin said that?'

'Yes. That is what he said. Was it true?' Hess said nothing. 'What annoys me,' I told him, 'is the repeated story in the newspapers that you are a poor old madman living listlessly in this prison. People, when they know I am a director of Spandau, say the same thing: "He's mad, isn't he?" I always tell people you are in fact a very intelligent man, very well read, and with a most inquiring mind. I tell them you are not insane.'

Hess leaned towards me and put his blue-veined hand on my shoulder. 'No. You should not tell them that. I would rather people believed I was insane,' he said, his eyes twinkling shrewdly. 'That way I might be able to get out of this damned place!' Then he laughed. 'Von Schirach used to tell me, and perhaps he was right, that I had a built-in trap-door in my mind that shut out unpleasant memories. Possibly that is what saves me.'

'Let's talk about the outside. Would you go to the theatre?'

'Oh yes. And the opera. And to concerts. But I would take care not to be recognized. I would like to see films, but none of these cheap sex films advertised in the newspapers. I would not waste my time watching rubbish. Censorship must have really deteriorated to allow them. And that magazine you showed me with Speer's interview in it! What photographs! I am surprised that Speer wore clothes in it. Perhaps he was the only one who did. I cannot see how anybody could concentrate in the Speer article without becoming quite diverted. You see, this sort of thing will eventually be your down-fall. There should be censorship. This is what the so-called "free Press" has led to. This is what happened to the Romans and caused the downfall of the Roman Empire. Too much pleasure and too much degeneration.' He added: 'You must realize that I have spent half my life in prison, a good deal of it in solitary confinement. I would not waste what time I have left to me watching rubbish.'

He told me he had lunched that day on lobster cocktail with a chicken dish to follow. He was allowed now to order virtually anything that came to his mind. Down in the tiny kitchen a Spanish chef and a Yugoslav tried their best to outdo each other on fine cuisine. Prisoner No. 7 sent his instructions on a child's 'magic-eraser' board, a plastic device on which he wrote with a stick, erasing what he had written to write again. He had the aid of Spanish and Yugoslav dictionaries. With the departure of the Turkish chef the German–Turkish dictionary had been replaced in the library.

He pointed to the plum-tree, almost groaning with fruit. 'I have asked the chefs if they would pick some and make some delicious plumcake. Thank goodness the plums weren't ripe in the Russian month. There would have been none left.'

The night before, the 71-year-old British chief warder, Chisholm, had suddenly been taken ill with a kidney complaint. He had been rushed from his comfortable flat in the prison to the hospital. Chisholm had been doing actual warder duty for the first time in seven years because of the illness of another warder. And his presence had been felt. 'They are all complaining that he has been an old grandmother,' said Hess. 'I for one will not be sorry if Chisholm retires and leaves the prison. None of the prisoners have ever been happy with him. Everything is done strictly by the regulations, so far as Chisholm is concerned.' Chisholm, I agreed, was old enough to give it up. But then so too were his British colleagues Swan, 72, and Belson, 68.

Colonel Ralph Banfield was soon to retire as British director. 'I've been here for thirteen years,' Ralph said to me over dinner in the director's dining-room. 'They told me when I came that it would be a temporary job for six months, then they would be closing Spandau down.' The conversation turned to the guard towers and he said: 'You know our fellows all feel Tower No. 3 is haunted? Ever since that Frenchman shot himself in it years ago. Well one

night just last year one of our sentries saw his ghost. He yelled and screamed and went berserk, firing off twelve rounds into the air before he was subdued. It was in my month of control. I kept it quiet.'
Over in the corner stood Schmokov, the Russian who had been acting Soviet director for almost a year. We wondered why the Russians had never replaced him with a permanent director of the rank of Lieutenant-Colonel. We also wondered why the Russians had suddenly relaxed regulations with Hess, allowing him extra time in the garden as the British, the French and the Americans did. One warder has even taken the prisoner out after dinner, at 7 o'clock in the evening, for a stroll. What were they up to?

32

The Haushofer Letters

THE NATIONAL ARCHIVES in Washington are crammed with the secrets of the living and the dead. Room after room is stacked with Nazi files and documents which detail the story of the rise of the Third Reich and the men involved in it.

I was in the reading-room scanning the micro-filmed file marked 'Hess, Rudolf', when I came across the first hint of the vital but tenuous link between Hess and the Duke of Hamilton. I asked for the file on the Haushofers. And when letters from this file were projected on the screen the last piece of the jigsaw fell into place. Here at last was documentary proof of the pressure that caused Rudolf Hess to take off for England. The behind-the-scenes moves by the Haushofers in Nazi Germany to contact the Duke of Hamilton in England were spelled out. Hamilton had the 'ear' of the 'highest authorities' in Britain; Hess had the 'ear' of the highest authority in Germany. The two must get together. Hess was to fly to see a man he had never communicated with in any way; a man he remembered vaguely as a face seen across a crowded reception during the 1936 Berlin Olympics, a man friendly with and trusted by Albrecht.

The Haushofers themselves were playing a dangerous game. Dr Karl Haushofer, Hess's old university professor, had given the young Hess asylum when he fled from the police after the 1923 skirmishes in Munich. Hess had never forgotten it, and now, as one of the most powerful men in the Reich, he had personally issued letters of protection to the Haushofer family: Dr Karl was married to a Jewess, and Hess ordered the Gestapo to let them alone. Albrecht, the Professor's son, hated the Party machine and what it was doing, and was walking a shaky tightrope, working part-time on Hess's behalf for Ribbentrop in the Foreign Office on one hand, and making secret moves to contact peace-minded Englishmen on the other.

In the middle stood Hess – code-named 'Tomodachi' (Japanese for 'friend') – in all the Haushofer communications.

Letter No. C002185, dated 3 September 1940, was the first in the Haushofer file to appear on the screen. Dr Karl was writing to Albrecht from Munich:

Dearest Albrecht!

Many thanks for your letter of 29th from the Hotel Imperial in Vienna, where by an uncertain feeling I had suspected you were. If you had written your birthday letter to me in an air-raid shelter, then I could have returned the favour today, in the night of the 1st and 2nd, because, when departing from your mother's mountain pasture I had promised to go and spend $1\frac{1}{2}$ hours down there doing gymnastics.

. . . but it was well worth it, because it gave me the opportunity to be with Tomo [Hess] from five o'clock in the afternoon to two o'clock in the morning, including a three-hour walk in the Grünwalder Forest, during which we had a long and serious talk. I have to tell you about part of it.

As you know, everything is ready for a very hard and sharp move against the certain island, so that the highest man just has to push a button in order to get everything moving. But before this perhaps unavoidable decision, the thought comes to mind if there really isn't a way to keep back this action which would bring unending consequences. In connection with this there is a series of thoughts which I must pass on to you, because they were obviously made known to me for that purpose. Can't you perhaps see a way in which one could talk about such possibilities at a third place with a middle-man, perhaps the old Ian Hamilton or the other Hamilton?

To this idea I answered that an excellent opportunity would have presented itself at the Zentenar ceremony in Lisbon if one could have sent well-disguised political people there instead of harmless larvae?

In this connection it seems to me to be a sign of fate that your old friend Miss V.R., obviously, even though with great delay, has found a way to send a note with dear and kind words of best wishes not only for your mother but also for Heinz and me, but also included the address to reply to:

Miss V. Roberts,
c/o Post Box 506,
Lisbon, Portugal.

I have the feeling that one should not omit any good chance, or at least think them over . . .

Tomo will probably stay here until Wednesday and would like to see me again once more. I had to pass on to him a new memoranda sheet and he promised me for sure to have the political and financial difficulties resolved through the highest SS authorities.

Albrecht, a day or two later, went to see Hess, where they discussed Dr Karl's letter.

It was Rudolf Hess who wrote next: on 10 September from Gallspach, to Dr Karl Haushofer:

Much honoured and dear friend!

Albrecht brought me your letter which mentioned our walk together on the last day of August, which I, also, like to remember very warmly, before starting on the official part.

Albrecht will have told you about *our* talk, which touched, apart from ethnic German matters, on the other matter which is very dear to both of us. I have thought about the latter matter thoroughly once more and have come to the following conclusion:

In no way must we overlook or ignore the certain connection. I consider it best that you or Albrecht write to the old lady who is a friend of your family and ask her if she would try to ask Albrecht's friend whether he would come to a neutral area, or where she lives, or has her cover address, in order to talk to Albrecht. If he cannot do that at the moment, he should in any case, through her, let us know at which place he will be in the future.

A neutral acquaintance, who will have something to do over there anyway, could look him up and give him a message with a referral to you or Albrecht. That person would not want to have to find out over there where he is staying, or to have to make trips in vain. You believe that the knowledge as to his whereabouts has no military value and we would promise not to use this knowledge in connection with anybody who would have use for it. What the neutral person has to transmit will be of such great importance that in comparison, making his whereabouts known would be of little importance.

It is understood, of course, that the certain question and the corresponding answer will not go the official way, because in no case did you want to cause your friend over there any kind of difficulties. The letter to the old lady would best be delivered by a confidant of the AO [Ausland Organization] to the address that is known to you.

As to the neutral I have in mind here, I would like to tell you in person sometime. That isn't very urgent as yet, since first an answer must be received from the other side.

Meanwhile let's both rely on our good spirits. Should success be the fate of the enterprise, the oracle given to you regarding the month of August would be correct after all, because the name of the young friend and the old lady friend of your family came to you on our quiet walk on the last day of this month.

With warm greetings to you and your wife Martha,

Yours,
R.H.

I can be reached by telephone under:
Linz – Gallspach A.

(File No. C002188
National Archives)

After Hess's meeting with Albrecht, Albrecht excitedly drew up his own memorandum of what had taken place. It was dated 15 September:*

Top Secret: ARE THERE STILL POSSIBILITIES OF A
GERMAN–ENGLISH PEACE?

On 8 September I was called to Bad G [Godesberg] to report to the Deputy of the Führer about the subject of this memorandum. The conversation, between the two of us alone, lasted two hours. I had the opportunity of speaking in a completely open manner.

I was immediately asked about possibilities of transmitting Hitler's earnest wish for peace to leading personalities in England. It had

* Memorandum listed as File No. C002193 in archives.

become quite clear that the continuation of the war would be suicide for the white race. Even with complete success in Europe, Germany would not be in a position to take over the inheritance of the Empire. The Führer did not want the destruction of the Empire, and still does not want it even today. Was there not somebody in England who was ready for peace?

I first asked permission to discuss fundamental things. It was necessary to realize that not only Jews and Freemasons, but practically all Englishmen who mattered, would consider a peace contract signed by the Führer a worthless piece of paper.

To the question as to why this was so, I referred to the 10-year term of our Polish Treaty, to the Non-Aggression Pact with Denmark signed just one year ago, and to the 'final' frontier demarcation of the border in Munich. What guarantee did England have that we would not break a new treaty whenever we considered the time was right? One had to understand that even in the Anglo-Saxon world Hitler was considered to be Satan's deputy on earth, and had to be fought. If the worst came to the worst, the English would rather transfer their Empire, bit by bit, to the Americans, than sign a peace that would give National Socialist Germany mastery in Europe. The present war, I was convinced, shows that Europe has become too small for its previous anarchic form of existence and it is only through close German–English cooperation that it can achieve an inner federated order which need not be built on the police-owner of an individual state, to keep its place in the world and maintain its security against Soviet-Russian Eurasia. France, for the time being, seems to have been broken completely, and we have had plenty of opportunity to observe the capabilities of the Italians. As long as Germany and England are rivals, the lesson of this war, so far as security on both sides is concerned, is this: every German has to say to himself, we have no security as long as provision is not made that the Atlantic gateways of Europe from Gibraltar to Narvik are free of any possible blockade. That is, there must be no English fleet. Every Englishman must, however, under the same circumstances argue: we have no security as long as there is an aircraft within a radius of 2,000 km of London that we can't control. That means there can be no German air force. There is only one way out of this dilemma: friendship intensified to fusion, with a joint fleet, a joint air force, and joint protection of property in the world: which is exactly what the English at the moment are preparing to conclude with the Americans.

Here I was interrupted and asked why indeed the English were prepared to seek such a relationship with America and not with us. My reply was: because Roosevelt is a man who represents an ideology and a way of life that the Englishman thinks he understands, to which he can become accustomed, even where it does not seem to be to his liking. Perhaps he is fooling himself – but at any rate that is what he believes.

A man like Churchill – himself half-American – is convinced of this. Hitler, on the other hand, seems to the Englishman the incarnation of what he hates, what he has fought against for centuries – this feeling includes the workers as well as the plutocrats. On the contrary, I am of the opinion that those Englishmen who have property to lose, those of the so-called plutocracy that count, are those who would be most ready to talk peace. But even they only regard peace as an armistice. I was compelled to express these things so strongly because I ought not – especially with my long-lasting attempts in the past to reach an agreement with England, and my numerous English friendships – allow it to appear that I seriously believed in the possibility of a settlement between Adolf Hitler and England in the present state of development. Thereupon, I was asked whether I was not of the opinion that maybe feelers had not 'come through' because the right language had not been spoken. I answered that – to be sure – if certain persons, whom we both knew well, were meant by this statement – then certainly the wrong language had been used. But at the present stage this was of little importance. Then I was asked very directly why all Englishmen rejected Herr von Ribbentrop so strongly. I suggested that in the eyes of the English, Herr von Ribbentrop, like some other personages, played the same role as did Duff Cooper, Eden and Churchill in the eyes of the Germans. In Herr von Ribbentrop's case there was also the conviction, precisely in the view of the Englishmen who were formerly friendly to Germany, that – from completely biased motives – he had informed the Führer wrongly about England and that he personally bore an unusually large share of the responsibility for the outbreak of the war.

But I again emphasized that the rejection of peace feelers by England today is not so much due to the personalities involved as to the fundamental outlook above.

Nevertheless, I was asked to name those whom I thought might be reached as possible contacts. I mentioned among diplomats Minister O'Malley* in Budapest, the former head of the South-Eastern Department of the Foreign Office, a clever man in the higher echelons of officialdom, but perhaps without influence precisely because of his former friendship with Germany; Sir Samuel Hoare,† who is half-shelved and half on the watch in Madrid, whom I do not know well personally, but to whom I can at any time open a personal dialogue: as the most promising, the Washington Ambassador, Lothian, with whom I have had a personal contact for years and who, as a member of the highest aristocracy and at the same time as a person of very independent mind, is perhaps in the best position to undertake a bold step – provided that he could be convinced that even a bad and uncertain peace is better than a continuation of the war – a conviction which he can only reach when he assures himself in Washington that English hopes of America are not realizable. Whether or not this is so could only be judged in Washington itself; and not from Germany at all.

As the last possibility, I then named the personal meeting on neutral ground with the closest of my English friends: the young Duke of Hamilton, who at all times has access to all important persons in London, even to Churchill and the King. I stressed in this case the inevitable difficulty of making a contact and again repeated my conviction of the improbability of success – whatever approach we took.

The result of this talk was that H. [Hess] declared that he would think the entire matter over very thoroughly once again and would send me word in case I was to take steps. For this very touchy case – in case I was to make the trip alone – I asked for very specific instructions from the highest authorities. The entire discussion gave me the strongest impression that it was not conducted without the prior knowledge of the Führer, and that I would not hear anything

* British Minister to Hungary.
† British Minister to Spain.

further about the matter until a new understanding had been reached between him and his Deputy.

As to the personal side of the discussion, I must say that – despite the fact that I felt myself compelled to say some unusually harsh things – it ended in all friendliness, and, yes, even cordiality.

Albrecht Haushofer, Berlin, 15 September 1940.

Three days after he had written his resumé of the discussion he had had with the Deputy Führer, Albrecht wrote to his parents from Berlin:*

Dear Parents!

In the middle of some rather hectic activity just these few words for today to let you know that I have received that certain letter. I am going to think about the whole case for 24 hours and then will write immediately to T. [Hess].

It won't really go the way he thinks it will. However I could formulate a letter to D.H. [Hamilton] in such a way that the transmission of it will in no way endanger our old lady friend; above all, I must make it clear to T. once again that my ducal friend of course can't write to me without the permission of *his* highest authority, no more than I can from the other way round. As I said, I'd like to sleep on that difficult case one night. In ethnic German matters, T. seems to have given pretty clear instructions to our friends in black uniform.†

My professorship has not yet been confirmed. I would like to know how much longer that will take. But what kind of worries are those compared to the big ones?

Much love,
Albrecht.

The next document I saw, projected on the screen by the archives attendant, was the enlarged image of micro-film No. C002202: an undated draft by Albrecht Haushofer of the first tentative approach to the Duke of Hamilton . . . DRAFT FOR A LETTER TO D.H. [Douglas-Hamilton].

* File C002196.
† A reference to protection from the Gestapo.

My dear D.,

Even if this letter has only a slight chance of reaching you – there is a chance, and I want to make use of it.

First of all, I wish to give you a sign of unaltered and unalterable personal attachment. I do hope you have been spared in all this ordeal, and I hope the same is true of your brothers. I heard of your father's deliverance from long suffering; and that your brother-in-law Northumberland lost his life near Dunkirk. I need hardly tell you how I feel about all that . . .

Now there is one thing more. If you remember some of my last communications before the war started, you will realize that there is a certain significance in the fact that I am, at present, able to ask you whether there is the slightest chance of our meeting and having a talk somewhere on the outskirts of Europe, perhaps in Portugal? There are some things that I could tell you that might make it worthwhile for you to try a short trip to Lisbon – if you could make your authorities understand enough, so they could give you leave. As to myself – I could reach Lisbon any time (without any kind of difficulties) within a few days after receiving news from you. If there is an answer to this letter, please address it to . . .

Immediately after he had written the draft – in English – Albrecht Haushofer hurried off a letter to his parents, on 19 September, from Berlin:

Dear Parents!

Enclosed I am sending you several responsible, important written pieces:

First, the letter from T. to father.

Secondly, my answer to T., which has already been sent, and which, hopefully, will still have your approval.

Thirdly, the draft of a letter to D., which I shall keep to myself and which I shall show to nobody, with the request to you to please examine it to see whether it will hold any danger for the person who may possibly hand it over. I believe it sounds harmless enough. I pointed to 'the authorities over there' as a security measure for the person who transmits it and the one who receives it. Please give me your honest opinion and make any possible corrections.

Fourthly, a report* about what I said on the 8th in G. – an account to history (to be kept by you).

The whole thing is a fool's errand – but that is not our fault. According to our latest news, the unity contracts between the Empire and the United States are shortly to be signed.

Much love,
Albrecht.

On the same day he had written to Hess:†

TOP SECRET

Dear Herr Hess!

Due to the old-fashioned postal service of Partnach-Alm your letter of the tenth only reached me yesterday. I again thoroughly studied the possibilities discussed therein and request – before taking the steps proposed – that you yourself examine once more the thoughts set out below.

I have in the meantime been thinking of the technical route by which a message from me must travel before it can reach the Duke of H. [Hamilton]. With your help, delivery to Lisbon can of course be assured without difficulty. We do not know about the rest of the way. We must take into account that foreigners might control it; therefore the letter must not be worded in such a way that it might be intercepted and destroyed or that it could endanger the sender or the final recipient. Because of the close personal contact and the exact mutual knowledge of each other which connect me with Douglas H., I can write a few words to him in such a manner that *he alone* will recognize the fact that behind my wish to meet him in Lisbon is something more important than a simple personal whim. (This would be enclosed with the letter to Mrs R.‡ without a place or full name mentioned in it – an 'A' as a signature would do.)

Anything further seems to be very dangerous and would be detrimental to the success of the letter. Let us suppose the case were the other way round: an old lady in Germany receives a letter from an unknown foreign source with the request to transmit the message,

* His memorandum.
† File No. C002198.
‡ Earlier referred to as 'Miss'.

the recipient of which in turn would be requested to reveal his whereabouts to an unknown foreign personality for a certain period of time – and this recipient would be a high-ranking officer of the Air Force (of course I don't know which office H. holds at the moment; judging from his past, I can imagine only three possibilities: either he is an active Air Force General, or he is supervising the air defence for an important part of Scotland, or he sits in an important post in the Air Defence Ministry).* I don't think you need much imagination to picture the faces which Canaris or Heydrich would make and with what kind of a smirk they would look at any kind of 'security' or 'confidential' offer in such a letter if a subordinate placed such a case before them. Their faces would not be their only reaction! Measures would be taken practically automatically – and neither the old lady nor the Air Force Commander would have easy times ahead of them! Matters aren't much different in England.

Now, a second matter. Here I would also like to ask you to reverse the case mentally. Let us assume that I should receive such a letter from one of my English friends. As soon as I had recognized its importance I would, of course, report the matter to the highest German authorities I could contact, as soon as I had realized the import it might have, and would ask for instructions on what I should do myself (after all I am a civilian and H. is an officer).

If it should be decided that I was to comply with the wish for a meeting with my friend, I would then be most anxious to get my instructions, if not from the Führer himself, at least from a person who receives them directly and at the same time has the gift of transmitting the finest and lightest nuances – an art which you yourself master, but which isn't mastered by all Reichsministers. In addition I should very urgently request that my action be fully covered, so far as other high authorities are concerned, of my own country, uninformed or unfavourable.

It is no different with H. He cannot fly to Lisbon – any more than I can! – unless he is given leave, that is unless Air Minister Sinclair and Foreign Minister Halifax know about it. If, however, he receives permission to reply or to go, there is no need to indicate any place in England; if he does not receive it, then any attempt through a neutral mediator would also have little success. In this case the

* The Duke of Hamilton in fact commanded an Air Sector in the East of Scotland.

technical problem of contacting H. is the least of the difficulties. A neutral person who knows his way around England and can move about there (it would be senseless to entrust anyone else with such a mission) will be able to find the first Peer of Scotland very quickly, if the situation on the island is still half-way in order. (At the time of a successful invasion all the possibilities we are discussing here would be pointless anyway.)

My proposal, therefore, is as follows:

Through the old friend I will write a letter to H. – in a form that will incriminate no one but will be understandable to the recipient – with the proposal of a meeting in Lisbon. If nothing comes of that, it will be possible (if the military situation leaves enough time for it), assuming that a suitable intermediary is available, to make a second attempt through a neutral going to England, who might be given a personal message to take along. With respect to this possibility, I must however add that H. is extremely reserved – like many Englishmen towards strangers. Since the entire German–English problem is based on a serious crisis of mutual confidence, this is not immaterial.

Please excuse the length of this letter; I just wanted to inform you completely. I have already tried to explain to you not long ago that, for the reasons I gave, the possibilities of successful efforts at a settlement between the Führer and the British upper class seem to me – to my extreme regret – infinitesimally small. Nevertheless I should not want to close this letter without pointing out once more that I still think there would be a somewhat greater chance of success in going through Ambassador Lothian in Washington or Sir Samuel Hoare in Madrid rather than through my friend H. To be sure, they are – practically speaking – more inaccessible.

May I please ask for a note or a call with final instructions; in case it should become necessary, would you also inform your brother [Alfred Hess], with whom I would then have to discuss the delivery of the letter to Lisbon and the setting up of a cover address for the answer in L.

With cordial greetings and best wishes for your health,
Sincerely yours,
A.H.

Albrecht wrote again to Hess on 23 September:

Dear Herr Hess,

After your last phone call I immediately got in touch with your brother. Everything went off all right and so far as I can report the letter* has been written this morning and sent off according to your wishes. Hopefully it will do more good than reasonable judgement allows one to dare to hope.

With cordial greetings,
Your
A.

On the same day he wrote to his father:

Dear Father!

Enclosed a copy of a short, but heavyweight letter, which is better kept by you than by me. I have just stated clearly enough that the action in question has not taken place on my initiative . . .

As before, I am convinced that there isn't the slighest possibility of a peace: I do, therefore, not have the least faith in the possibility about which you know. However I also believe that I could not have refused my services any longer. You know that for myself I do not see any possibility of any satisfying activity in the future. If the 'total victory' from Glasgow to Cape Town were to be achieved for our savages, then the tone will be set by the drunken sergeants and the corrupt exploiters anyway; experts with quiet manners will not be needed then. If that does not happen, and the English succeed in resisting the first blow, and then, with the help of the Americans and by using the insecurity of the Bolshevists, create a long-term war equilibrium, then, however, there will sooner or later be a demand for the likes of us – but in conditions in which little enough will be left to salvage any more. So if I am being used now, that only means running the danger of senseless wear and tear. I can only meet this danger if I make it very clear from the beginning how little chance of success any attempt will have. I have tried to do that. If the order comes anyway, there is nothing I can do. But there is one thing which must be very clear

* Filed in the Washington archives.

to me: *I* will only have a political future if I, with my Cassandra warnings can *be in the right* (hopefully in a more limited way than I fear deep down).

Many greetings to both of you!
Albrecht.

His father replied on 4 October:

Dearest Albrecht,

. . . somewhere around T. [Hess] there seems to be a counter movement, which has not been revealed. Or the fear of such a movement.

A *fool's errand* stands . . . in the stars – which are beginning to twinkle beautifully again. In their sign I send my greetings, with a willingness to hope even at the edge of the grave.

What I had seen on the micro-film viewer was documented proof of the driving-force of Rudolf Hess's flight to Scotland. He had let Albrecht Haushofer prepare the groundwork, and when, as he thought, Britain had had time to absorb the letter and its implications, and various backdoor talks had been going on in neutral Switzerland sounding out sympathetic Britons, he decided there was only one man important enough to bring things to a head – Hess himself.

Back in Spandau, armed with photo-copies of the original letters from Washington, I walked once more into Hess's cell. Would he still claim he couldn't remember?

Hess sat on the chair by his bed, studying the letters I had handed to him. He glanced at the top of the first page to see to whom the letter was written, and then over to the last page, to see the signature. He read slowly, his lips moving now and again with the words, his left leg quivering a little, showing his excitement. Wordlessly he handed me one letter and took the next, his face serious, brow furrowed; both hands gripping each page as he read.

At last when he had finished them all and the light of the late afternoon sun had begun to fade in his cell, he turned to me, his hands shaking slightly as he handed over the last page. 'Where did you get these letters?'

'From the Archives in Washington DC. Do you believe they are authentic?'

He nodded, his spectacles flashing as they caught the overhead light I had just switched on. 'There can be no doubt about that. It is my signature. The others are certainly the signatures of the Haushofers.' He was silent for a long time, sitting staring vacantly ahead. Then he said: 'It was all such a long time ago. My memory has faded so much . . .'

'But there is no doubt from what you have read this afternoon that these letters are genuine and that you were working with the Haushofers for a peace agreement with England?'

He shook his head. 'No. That is quite true.'

'And they knew all along that you were flying to see Hamilton.'

'*No!*' exclaimed Hess angrily. 'They did not know. Look – I will explain. The Haushofers were definitely working to find a basis of negotiation. You can see by the correspondence that took place between us that I was working with them. But the Haushofers did not know – and couldn't have guessed – that I would myself fly to conduct this negotiation. You see, Colonel, the problem was to find somebody sufficiently high up in the Government here that I could trust; somebody who was in the position to negotiate. Who could we turn to? We had to choose a man and have him meet the British contact on neutral ground.

'At the same time there was a stepped-up war situation. And there was great difficulty in choosing neutral ground in Europe.

'We had not heard from the Duke of Hamilton and it was becoming urgent that something had to be done soon or it would be too late. There was the danger that England would make her pact with America (which she later did) before we could get someone over to talk to her highest authority.

'That is why I decided to take it on myself to fly.'

'Did you talk to Hitler about it first? You see, your wife has written in a book that you tried to get in touch with prominent people in England, through Spain and Switzerland, and that it was done with Hitler's knowledge. In that memorandum you have just read, where Albrecht Haushofer wrote it all down for history, he had the impression that you were talking *with* Hitler's knowledge and agreement; that Hitler actually knew what you had in mind and agreed to it.'

'Let me tell you. Hitler did not know I planned to fly to England myself. But I knew what I had to say would meet with the approval of the Führer.'

'Are you saying, then, that Hitler gave you a measure of approval to make inquiries to find a peace-contact through Albrecht Haushofer?'

'Yes. That is true.'

'It may explain, then, this protection you organized for the Haushofers. They refer to it in their letters. You gave them letters of protection, did you not, shielding them from the Gestapo? Wasn't it true that Karl Haushofer had married a Jewess, and that made your adviser and friend, Albrecht, half-Jewish?'

Hess nodded.

'It was odd, knowing how the Nazis – and you yourself – felt about Jews.'

'Yes. I know.'

'I have always believed this was a dangerous move on your part to shield a friend. But if in fact Hitler knew what you were doing, and wished to use the Haushofers, that would have been a different story ...'

'Hitler would certainly have known about it.

'As I recall, he would certainly have been involved. I did very little without informing him. But I want to stress this – it was the Haushofers who knew the Duke of Hamilton. Contrary to what books have said since I flew, I had never met the man. Maybe I saw him across a room at a reception in Berlin, and I certainly knew about him and his flying exploits. But I did not meet him, and did not correspond with him. When I flew I took Haushofer's visiting-card with me to present to him.'

'Hess, when was the precise moment that you made your decision to fly over yourself? Can you recall it?'

'We had waited a long time for a reply to the letter sent by Albrecht Haushofer. Months went by and the reply did not come. I suspected, but did not know until I read it recently, that the British Secret Service had intercepted the letter and retained it. I did not suddenly make up my mind. I thought a lot about it.'

'Where did you write your letters to the Haushofers? Did you dictate them to your secretary, Fräulein Fath?'

'Oh no!' Hess chuckled. 'Hildergarde Fath was an excellent secretary and a nice person, but these letters were extremely secret and confidential. I typed them myself at home or in my office.' He picked up a photo-copy of one of his letters again. 'That they should have been kept over all these years . . .'

I interrupted another long silence: 'Hess, I went right through the Haushofer file in Washington, through literally hundreds of letters; I also went through the papers of everybody you saw in England. What astounded me most was that having flown to England, and got your hearing with British officials, you then said Germany would refuse to negotiate with the Churchill Government; that Britain would have to change her government and get rid of Mr Churchill before you would talk terms. Was that true?'

'Yes. That is where I made my great mistake. I should never have insisted that they change their government. That was a foolish move on my part. Of course they would not change their government just because I demanded it.'

'Talking of negotiations, Hess, it is puzzling to me that the peace terms you offered were never made clear. Some of the British who saw you say you came over with specific terms and then started adding others as you went along.'

'Lies!' said Hess. 'Deliberate untruths put out by the British and repeated by historians ever since. I did no such thing.'

'One historian said you demanded the British withdraw from Iraq before you would agree to peace; and that you threatened to blockade England and starve her people.'

'Both statements are lies. I never at any time asked for a condition on Iraq. And it is against my nature to threaten to starve anybody. They are deliberate lies, possibly put about to gain sympathy for the British cause and stir the British public against me.

'The Führer never intended to fight against Britain. He had not expected Britain to declare war, and he had no designs on her Empire.'

'Well I find it difficult to understand – if what you say is true about Hitler wanting peace – that in July 1940 he was working out the details of Operation Sea-Lion, the invasion of Britain, and at the same time, through you and the Haushofers, putting out peace feelers. It doesn't add up.'

'Well, it is true.'

'What about Dunkirk? Is it true that Hitler deliberately restrained himself from attacking the British waiting for evacuation on the beaches?'

'Yes. He could of course have crushed them. I am quite sure of it. He deliberately held back, as you say. He believed there was still a chance of negotiating peace with England.' Then Hess said: 'I have read enough today, Colonel. And have a lot to think about. May we talk again tomorrow? I want to say something then about Churchill.' I agreed; the old man had gone through enough of his past in one day. I left him.

'Colonel Bird,' said Hess, bright and chirpy as I met him in the garden the next morning, 'I have made a statement and I wish it to be handed to the world Press, and included in your book. It is about Churchill, and it is timely, because next month is the 25th anniversary of my sentence at Nuremberg.' He drew out of his jacket pocket two pages of quarto writing paper, covered with his firm, neat handwriting.

'*From many sides it has been noted,*' the statement said, '*also from Churchill, that Rudolf Hess did not fly to England by any prompting from Hitler. Rather it was his own decision. He risked his life, with the intention of being the initiator to end the war as quickly as possible by a mutual understanding.*

He believed that he would have done a great service to all mankind and to the two nations involved. It is totally incomprehensible that the British brought him to Nuremberg to stand trial by a court, and at the end of the proceedings, they even agreed that he be transferred to Spandau Prison. With that they handed him over to the hands of the Russians. The Russians were given the right to keep him there as long as they wished, due to the fact that they were given a right of veto against his release. Also Sir Winston condemned that. Surely it can, above all, be expected from Great Britain that she will publicly, and in front of all the world, apply herself again and again for appealing for the release of Rudolf Hess.'

(*Given to the hands of Colonel Bird, 20 September 1971.*)

Hess stood waiting for me to finish reading. 'I have studied all that has been written about Churchill's attitude to my flight. He has even said that he was glad he was not responsible for the way Hess had been and is being treated. He did not agree that I should have been kept here for life. He is dead now. But the British still have a responsibility to do something about it.'

'It seems astounding to me,' I told him, 'that you can recall important things like this – things that are important to you – yet you cannot remember things that are vital to history: like whether or not you knew about Barbarossa before you took off. Sometimes you give the impression you really didn't know.'

'I do?' said Hess sharply. 'I give you this impression? If you believe it is the truth *and you have proof*, write it down in your book. I do not really care now. Before the Nuremberg trial I cared because I knew such a thing could be held against me. But I do not care now.'

I looked hard at the old man. What *was* going on in his mind? Was it true that his memory was shutting him off from most of the past? I felt there was, more than anything, an overall embarrassment. He was still embarrassed that he had given such blind devotion to Adolf Hitler, a man who had turned out to be inherently evil. Hess was embarrassed about being connected with and reminded of so much evil: evil that had been done by his colleagues and by the Party to which he had belonged. Hess, unlike Speer, had not made a complete break with the past. There had been no public repentance, as there had been with Speer. Hess was still proud, still arrogant. And because of this position – poised between guilt and arrogance – he had maintained his silence. It was easier to say: 'I cannot remember.'

I said, 'There is so much you could tell, Hess, if only you would dig genuinely and deeply into your memory. Those letters surely brought it all back to you? You have said before that your so-called loss of memory in England, and later at Nuremberg, was faked. Is it now?'

Hess's mouth tightened as I said it. 'You are not the first to accuse me. I told people I was putting on an act about my memory, I volunteered it to the court. But the reason was that it was so terribly worrying to me that I had indeed lost my memory that I pretended it was an act, a fake. But in reality I had forgotten. Call it escape mechanism if you wish; call it self-protection, whatever you will. Von Schirach said of me that I had a curtain I could pull down on the past –

that it was an act of self-preservation, a way of preserving my sanity. Perhaps he is right. And in doing so I genuinely forget.'

'Perhaps the memory of the Nazi crimes still embarrasses you today?' He nodded. 'There is probably a great deal of truth in that. But I have lost a lot of my memory. That is why I would never sit down and write my memoirs.'

'That is why it is so frustrating for me,' I said. 'What a great gift to History it would have been if Napoleon in his exile had had someone beside him, to chronicle what he had to say. Now here I am with you, ready to write down what *you* recall of the past and you cannot remember the facts about an important thing like Barbarossa!'

'I know, I know,' he shrugged. 'I agree it is a pity. But believe me, I am trying.'

Shortly before 1 pm the next day I went in to see Hess again. I had decided on a bold move to jolt his memory. I rang the bell at the prison door and waited for the duty warder to first scrutinize me, and then come and let me in. I could tell by now, by the sound of each man's step, which warder was on duty. If it was a fast, running step, it would be Swan, the elderly but fit British warder. He would jump down the stairs taking two at a time. Chisholm would pad softly, but purposefully to the door, every step saying 'I am doing my duty'. Jim Belson limps, and so does the fat French warder Barcanan, but with a different type of limp. I knew by the way that he rattled the keys all the way from the chief warder's office to the door that today Kyle was on duty.

Hess was sitting up on his bed eating his salad when I entered his cell. I said: 'How would you like to see your flying outfit today? The one you wore when you took off for Scotland?' His eyes widened. '*Mein Gott!* Now?'

'Come on.' He quickly slipped his feet into his shoes and we walked briskly along past the empty cells and the aide-room to the prison store-room. Earlier in the morning I had taken out the blue-grey Luftwaffe captain's uniform and the brown leather flying-suit and hung them on the cupboard door. Hess took a quick step ahead of me when he saw them and reached out to feel the leather. 'Fantastic! That is my suit. That is the one I took off from Augsburg in.' He fingered the arm of the suit, running the zippers up and down in the sleeves. 'All working perfectly. Good German craftsmanship there, Colonel.' He then took down the soft leather helmet and stood with it in his hands, thinking, his mouth a thin line, turned down a little at the corners, his eyes downcast, hidden by the black bushiness of his eyebrows.

'Ach! It has kept well. And the uniform has been dry-cleaned. It is in excellent condition.' He touched the bright, unfaded yellow and silver lapel flashes that had survived 30 years of storage in Britain, Nuremberg and Spandau. 'No sign of moths here.' He felt inside the fur-lined leather suit and brought out a soft, air-force forage cap. 'Look at that. Just where I left it. I carried it there with the photographs of my family. The last time I saw that was on 10 May 1941. It was then taken away from me.' He picked up one of the fur-lined flying boots. 'I had these in Nuremberg, but they took them away from me when I came here. They would be good to have in the winter. Colonel, what is going to happen to the uniform and flying suit when, for whatever reason, the prison closes down?'

'The regulations say that they will be burned.'

'Oh that is ridiculous – why?'

'Well I imagine it is considered that they could become a relic, or some sort of Nazi shrine.'

'But surely they could go to the Imperial War Museum where they have a motor from my plane. That would be far more sensible. To destroy them would be stupid. Colonel, would you please take a photograph of me with my suit?' He was searching around inside it again. 'I can see no name.'

'It has always been said, Hess, that the suit is not your own – that you picked it up in a hurry before you flew away from Augsburg and that it belonged to somebody else.'

'Ah! That is right. I snatched it off a peg in a hurry when I could not find my own. I always used to change in the dressing-room in the Augsburg hangar. I suppose the man who owned it is having a long wait!'

We walked back along the cell-block passage, talking. 'Perhaps you are right about the suit,' said Hess. 'There are these crazy people with a lot of money and nothing to spend it on; somebody would probably pay $50,000 for that suit and uniform today. Why, one man bought the London Bridge and put it up again in a desert in America, so I suppose anything is possible.'

Then he said: 'Before you came in I was studying these amazing reports about Bormann. Have you read them?' I said indeed I had. A former head of the West German Intelligence Service, General Reinhard Gehlen, was proclaiming to the world that Martin Bormann, Hess's one-time secretary and later Hitler's top lieutenant, had been a Soviet spy. General Gehlen had written his memoirs and had let it be known that he had proof to substantiate the allegation he was making about Bormann, who, he said, had not only been a Russian agent during World War II, but had fled Germany for Russia where he had become an adviser on German policy. He had died, said Gehlen, only three years before in Russia. His memoirs would prove that Bormann did not (as had been supposed) flee to South America when the Russians advanced on Berlin. When they had surrounded Hitler's bunker, Bormann had gone through their lines and had been given sanctuary in Russia.

Hess shook his head. 'Bormann a spy! Amazing. Unbelievable. There was no suspicion of any such thing: if there had been he would certainly no longer have worked with me or the Führer. The position of confidence he had until the end with the Führer shows that no such suspicion arose – or if it ever did it must have been proven false.

'Bormann was rather a treacherous individual. This came out more and more after I left. He certainly was not kind to my wife. Speer said he even tried to prevent my wife getting any money. He ran me down when I departed and used every chance to make himself closer to Hitler. I knew all this, but I could never believe he was a Russian spy!

'My wife, you know, never cared for Martin Bormann, and often women have intuition with these things. They are often able to judge men better than other men can themselves. Bormann just seemed to me a man who always was capable of unpleasantly using his elbows to get to the top and gain whatever it was he was after.

'But a *spy*! No. It must have been almost impossible. Yet – he was so close to the Führer that who was going to point a finger at him and accuse him of such a thing? I am terribly interested in this development. Please tell me anything that happens. I would very much like to read Gehlen's book when it comes out.'

He went back inside his white-painted cell. Outside in the passage, lying on a food-trolley, the 'magic-marker' board lay waiting for the cook. The once second most powerful man in the Third Reich – Bormann's superior – had written: 'Too much salt on potatoes. No potatoes tomorrow, rice instead. Wiener schnitzel tonight.'

33

Barbarossa – The Question-Mark

HESS WAS BUSY writing when I walked into his cell. He peered over the top of his spectacles at me and then climbed off his bed, rummaging through his papers. 'Colonel, I would like you to read what I have written to NASA. It is in regard to the problems of heart-strain on re-entry into the earth's atmosphere.' He handed me the letter.

'Subject: *Recommendation to strengthen the heart muscle while in space.* Medical specialists agree that it is of decisive importance for the health of the space-ship crew to eliminate the bad effects of the absence of gravity. As the heart in the absence of gravity has not to be very active it becomes slack quickly. Therefore, it is necessary to force it into working at least for a short time daily during the flight and during the stay on the moon. This may be accomplished by exposing the body of the astronauts to a legward directed centrifugal force, accordingly administered, which has about the same effect on the blood circulation as the gravity has on men upon the earth with corresponding heart activity. The centrifugal force can be produced by a fast rotatory disc upon which the astronaut is placed, the heart near the centre. A short daily use would be sufficient, as it is known that the health of the heart can be maintained by three minutes' training daily, when it is tasked to the utmost degree. By various rotatory speeds the heart can be trained as required. Thus there is the chance of developing an enlarged heart of the astronauts, a so-called "athletic heart" as is common among athletes. Such a heart could better resist the high requirements of the landing and reacting of the gravity on earth. This method could also be useful to train the heart before

258

the flight to help fulfil the high requirements of the start and as a reserve on the way.

The disc can be set in motion by a hand-operated winch or by pedals, which would also provide additional training for the arms and hands. Since in the absence of gravity not so much energy would be required on the disc rotation after it is set in motion, brakes should be put in. So as not to keep two astronauts busy with the disc, generators, accumulators, and a motor could be installed.

Should the installation of a disc of 4m diameter not be possible with the dimensions of the present space-ships – with the dimensions of the Russian space-stations as "Salyut" it would be no problem – a crouched position of the astronauts is recommended so that a disc of $2\frac{1}{2}$m diameter would do. If a longer stay on the moon is scheduled, a training disc should be erected there. In consequence of the low gravity of the moon, disc and man have only light weights, this makes a light construction of the disc possible, which could easily be placed in the moon-craft.

Longer space-ship and space-station programs are depending on the solution of the problem to simulate absence of gravity. That is proved by the experience of the latest Apollo crew. Already the difference from eight to 12 days of absence of gravity was such that the Apollo-15 men needed much more time to recover.

(Irwin, who was in relatively better health, had perhaps more physical training before the flight and so could task the reserve of his "athletic heart" – or had strained his heart more in unloading the car and in pulling out the obstinate geological probe.)

It is questionable whether the "walking" on the running plank of the Salyut-1 crew (who died in vacuum) would have been sufficient to avoid heart failure which the impact of the braking action or the earth's gravity might have caused after a three-week absence of gravity.'

'Signed Rudolf Hess.'

He said when I had finished: 'I would appreciate it if you could send that on to NASA urgently for me. It might very well help.' I promised I would.

He pointed to an article in a newspaper on his bed. 'I have been reading about the problems of youth. You know, with all the criticism that was levelled at von Schirach and his Hitler Jugend, it is forgotten that he did a fantastic thing with Germany's young. He kept them busy, he kept them out of trouble. He had a health programme and health camps for them to enjoy. In those years we did not have to concern ourselves with the worry of youths taking drugs, getting involved in crime, and sexual permissiveness. We did not have the burning of national flags and draft cards. We had a healthy young with healthy minds, all pulling together under one flag to build a nation. That is what we need today,' he said, waving a finger, 'we need to get them back on the right track.'

'But surely,' I said, 'you were doing all this with youth for a different purpose. You were building a super-race for war, for conquests; to make Germany the strongest nation in Europe. Today youth is rebelling because we made a mess of their world.'

'Maybe, but they won't make a better world with drugs,' he growled.

I had brought with me a further batch of pages from the manuscript of this book, which Hess was assiduously going through. I had allowed him to keep 44 pages of it overnight in his cell. He turned to page 30 of the manuscript and said: 'I want to talk to you about this paragraph on Barbarossa. You had written that Hitler was worried – when I flew – "*that Hess might reveal his Führer's plan to attack Russia. Hess was one of the few who knew of the planned attack to take place six weeks later. And Hitler was horrified that Hess might betray it.*" Then you drew a line through it all. Why did you do that?'

'Because when I wrote it I believed it to be the truth. But after talking to you to check it out you emphatically denied it. I crossed the whole paragraph out. If you say something I have written in that manuscript is not true – not as it happened at the time – then it will not go into my book.'

Hess looked at me steadily. 'Colonel I want you to have that paragraph in, just the way you had it.'

I asked him to repeat what he said. 'I want that paragraph to stand,' said Hess.

'Do you realize what you are saying? You are admitting to me that you knew about Barbarossa before you flew off to Scotland.'

'Colonel – I am asking you to leave what you had originally written.'

'Then you did know about Barbarossa?'

'*Yes. I did.*'

'Then tell me about it. You have just made an extremely important statement – important to History.'

'Not now,' said Hess. 'It suffices to say that I wish you to record that fact as you originally recorded it before you struck it out. Now, if you will excuse me . . .' And stepping into his down-at-heel carpet slippers he shuffled off to the toilet to urinate.

I saw him again the next day, hardly daring to broach the subject again. 'I made that alteration in the manuscript,' I said casually. 'Yes,' he replied. 'Yes, I did know. We can discuss it fully at a later date.'

I had with me the latest biography* of Hess which had just come out in England. I took it out of my brief-case and he looked at the cover picture, the old, much-used portrait of a gaunt, staring Hess, taken in his Nuremberg cell. '*Mein Gott!* Not that picture again. It makes me look so crazy! I wish in a way your book would come out now. It would show that I am not the sick, crazy old man people in the outside world think I am.'

'I have been reading everything that anybody says about you. This latest biography is said to have had your wife's help. Your wife has said you were "the conscience of the Party", back in the old days.' He chuckled. 'Yes, in many ways. I was very much against treating the Jews the way they were treated.'

'It also says that you helped Hitler rehearse his speeches. Did he rehearse all of them?'

'Oh certainly. The Führer went to great trouble to meticulously rehearse every point. He spent hours before a speaking occasion – and every occasion was important to him – going over the emphasis of points, and the gestures he would make. He was an hypnotic speaker. He swayed his audiences, holding them in the palm of his hand. I cannot say as much for his writing ability, but when it came to speaking there was nobody who could put such a spell on his audience as did Adolf Hitler.'

'It is also written that Hitler suggested your marriage to your wife . . .?'

* Roger Manvell and Heinrich Fraenkel, *Hess* (Drake, 1973).

'No! That is *not* true,' he said angrily. 'It has been said before and it is a lie. Maybe he agreed that Ilse would make a fine wife, but that is altogether different. No man marries a woman simply because another man – no matter how highly respected he is – suggests it. Love is not suggested by anybody. We have had a long and lasting love, my wife and I; she has been loyal and true to me for all these years. Look what a fine young man my son has become, and she had to take it on herself to provide his education. Something like this could not be built on a suggestion.' He obviously then wanted to change the subject.

The next day Hess's wife and her sister arrived to see him and I chatted to the elderly Fräulein Prohl while she waited to go inside. She told me: 'Flew today for the first time since the war years, when I used to fly with Rudolf in one of his ministerial planes; we used to go from Munich to Berlin. He always had his own pilot with him but he would take over the controls of the plane himself. One day he was demonstrating to Ilse and me how to handle the plane if it stalled and the motors cut out. He switched off the motors to show us, and when he went to switch them on again nothing happened. He had to go ahead and make an emergency landing! After that I believe Ilse never flew with him again.'

Frau Hess came out, wearing a new dress she said she had bought for the occasion. 'A rare thing for me,' she said. 'He looks fine. Very smart, very alert.'

I told her I was arranging at Hess's request to get him a tie for Christmas. He had also asked for a suit so that he might look well-dressed if he was released. Frau Hess's face saddened, and she put her hand on my arm. 'Oh Colonel, I really don't think we can hope for that any more. I think we must resign ourselves to the situation. My husband will die in this prison.' And she turned away.

Back in the garden I thought the old man's elation over the visit might well have put him in the mood to expand his conversation about his Barbarossa bombshell. I had a copy of my re-written page – *re-instating* the important paragraph that had been crossed out. He had been signing each page as he read it and I asked him to check what had been written and to sign this if it was accurate. His brow

furrowed and he read it through several times. There was a silence
for a long time and he then said: 'I do not believe I can sign that.
You see, I do not remember.'

'But that is exactly how you told me it was! That is what you
told me three days ago!' He peered at me beneath his bushy brows.
'If you have papers by historians confirming that I was in on the
discussions then you may write it. But I do not remember. I cannot –
at this stage – sign that page of your manuscript.'

I shook my head in exasperation. But I agreed to let the matter
drop for the time being. Four days later I was going through the
manuscript with him again and he stopped at the controversial page 30
and asked to read it. With a gnarled finger following the line as
he read it he spoke the words out loud. 'I see you have crossed it out,'
he said.

'Yes. You asked that this be done.'

'Leave it in,' said Hess abruptly. 'I just don't care about it.' I said:
'Mr Hess, I am going to ask you this question once more and once
more only. We must be factual. Do I leave that paragraph in, or do
I take it out? You must answer this clearly.' He said: 'Leave it in,
as you had it originally.'

I shrugged, and closed the book. He was in a mood that would
obviously add nothing constructive to what had been written.
Instead we discussed the latest that had been published about him.

'Is it true that you once vowed never again to keep a bird in a
cage if you ever got out of prison?' 'Yes,' he said. 'I recently read
an article written by a man imprisoned in Greece. He had two
mosquitoes in his cell, and he made friends with them, allowing
them to suck blood from his arm. Well, I had a spider for a long time
living in my bath in the prison. I could not kill it. I would gently
move it out while I had my bath, and if he wished to go back after
I had finished that was all right.'

Earlier, Hess had been posing in the garden for photographs. I
asked him if he used the exercise bicycle in the cell-block I had given
the warders. 'No,' he said. 'And if I did I would not sit for a photograph on it! I do not want to be part of some sort of monkey theatre.
I prefer to be shown studying my books, or my wall-maps of the
moon, or reading. I want to be shown to the world for what I am –
a man who is mentally active and alert.

'I have been thinking,' he smiled, 'of Willy Brandt and the award made to him of the Nobel Peace Prize. You see, Colonel, it depends very much on the times you live in, and the circumstances. A great deal of luck is involved.

'Now let us draw a parallel. Let us say that back in the time I flew to Scotland on my peace mission I had succeeded. What would have happened?

'During the war Willy Brandt went underground and if he had been found he would have been shot. If I had been sent back to Germany I might also have been shot.

'It is valid to ask what would have happened should I have succeeded with Churchill? I would have accomplished something far bigger than Willy Brandt has accomplished today. I could well have been a candidate for the Nobel Peace Prize.

'We live in strange times, Colonel.'

EPILOGUE

SINCE I WROTE the words on the preceding page, much has happened.

In early March 1972 I had been to the United States where I had left my wife, Donna, seriously ill, continuing with her medical treatment. On the way back, I had called into Washington where I spent some days in the Archives building going over the Hess File and copying the Hess–Haushofer letters.

I was putting my key into the door of our Fischottersteig, Berlin, home when the phone began to ring. It was Donna from Florida. There had been a strange telegram from my Berlin superior officer, asking when I was likely to return. 'It sounds odd, Gene,' she said.

I put down the phone and then called Spandau Prison to talk to Warder Donham, the man I had left in charge. He sounded strangely stiff and formal. He assured me all was well with the prisoner and that Hess had been missing me. But there was none of our previous easy-going relationship. I felt uneasy.

Next morning I drove through the slush of winter Berlin to the US Mission Headquarters and went to the office of my superior, Mr Small. He said: 'Gene, I have some questions for you and I want them answered.' There were tapes in existence concerning Rudolf Hess which had been taped inside the prison. There was also, he understood, a manuscript which had been written with Rudolf Hess's full cooperation. Only one man was close to Hess. Had I been responsible?

I told him yes, I had.

I was then interrogated for several hours. I was allowed to go home but placed under house arrest. My house was kept under 24-hour surveillance, my phone was tapped, a team of officers came and made a thorough search of every room. They took away documents, letters, photographs and negatives dating back to 1934. Every page was then laboriously cross-indexed with the information which appears in this book. I was allowed to travel about Berlin in my car, but when I did, three cars, each containing two Secret Service men, followed.

I was put under oath when I made the following statement (see Appendix) before the US flag and a portrait of the US President, and I was asked to resign my job as US Commandant of Spandau. This I did. I was also made to sign a Secrets Act, a document I, as a retired Army officer, had not signed before.

Later in Washington, while staying at the same hotel from which the Watergate raids were made, I went before a Board of State Department officials. Sitting opposite me I recognized with some amusement the man who had flown to Berlin and asked me if, for the sake of the US historical record, I might be able to persuade Rudolf Hess to divulge his secrets before he died. (I had told him I would do my best.)

They told me that several copies of the 160,000-word manuscript had been made. One was being kept in a sealed vault, another was sent to the Department of the Secretary of State, a third was with the Department of the Secretary of Defence, a fourth was in the Archives in Washington, and one had been sent to the office of the US Commander, Berlin. Again I smiled to myself. It was this same gentleman's Chief of Staff, who had been reading my manuscript, chapter by chapter, from the time it was three-parts completed. He had even allowed his wife to read it. Both had told me it was 'terrific' and all had offered several constructive suggestions to add to its scope. The Director of the Archives in Berlin had been allowed by me to read it as it was written, and so had several other officers. In short, if it had not been the subject of conversation in the general officers' mess and at the officers' wives' bridge parties I would have been surprised indeed.

But now I was going through questioning and rebukes by men who, if the US Secret Service has efficiency at all, must have known about my book's production for years and had done nothing whatsoever to stop its compilation. I told them that they must have realized there was nothing in it which breached any secrets act; nothing that could be used against the US by a future enemy. I believed – and they should agree – that it was an important and unique historical document. They said nothing other than I would have to await their permission to publish it.

I told them its publication might well do something that the Heads of State of Britain, the United States and France all wanted, but had failed to achieve: force the Russians to bow to the weight of sheer public opinion and release Hess.

This I believe could happen as millions around the world read for the first time the true story of the old man's incarceration for year after year purely because a country is using him as a political pawn for its own ends.

Only the future will tell.

APPENDIX

MY STATEMENT SUBMITTED on 27 March 1972 read:
I have prepared a sober, factual, historic record of Spandau Prison as I know it, with particular reference to the last seven years and my contact and dealings with the prisoners who were there when I arrived in 1964; and finally with Hess who is still there.

The book was originally to have been published after Spandau Prison had closed down, i.e. after death or release of Hess, and then only after the script had been properly cleared and approved.

The manuscript has been written with all the facts at my disposal – as fully explained in my foreword to the manuscript. It has in no way been written for the sake of sensation, or in any way that could be damaging to any one nation.

I decided to write this book very early, when I was assigned as Director of Spandau Prison on 5 September 1964. The seed was well planted in my mind. Since then, I have been asked by many people, my superiors here in Berlin – people have said, 'You should write a book one day and tell the TRUE story'.

It is something that should be recorded for the sake of history. There have been speculations in newspapers and magazines in every language in the world of what is going on. They have said, here is a madman being kept in chains and starved; or, here is a man living off the fat of the land. It has been speculation because nobody knew what was going on. If Hess died tomorrow and no one had taken the trouble to set down the true, factual record proved by documentation of medical and psychiatric reports, first-hand conversations with Hess, etc., *the true story would never be told*. The question-mark over Spandau would remain forever after Hess died. Were they being cruel to Hess? Humane to Hess? Was he mad? I am trying to show the world the real story of what went on in Spandau. Further, I am trying to show the world, with the help of Hess himself, what was really behind his flight and what went on in his inner thinking. Many of these questions, which I have been able to answer with the help of Hess, have been
268

asked for years by the leading historians of the world. I, at last, can provide the answers.

I became more convinced than ever that I MUST write this book after Speer and von Schirach were released at the end of September 1966; when Hess was left in prison alone, practically in solitary confinement. He *was not* sentenced to that.

That was when I started to put my material together.

Hess has been called the most examined man in the world, medically and physically. If you have some 200 different psychiatrists over the years come to try to understand you, it must have some effect on you.

In collecting information and reading material, I have often thought that here is a man *who has only been surrounded by people trying to figure him out.* As a result, he has withdrawn more and more into his shell where he lives. Many have thought and still think he is insane. In my many hours of talking to him, reading letters he has written, etc., I have found him to be an intelligent man. What he did in flying to England was, indeed, no simple thing.

I have come most close to the answer of Hess because I have taken the trouble to talk to Hess not as someone who has come to examine him, but as close to the man as my job would permit so Hess could talk to me normally and not as a psychiatrist who was examining him for a limited period of time. I have faithfully recorded these conversations. If I were to try to put anything into them or subtract anything from then, I would, like the rest, be trying to read things into what he says – as a psychiatrist. I am not a psychiatrist and I am therefore trying to report as a reporter what he has said to me in his cell, in walks in the garden, and when he lay close to death in hospital.

When he was afraid of dying, he called me to his bedside. It was I who convinced him that he should allow his family to visit him after nearly 29 years of not seeing them. I have come to know him, I believe, better than any living person since 1941.

My book is the story of a man who helped start a war, who once vainly tried to stop it, and who now lives in virtual solitary confinement in a prison.

I feel that if my book were published at this time or in the future (with some minor changes or deletions), it could well serve to rally public sympathy throughout the world, which could in turn aid in his possible release. If this were possible, I would gladly accept any and all blame or criticism levelled against me, and the consequences thereof.

I fully realize, however, that due to many circumstances this is perhaps not possible. It is my sincere plea, therefore, that my manuscript be read with an open mind, so that one day it can be published as is, and in so doing cover an important gap in history.

I thank you.

EUGENE K. BIRD